Alternative Strategies for Coping with Crime

Aspects of Social Policy

General Editor: J. P. Martin

Professor of Sociology and Social Administration,
University of Southampton

Also in this series:

The Poverty Business:
Britain and America
JOAN HIGGINS

Social Policy
A survey of recent developments
edited by MICHAEL H. COOPER

Provision for the Disabled
EDA TOPLISS

Efficiency in the Social Services
ALAN WILLIAMS AND ROBERT ANDERSON

The Child's Generation
JEAN PACKMAN

Capitalism and Social Welfare
A comparative study
ROGER LAWSON

Penal Policy
A. E. BOTTOMS

Alternative Strategies for Coping with Crime

Edited by

NORMAN TUTT

BASIL BLACKWELL · OXFORD
MARTIN ROBERTSON · LONDON

ISBN 0 631 16240 2 (Hardback)
      0 631 16250 X (Paperback)

First published in 1978 by Basil Blackwell
& Mott Ltd. Oxford, and by Martin Robertson
& Co. Ltd. London

British Library Cataloguing in Publication Data

Alternative strategies for coping with crime. – (Aspects
   of social policy).
   1. Corrections
   I. Tutt, Norman
   364.6   HV8665

   ISBN 0–631–16240–2
   ISBN 0–631–16250–X   Pbk.

Printed in Great Britain
by Western Printing Services Ltd, Bristol
and bound by the Kemp Hall Bindery, Oxford

Contents

v

CHAPTER ONE

Introduction

NORMAN TUTT

At the initial planning meeting for this book it soon became obvious that all the contributors were closely identified with attempts to reform or improve the criminal justice system. For the majority that identification took the form of a firm commitment to strategies for coping with criminal behaviour alternative to traditional forms of incarceration and use of institutions, even though we recognized that custodial disposals are used in only a small proportion of all cases. However, further bonds amongst the contributors were also evident, the most significant of these being a firm belief in objectivity and a common political awareness.

The belief in objectivity was illustrated by the way in which each contributor was prepared to describe and discuss his own particular alternative only if allowed to do so critically. No one was prepared to say alternatives were 'good' because they are alternatives, but rather, each felt it essential to illustrate the difficulties and disadvantages of an alternative, the problems of its implementation and the strain on staff and the community. Also, if possible, all the contributors wished to present some hard factual evaluation of an alternative. In all cases this evaluation was seen primarily in the form of a reduction of incidence of reconviction amongst the population exposed to the alternative. The establishment of reconviction data as the criterion for assessing success was easily agreed; this is somewhat surprising since the contributors came from such mixed backgrounds as law, social work, sociology and psychology. Each contributor identified the reduction of criminal behaviour as the objective of any intervention aimed at a delinquent or criminal individual. We were not concerned with treating maladjustment, improving an individual's ability to relate, or even providing good experiences. All these aims are no doubt laudable but are not

1

important to this book unless they can be shown to be intervening variables affecting the vital outcome of reducing offending.

The second major bond amongst the contributors was that of political awareness. There seemed little point in writing 'just another book' which outlined an exciting new development, which after publication became of only historical interest because the idea was never generalized or taken up by others. We therefore wanted to write a book which would not only describe a number of alternatives, but would also indicate how they were developed and how they could be generalized. This book therefore concentrates as much on how social change is brought about as on the direction we would wish to see such a change take. This is important, since comparatively little has been written about the process of social change, and it appears that there is little formal knowledge of this topic in the fields of social welfare and social control policies. Policies in these fields often appear to be based on a current social or psychological belief. For example, the Children and Young Persons Act (1969) was based on the belief that delinquency was caused by deprivation and could be alleviated by treatment—yet there is little understanding of the process whereby that belief was transferred into practice. The importance of examining the process of social change emerges throughout the book and is particularly evident where examples are given of progressive legislation which has led inadvertently to retrogressive practice. This has occurred in the field of delinquency, criminality and mental illness. Hopefully this book successfully demonstrates that alternatives to incarceration can be developed, that they can be generalized, and more importantly, that the outcome desired of the alternative can be ensured without adverse spin-off.

All the contributors recognized that if social policy is to be moved into new directions away from the development of institutions those new directions must be shown to be effective. Effectiveness, for the majority of politicians, resource controllers and most importantly for the general public, means the ability to control criminal behaviour during the period immediately after arrest and court proceedings, and the ability to reduce the incidence of criminal behaviour by the individual in his future life. This is a great demand to make of any project but nevertheless is the yardstick against which any alternative will be measured.

This book appears in an unusual climate. The decade of the sixties, in simplified social terms, was characterized by the youth culture. The Beatles ruled, their music was reviewed in all the best newspapers. The youth culture permeated the ranks of middle-aged policy makers and educational and social policy was aimed at accommodating youth rather than controlling it. Penal policy was based firmly on beliefs in rehabilitation and treatment, there were demands for more psychiatric facilities, group therapy and work training. But now, in the latter part of the seventies, the climate appears to have changed dramatically. First, population trends in the United Kingdom have changed—a declining birth rate and increased longevity have led to a noticeably ageing population. The percentage of the population over 65 years of age had grown to 25 per cent although the total population had grown by only 7 per cent. This has had the effect of turning adolescents into almost a minority group. In retrospect the seventies may be characterized as an era of control. In Great Britain the adult prison population had risen to record heights. Similarly there were more children in residential care than ever before. Also, contrary to the aims of legislation, there were more children and young people in prison department establishments than for many decades. Moreover, there was strong pressure from many quarters for increased use of secure facilities in the control of delinquent children, adult offenders and the mentally disordered. This response may have been inevitable given a continuous growth in crimes committed and persons convicted (see graphs later in chapter). Those of the contributors from North America and those with contacts in Western Europe reported that the trends in Great Britain were being repeated elsewhere as communities began to demand greater control of their deviants. The contributors were conscious of the fact that some of our parent disciplines and indeed some of us personally were partly responsible for these changes. For example, a good deal of research by psychologists and sociologists in the past decade had been aimed at evaluating the treatment of delinquent and criminal behaviour. In most cases it had shown the ineffectiveness of treatment and by so doing had been used by those who wished to discredit treatment. Some of the contributors, being concerned about the adverse effects often generated by a social welfare intervention, had found themselves adopting a reactionary stance by saying that the best protection for the child or adult was to ensure his legal rights against administrative or executive decision. (It is interesting that this stance is being adopted by some states in the U.S.A. as a progressive improvement on previous apparently progressive methods of professional social welfare decision making.) The group therefore were aware that they were involved in producing a book which advocated policies which may be contradictory to the developing underlying trends in various communities. Also, they were aware that their contributions could be misinterpreted; perceived either as more 'liberal hogwash' removed from reality, or as reactionary, opposed to the development of professional social welfare agencies and wishing to replace treatment with control and the rule of law.

The book is based on certain assumptions or ground rules which need to be made explicit. The first of these rules is that the term 'criminal justice system' is used without separating specific areas of juvenile justice or child welfare although it is essential to remember that only a small fraction of the child welfare system is concerned with delinquent children. (See Table 1.) The criminal justice system is a title given to several branches of statutory intervention which only fit together as a system in as much as they are all part of a process through which an offending individual of whatever age may pass. The label 'criminal justice system' includes the police, the courts (both lay, as in magistrates' courts, and professional, as in the judicial system), the social welfare agencies (e.g. probation and other social work agencies), residential treatment centres and adult penal institutions. There are a number of reasons why no differentiation is made between aspects of the criminal justice system and the welfare systems and these need to be explained:

(a) Nearly all the contributors took the view that in many cases the outcome of a social welfare intervention is in fact social control. There is a major philosophical debate over the boundaries of welfare and control and indeed over whether a boundary exists, or whether welfare necessarily subsumes some form of control. Not all of us would resolve the dilemma with such a forthright statement as that chosen by Allison Morris: 'Indeed social welfare is an euphemism for, and one of the most efficient modes of, social control!' (Chapter 3). However, most of the contributors recognized that the differences between welfare agencies and control agencies is more often administrative than practical.

(b) It is obvious that the boundaries between the child welfare system and the criminal justice system are highly permeable so that the actions initiated in one system rapidly produce reactions in the other. For the individual delinquent the two systems are often inseparable as he passes through his career. In England a fourteen-year-old offender can be remanded in custody to a prison department establishment after his first appearance in court if he is felt to be of too unruly a character to be placed in the care of the local authority. After the committal hearing he may well find that he is placed in the care of the local authority and duly placed in a community home which forms part of the child welfare system. However, he may then abscond and commit further offences for which, after arrest and arraignment, he may find himself committed to a junior detention centre—a prison department establishment—for three or six months. After serving this sentence, he may well return to the community home, since he may still be in the care of the local authority. Moreover, the children's legislation in the United Kingdom allows the possibility of transfer from the child welfare system to the penal system by executive action. This rarely happens except in extreme cases but clearly illustrates the permeability of the two boundaries.

The interaction of the varying social control systems is illustrated by the outcome of social policy as well as by individual case studies. As David Thorpe shows in Chapter 4, trends in sentencing policy away from the use of child welfare services (supervision by a social worker or committal to the care of the local authority in the case of the care order) are mirrored almost directly by the trend towards the penal and custodial sentences of detention centre or borstal training. Similarly, Otto Driedger from Canada illustrates in Chapter 7 the interaction between the other major social control systems, namely, the mental health system and adult corrections. He shows how the laudable shift to community care within the mental health system has led to the adverse effect of more of the mentally retarded and the chronically mentally ill finding their way into the adult correctional system—if only for 'asylum'.

(c) It was irrelevant to differentiate between separate systems dealing with the offending individual because often the difference is one of the semantics rather than reality. As stated above, for the individual it often all looks the same. If one examines the processes through which any offending individual passes they are often the same. Thus no matter what the age of the offender his initial contact as an offender with the social process is a police officer, although he may have been known previously to social welfare agencies as a 'welfare case'. The next part of the process is the court which, although differentiated to some extent for juveniles (i.e. with more informal proceedings, protection from public viewing, etc.) nevertheless follows the same basic procedures: the offender must make a plea, the evidence is presented and a disposal made. In a substantial proportion of cases the disposal will involve a financial penalty and no further action taken. Indeed the use of financial penalties is probably the most effective and widely used alternative to custody for the purpose of reducing reoffending. Otherwise after the court stage the offender may proceed to receiving non-custodial social work support. It was hoped that eventually this would be administratively differentiated, a child receiving support from a social worker employed by a social services department, an adult receiving help from a probation officer employed by the local probation and after-care service. At the moment this is not fully implemented, and probation officers still play a major role in supervising children and young people. However, the two alternatives are not as different as they may first appear because in fact both workers will have undergone very similar if not identical training and will share the same professional qualification. It can be safely assumed that the offender will be exposed to much the same system of attitudes and advice whoever his supervising officer. (It is interesting to note that in Scotland probation officers have been fully integrated into the social work departments whose social workers provide, amongst other duties, a service for the courts and penal system.) If, on the other hand, the offender receives a custodial disposal, be it penal or welfare, from the court, the differences are again marginal. Whilst accepting the fact that the regimes of child welfare establishments and penal establishments are vastly different there is nevertheless some commonality in terms of process. Both involve segregation, i.e., removal of the individual from his normal contact with his normal community, which is involuntary on the part of the individual. Both the child and adult systems have recourse to the use of secure accommodation, if they consider it necessary, in which the individual can be isolated and confined.

(d) Although generally the methods employed within the child welfare system and the penal system differ, whenever a method is a proven success in one system there is persistent public and professional pressure to implement the new method in the other system. This interaction has been seen most recently in the United Kingdom with the success of community service orders (see John Harding's discussion in Chapter 9). This policy, developed as an alternative to prison, was implemented with a combination of good publicity and good practice. Its apparent success has captured the imagination of both the public and professions, who are demanding that a similar practice be developed for juvenile offenders.

(e) Not only are methods transposed from system to system as suggested above, but the close interaction of the systems limits certain areas for innovation. For example, it would prove extremely difficult to 'decriminalize' certain behaviour for children and juveniles and yet regard the behaviour as an offence for adults. Obviously this does happen at the extremes of the age range— young children not being held criminally responsible for their behaviour—but in most instances the juvenile behaviour defined as offences is the same as for adults. Similarly, grave difficulties arise when changes in the penal system produce a more liberal treatment for adult offenders than for children committing the same offences. For example, one of the current problems in the child welfare field in England and Wales is the length of a detention centre order. A young person over the age of fourteen years found guilty of an offence may be made subject of a care order and dealt with by the local authority's child welfare system. The care order which removes the parental rights to the local authority would normally remain in force until the young person's eighteenth birthday. Theoretically the young person could therefore be placed in residential care away from home for 4 years. However, for the same offence, with the same child, the same court could decide to make a detention centre order for 3 months. The detention centres are run by the prison department and operate a system allowing remission for good behaviour. The percentage of the sentence which can be remitted was recently raised by executive decision to 50 per cent. The boy sent to a detention centre could thereby be released after 6 weeks. If, as suggested above, the basic processes of the welfare and penal systems are perceived as the same even though the regimes differ, then the variance between a 4 year 'sentence' and a 6 week 'sentence' is inevitably viewed by the juvenile offender, public and professions as inequable.

These five major reasons convinced the contributors of the similarities of the child welfare system as it pertains to offending children, and the penal system. Given such similarities it seemed economic to define all parts as sections of the criminal justice system. The contributors have chosen to concentrate on the similarities of the systems rather than highlight the differences, although all have been aware of them. However, the reader may reasonably question why, in a book on alternatives *within* the criminal justice system there should be a chapter on the role of the educational system. Our reasoning was that the most important alternative is prevention, and that it was much more relevant to prevent crimes and thereby a great deal of personal suffering than to find alternative ways of processing the individual after the event. It will be clear from David Reynolds' and

Dee Jones's chapter that schools can have a major preventive role. Secondly, the educational system is the only statutory system through which every child and young person passes: there is no adult equivalent. The welfare, penal and health systems are all by various means selective in that only a minority of the total population passes through those systems. This places the educational system in a unique position for influencing social behaviour. It seemed important to comment on that influence in a book which deals with deviant social behaviour.

The other major ground rule that needs explanation is that the contributors have attempted as far as possible to ignore arbitrary divisions. For example, age groups which are created by legislation are ignored. Instead, the general structure of the book is such as to lead the reader through the age bands, starting with children and young people, moving on to alternatives for young offenders and finally for adults. This structure has been used to try to illustrate that the alternatives are widespread and that they occur for all age groups. Similarly, cultural boundaries are ignored in an attempt to show that alternatives are occurring within different social and political settings. Moreover, by drawing on the experience of these other countries it soon becomes obvious that the development of alternatives is controlled by the social and political will of the country rather than being influenced by levels or styles of crime. Nancy Hazel (Chapter 5) clearly illustrates this point by referring to the different levels of fostering in England and Wales, Belgium and Sweden. It is difficult to believe that these differing levels are the result of different patterns of offending amongst juveniles, since basically all three countries have similar socio-economic structures and similar cultures. The difference more obviously reflects varying levels of commitment to a policy of fostering, and suggests that, given the social and political commitment, alternative strategies can be viable whatever the cultural context.

The experience recorded from North America—Otto Driedger's from Saskatchewan, and more specifically Andrew Rutherford's from Massachusetts—suggests that in some situations the term 'alternative strategies' is a misnomer since the alternative is now the only option. In Massachusetts, where the traditional institutions for juvenile offenders were closed, community-based activity became the established strategy. This is very important because alternatives are only of interest if at some point they can become the mainstream strategy for dealing with that minority of cases that enter custodial institutions. Whilst they are small scale experimental projects, it may be argued they serve a useful purpose as 'gadflies' to the established methods, stimulating them to more innovative methods of working. However, to be of any real value an alternative strategy should be capable of expansion and generalization, and ultimately, of becoming the major method. We hope to demonstrate that alternative methods of coping with crime, other than the use of institutions exist for all age groups, exist within a number and variety of cultural and political contexts, and in some instances have become so widespread and generalized that they represent the formal policy. If we are successful in so doing, then alternative strategies may no longer be condemned as experimental, shortlived and unstable, but will have to be taken seriously and integrated into the mainstream of disposals for offenders.

So far the value of alternatives has been implied, but no explanation given as to the target group for alternatives or why alternatives are needed. Conventionally this question is answered by an attack on institutions, illustrating their detrimental effects on the individual, their enormous costs and their failure to attain their objectives. To do so ignores historical and social reality. Indeed the crucial fact so often forgotten in the debate over institutions is that the majority of institutions which were established in the last century were themselves established as alternatives to harsher and less acceptable methods of coping with deviants. As David Thorpe (Chapter 4) points out, the reform and industrial schools set up for child offenders and children in need were established only after furious crusades by reformers who wished to rescue children from the perils of adult prisons. It is ironic that Massachusetts, the first state to close its training schools for juvenile offenders, had in the nineteenth century been the first state to take the progressive step of establishing the training schools as an alternative method of dealing with juvenile offenders (Chapter 6). It is also forgotten that the long term adult prisons were established at a similar point in our history, to replace the hulks, transportation and public executions, although, of course, prisons serving a remand function for the courts have a much longer history.

Therefore, it needs to be remembered that historically institutions were established as an act of humanity. Many still serve such a role in current society, offering shelter, assistance and support to many of society's casualties. For example, the vast majority of children in residential care are so accommodated because their home conditions are inadequate in some way. Very often no home exists at all. Similarly, the prisons and mental hospitals shelter a number of homeless, often socially derelict adults who would otherwise be left to survive on the streets. This is not to say that these groups are ideally placed in such establishments, but to recognize the reality that, due to lack of adequate alternative accommodation, the only 'security' available to many people is provided by institutions.

The other major aspect of social reality which needs to be considered is that society has a right to protect itself against its more disruptive members, and our society has chosen to do this in extreme cases by placing the disruptive member in an institution which thereby isolates him from society. Institutions may therefore be necessary to protect the public from dangerous, or otherwise serious, offenders and to give the public reassurance.

However, changes in social attitude, economics and employment have led to major changes in social policy. Social attitudes towards institutions have changed markedly since the era of industrialized Victorian England which thrived on institutions, with its boarding schools to educate the expanding middle class, institutions for effective industrial production as well as for all social deviants. Attitudes have moved away from the 'paternalism' of the Victorian period towards 'participation and consensus', and with that have moved away from admiration for institutions to a search for alternatives. The costly development of institutions in Victorian England reflected an expansionist economy. As changes in the economy put pressure on public spending, so alternatives to the huge capital costs involved in developing a new institution are sought. Changes in employment have made it more difficult to find people who are prepared to work the unsocial hours, and often live in the unsocial conditions, demanded by institutions.

These changes have led to a social policy aimed at creating alternatives to institutions for deprived children, the mentally ill and handicapped and the criminal. This has to some extent been effective; for example, in the criminal policy field it is a Government objective to develop alternative penal measures, and build up public confidence in them in such a way as to make it possible to reduce reliance on penal institutions (see Chapter 9, on the development of community service orders). The greatest portion of this change has come during the last two or three decades, in 1957 approximately a third of males over 17 years of age found guilty of an indictable offence were received into custody. By 1976 this had dropped to about one sixth.

However, it is a continual struggle, for as the number of social casualties and the numbers found guilty of offences continue to increase, there is a tendency to revert to institutional methods. If these two areas are examined separately, taking the numbers of children in care (although not necessarily delinquent) as one index of social casualty, in 1976, the last year for which figures are available, there were over 100,000 children in the care of local authorities, of these only about 6·4 thousands would have been committed to care for offending behaviour. As Table I illustrates, not all of these 100,000 children were in residential care, many thousands were boarded out (33,000) and many more thousands were allowed to remain living at home with a parent or guardian whilst the local authority retained parental rights of the child (this figure, which had risen each year between 1972 and 1975, remained the same in 1976). The very substantial minority (40,100) who remained under residential care (categories (b) and (c) in Table I) showed a growth of some 3,000 children between 1972 and 1976. This increase occurred despite a *decrease* in the numbers of children entering residential care and arose because there was an even greater decrease in children leaving, thereby producing a build-up of children in residence.

TABLE I

Children in care at 31 March 1976—Manner of accommodation
(thousands)

	England and Wales				
	1972	1973	1974	1975	1976
Children in care: total	90·6	93·2	95·9	99·1	100·6
Manner of accommodation:					
(a) Boarded out	29·9	29·8	30·7	31·9	33·1
(b) In community homes:					
with observation and assessment facilities	4·2	4·7	4·8	5·3	5·0
with education on the premises	6·8	7·1	6·7	6·2	6·8
others	18·9	19·3	21·4	23·1	23·4
(c) Voluntary homes and hostels	7·2	7·2	6·4	5·0	4·9
(d) Under charge of parent guardian relative or friend	15·2	16·1	16·6	18·0	18·0
(e) Other accommodation	8·3	9·0	9·2	9·6	9·6

Note: Figures may not add to total because of roundings.

B

This gives some indication of the difficulties involved in returning children to their families and to communities. This growth obviously made substantial demands on both capital and staff resources, since if an average number of children per establishment was taken as twenty children it would mean the creation of 150 new establishments in five years. At the same time the proportion of children boarded out has remained stable.

A similar trend is seen when offending behaviour is examined. Tables II and III set a backcloth for the reader, illustrating the growth in offences in the past two decades. These figures show a steady and dramatic growth until 1974. Since then there has been a slight but extremely encouraging drop in the numbers of juveniles and young offenders cautioned or found guilty of an offence. (Home Office, 1977.)

Similar worrying increases in juvenile crime are reported from Europe and North America. For example, in the United States between 1960 and 1975 offences involving property committed by

TABLE II

Males found guilty of, or cautioned for, indictable offences per 100,000 population—England and Wales (Home Office 1977)

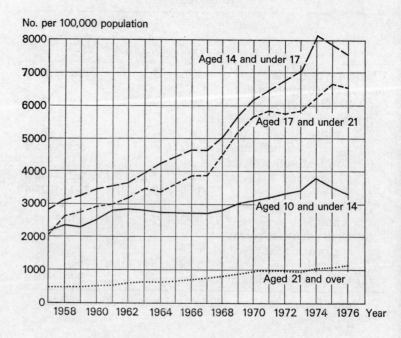

TABLE III

Females found guilty of, or cautioned for, indictable offences per 100,000 population—England and Wales (Home Office 1977)

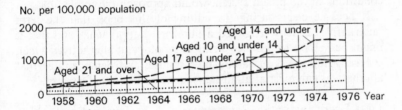

young people under 18 years increased by 132 per cent; of even greater concern, crimes of violence increased by nearly 300 per cent. Although people aged 10–18 years form only 16 per cent of the population they accounted for 43 per cent of the arrests for serious crimes (i.e. Part 1 offences as defined by the FBI, which include murder, robbery, rape, assault, burglary, larceny and taking and driving away a motor vehicle). In the United States approximately one million juveniles came in contact with the criminal justice system last year (1976).

In the United Kingdom the increase in offending behaviour has led to a growth in the number of young people held under custodial conditions. The official figures (Home Office 1976) for the last few years are shown below. Detention centres accept 'young people' between the ages of 14–17 years, and young people between the ages of 15 and 17 years are also accepted for Borstal training, although it should be remembered that both detention centres and Borstal training are primarily for those aged between 17 and 21 years.

TABLE IV

Number of young people receiving custodial sentences excluding those convicted of grave crimes and placed in prison

Year	Number under 17 years sentenced to Detention centre	Number under 17 years sentenced to Borstal training
1969	2,228	818
1974	4,451	1,622
1975	4,793	1,854
1976	5,388	2,008

For adult prisoners, suffice it to say that in October 1976 for the first time ever the adult prison population of England and Wales exceeded 42,000 prisoners, a number which had previously been identified by the Home Secretary as being that point at which conditions in the prison system would approach the intolerable.

It became clear during the editing of this book that the term 'alternative strategy' engulfed a number of approaches and that it might be helpful to produce a simple typology of alternatives which generally follows a hierarchy of response, and demonstrates that alternatives can exist at almost any stage of a criminal career:

(a) Decriminalization—acceptance of behaviour and recognition of legal action as inappropriate.
(b) Non-intervention—acceptance of need for prescribed and limited statutory intervention.
(c) Legitimization—developments in practice aimed at strengthening 'informal' practice.
(d) Radical intervention—attempts to avoid the traditional institutional responses which is seen as damaging.

(a) *Decriminalization.* Recently there have been a number of proposals that certain offences be removed from the statute book, thereby removing the stigma of criminal behaviour from those 'offenders'. This does not necessarily mean that no action would be taken against the offender, but that the offender would instead be put in touch with a more appropriate service than the criminal justice system. Normally it is suggested that offences suitable for 'decriminalization' are the so-called victim-less offences, for example prostitution. In the children's field there is certain behaviour which may bring the child to official notice which arise from the child's position in society and have no parallel in the adult field (e.g. truancy in the U.K. and status offences in the U.S.A.) and these may be more suitably dealt with by other means. Saskatchewan (Chapter 7) provides a very interesting example with the use of peace officers being sent into violent domestic crises rather than the police. This recognizes the fact that most domestic violence is not resolveable or even adequately dealt with by the criminal justice system and that it is more sensible to aim at a reconciliation between the partners than a criminal prosecution.

(b) *Non-intervention.* This heading is used for any procedure that is severely limited beyond the first contact and thereby avoids any prolonged contact between the offender and the criminal justice system. Non-intervention does in fact have an extraordinary long and respectable official history in English law if the power to 'bind over' is seen as non-interventionist measure. Since as far back as the fourteenth century the courts have had the power to 'bind over' an individual whereby in effect they establish a contract with the offender to take no action, if in return the offender is of good behaviour. A more recent development within the courts system has been the conditional discharge whereby the offender is discharged subject to no reappearances within a prescribed time limit. If a person subject to a conditional discharge is convicted of a further offence during the period of the order, he is liable to be sentenced for the original offence as well as the fresh offence. The last decade has seen an expanded adoption of non-interventionist procedures. As Allison Morris (Chapter 3) shows, the panel system in Scotland has made extensive use of the disposal of 'no-action'. She goes on to illustrate the increased use in England and Wales of police cautioning with first offenders who admit to being guilty.

(c) *Legitimization.* Some alternative measures are in fact a strengthening of current procedures and practice; very often the method has been employed for some time, but new legislation allows the idea to be generalized and resources made available. Before the intermediate treatment attachment to a supervision order or its equivalent existed, some supervisors chose to base their supervision on an activity programme (see Chapter 4). Intermediate treatment as provided by the Children and Young Persons Act (1969) accepted such procedures as good practice and hoped by legislation to generalize and strengthen such good practice. A parallel exists with community service orders. For some time both the public and professionals had believed there was a role for reparation, other than by a compensation order made by the court, in the treatment of offenders. There were a number of ad hoc schemes aimed at reparation, a number actually based on the prisons, used outside working parties to help on various community projects. The creation of community service orders (Chapter 9) allowed the court to direct an individual offender to make reparation by working unpaid in the community.

(d) *Radical intervention to develop alternatives to incarceration.* This is the biggest category of alternatives. They are developed because of the widely held belief amongst professionals that incarceration is not an effective way of dealing with offending. It is not effective when the offender is a product of a disrupted social environment and nothing is resolved by removing him from that environment for a period in an institution. At the end of his sentence he returns to his environment, is subject to the same pressures and reoffends. Moreover, it is held that placing an offender in an institution where he lives with other offenders, far from helping him, gives the opportunity of learning more about crime, and anti-social attitudes become reinforced. This is a point widely understood and accepted by the public.

Alternatives aim at providing a system which avoids the brutalizing effects of large institutions, breaks down the anti-social subculture into smaller and less cohesive units and keeps the offender in contact with his community. Chapter 5 describes the attempts of one local authority in England to use professional foster parents to help disruptive adolescents who would normally go to an institution. Chapter 6 describes the attempt of one American state to manage its juvenile offenders without recourse to institutions at all, and Chapter 8 describes a new careers project set up by a voluntary body aimed at offering young offenders a more satisfactory and socially productive experience than incarceration.

However, we hope to do more than just describe alternative strategies and draw some conclusions as to how alternatives arise and are implemented, and what sort of structures make for successful alternative strategies. To this end, a simple analysis is offered to the stages through which the alternative policies pass. This 'guide' is drawn from the ensuing chapters, wherein a much more detailed and academic description is given. The inception of alternatives passes through a number of phases and processes which seem to be common to all. These phases which have profound implications for the nature and structure of professional social work agencies are described in detail in order to throw light on a shadowy aspect of social policy.

The first phase may seem extraordinary given the complexity of modern bureaucratic states. It is *the appearance of a crusader*. For nearly every alternative strategy given in this book it is possible to identify an individual or small group of individuals who set out to challenge and change the prevailing system. In each case the individual acts as a catalyst by creating a crusade and polarizing opinion around himself or herself. Such a crusade is obviously easier in the case of children or young offenders when it is possible to create a public image of the offending child as being the product of a bad home, abused by the system and a hostage to fortune whose only hope of salvation lies with the crusader. However, similar tactics have been developed with adult offenders—for example by characterizing them as inadequate drunks who are more unfortunate than dangerous.

The development of a sympathetic stereotype of the offender is crucial to the next stage in the development of alternatives. After the crusader emerges and begins to polarize opinion he turns to *the media* which he uses extensively to convince the public of the strengths of the alternative. In the illustrations presented the crusader has been successful in winning the support of the media and has been of such a character as to be able to handle the media personally. He misses few opportunities to promote his ideas by public debate. He takes part in phone-in programmes and articles in the popular press. It is important to highlight this because it is in this way that the crusader argues his case directly to the public. Therefore he keeps the argument simple, polarizes the issues and uses uncomplicated, emotive case studies. The crusader normally avoids protracted professional debate in the learned journals, thereby avoiding the statistical argument of scientific debate. Often this avoidance is essential since the alternative strategy will have few results on which to base any academic argument.

Once the media has taken up and promoted the alternative a new phase of development is entered which is characterized by *the establishment of myths*. Because of the very nature of the crusader's appeal he generates a great number of myths within the professional social work agencies. Many of these myths will be antagonistic to the project but a number will be sympathetic. The sympathetic myths will attract a number of like-minded, normally radically inclined, professional workers with a high motivation to develop different ways of working with their clients. This core of workers will be highly committed and supportive to the alternative and consequently prepared to invest a great deal of enthusiasm and energy in making it work. This investment is essential. If the project is to be successfully taken through the invariable crises which arise, the staff must have a committed belief in the project to maintain morale.

After a limited period many of the core staff will move on to new posts and *generalization* occurs. Generalization gains momentum as other professional authorities recognize the attention captured by the crusader and after a respectable period to insure that the alternative is not too extreme to become counterproductive, other authorities begin to take up the idea to demonstrate they are as progressive as the initiator. These later authorities will often recruit staff from the initial project, thereby accelerating the bandwagon.

However, at some point the alternative projects come into conflict with the established professional authorities. Some alternatives are defeated by the confrontation, while others manage to survive, albeit in an adjusted fashion. The reason why conflict with the professional authorities arises is simple since by definition any alternative project is a move away from professionalization and many are indeed attacks on the supposed expertise of professionals. Each of the alternatives outlined in this book suggests that the layman has much if not more to offer the offender than the professional social worker. Nancy Hazel (Chapter 5) suggests that motivated lay couples with reasonable professional support are able to help and modify the behaviour of the most disturbed and disruptive adolescents. In Massachusetts a firm belief in the 'deprofessionalization' of the services was developed, with the professionals charged only with the monitoring of services. Similar implications arise from John Harding's chapter (Chapter 9) in which it is suggested that offenders placed in a situation working alongside lay people need only minimal professional supervision to achieve changes in behaviour.

It is also possible to draw out from the examples of alternatives presented a number of features which are essential if alternatives are to be successfully tied into existing strategies. The first of these is *the networking of services*. No alternative will achieve success unless it is built into a network of services to which it can pass clients and from which it can receive clients and support. The successful fostering scheme described is linked with residential and observation and assessment facilities. The latter are essential since they are the intake point to the system and their commitment is vital if the alternative is to have any clients passed to it. Similarly if the foster parents are to survive they need to feel part of an established system which can offer some support at times of crisis which often takes the form of 'back-up' from a residential facility which can give some respite by taking the foster child 'in' for a few days. In the table in Chapter 4 on the range of intermediate treatment facilities, David Thorpe shows the way in which the facilities will interact, providing lesser or greater attention to the young person as required. Andrew Rutherford makes a similar point in his chapter on Massachusetts, stressing the way the offender needs to be passed across a network of services until he 'fits' a facility rather than the traditional strategy of passing the offender upwards through a tariff system ranging from supervision in the community to secure incarceration.

The second requisite for integration of an alternative is *flexibility of funding*. This is often the most difficult to achieve since authority budgets are based on institutions which are relatively static organizations allowing long range forecasting and estimates. Alternatives require flexibility, since they often involve short life projects which require an injection of cash for a short period and then disbandment. Moreover, alternatives often require unorthodox payments—for example a 'salary' to a foster parent or part-time lay worker who is not a staff member, the purchase of equipment at short notice or payment of tuition fees for an offender. All of these unorthodox payments raise budgeting difficulties.

Third, the authorities, central or local government, must be committed to the alternatives and to restricting or at least holding steady, the development of institutions. This is essential for several reasons. It polarizes the issues and strengthens the staff of the alternative in their resolve to make it work since they have no 'way out'. If the institution option is retained there is an inevitable imbalance in budgeting, and resources are continually 'bled off' to the institution, while the alternative has to compete for resources against its established opponents. Finally, if the institutional option is removed, a 'deep-end' strategy is ensured: the alternative project has to take on and cope with the most difficult and disruptive client. This means that the alternative does not merely draw into the welfare net a number of clients who would otherwise not have been identified and processed. The danger of merely drawing into the alternative a new population of less troublesome clients is amply demonstrated in the chapters on diversion, intermediate treatment, Saskatchewan and community service orders. Moreover, if a 'deep-end' strategy is adopted, then it can counteract the 'drift' to the easy end, a process whereby a facility designed to cater for 'difficult clients' gradually accepts the less difficult.

This drift seems to happen with all client groups and with all social disorders. The young people's secure units and mental hospitals wish to admit only those clients with whom there is some hope of success—an understandable aim but one which guarantees the admission of the less difficult client. By the same token, intermediate treatment schemes show a greater willingness to deal with those children 'at risk' rather than known juvenile offenders. To avoid this pitfall the alternative must adopt a 'deep-end' strategy and accept the most difficult group, thereby demonstrating its ability to work with all the 'easier' clients in the spectrum.

Any book concerned with offenders and society is inevitably

concerned with justice—both natural justice and legal justice. It is hoped that this book makes recommendations which are just both to the offender and to the community. Justice to the offender is attempting to offer him an opportunity to change his behaviour and develop alternative adjustments to his life style while avoiding 'double think' and brutalization. But equally important is justice to the community in offering it protection, freedom from exaggerated claims and value for money.

Views expressed or implied are those of the author, and do not necessarily reflect those of the Department.

CHAPTER TWO

Education and the Prevention of Juvenile Delinquency

DAVID REYNOLDS AND DEE JONES

> It is the great weakness of most schools that they so seldom
> trouble to analyse the reasons for their failure. Why is it that
> the school is not blamed for a child's delinquency more fre-
> quently than his home?
>
> Sir Cyril Burt, 1952

We live in a society characterized by a dramatic and continuing
rise in the educational and social problems of its young people.
Rates of juvenile delinquency, drug abuse, maladjustment, school
violence and educational failure are widely believed to be rising
rapidly (Cox and Dyson, 1975). Even allowing for the natural
paranoia of an older generation who are alarmed at how children
are growing up to be different from themselves and even allowing
for the fact that simple statistics may exaggerate the extent of this
rise, there is rightful concern both in this country and in other
industrialized societies like the United States (Bronfenbrenner, 1975)
both as to what the causes of this rise may be and also as to what
practical policies can be followed to deal with these problems.

For many years now, we have attempted to combat these problems in a remarkably stereotyped and ineffective way. Like the
physician who, upon seeing that his drugs are not working, simply
increases their dosage, we have simply gone on increasing the
amount of education that we give young people, assuming that the
reasons for their delinquency, rebellion or maladjustment is that
they are not getting enough of this 'good' thing. More and more

young people now spend more and more time at school. More and more teachers employ ever more sophisticated examples of educational gadgetry to teach ever more attractively packaged courses in the attempt to interest students once they are there. For those who somehow manage to resist the attractions of the schools, an ever increasing army of educational welfare officers, school-based social workers and educational psychologists now exists to 'help'—or rather force—them to adjust to the demands that the schools make of them. Education we believe to be something good for children—and we believe that their educational and social problems will be ameliorated by more of it.

However, it is my contention that, far from being an effective antidote to juvenile delinquency, aspects of our educational system in general and particular aspects of schools within that system are actively functioning not to *prevent* delinquency, but to create it. Although we shall see that the reasons why society has backed the school as an antidote to juvenile delinquency are entirely understandable, the policies of social engineering that have been followed in our schools to combat young people's problems represent only minor adjustments of an educational system; and part of its basic structure is bound to continue to produce stresses, strains, alienation, and therefore delinquency, in some of its young consumers. The chapter finally aims to review those structural features of many schools that existing reforms have left substantially untouched and concludes by discussing the implications of these views for current educational, social and correctional policies concerned with the welfare of young people.

Why Prevention By Education?

The principal reason why our society—or, more properly, elite groups within our society—have been drawn towards the school as an antidote to the problems of young people is a very prevalent belief that schools possess great power to socialize their charges and to 'mould' young minds, a power that has been emphasized by governments from the Victorian era right up to the present day.

For the new Victorian middle class, for example, education was to impose habits of restraint, punctuality, discipline and obedience on a young labour force that had been unaccustomed to such necessary capitalist values in their formerly rural society. Victorian Blue Books, inspectors' reports, government enquiries and philanthropists' tracts were evidence of an obsession with the condition of poor children. As Johnson (1977) notes, in his discussion of the 'monitorial' system of British education in the Nineteenth Century,

> Monitorialists tended to speak a common language. The key phrases emphasised restraint—'check upon delinquency'; 'enforcing the observance of religious and moral principles'; 'the laws of the school'; 'the Will of God'; 'accustom them to obedience under control and command'. Or habit: 'many beneficial habits of an indelible nature'; 'steady habits of industry and integrity'; 'a right bias to their minds'. Or order (the product of habit and restraint): 'the children inured to habits of order and subordination'. The analogies used to describe the working of the school were often mechanical: 'the whole machine'; 'a grand intellectual factory'. Or military: 'non-commissioned officers selected without trouble, and serving without pay' (Bell of his monitors), and Lancaster again: 'the firmness, promptness and decision attendant on military order'. The similes employed to express the effects of education were medical, purgative, even sanitary: 'vaccinate the rising generation'; 'the alternative medicine'; 'as a preventative against the poison of infidelity'; and, finally, of a school's influence on its neighbourhood: 'as a salutary stream pervades every part of the parish'.

The teacher was, therefore, to be 'in loco parentis', as a substitute for the natural parents of the child, parents whose influence was seen as inimical to the foundations of public and moral order. The school was to be a sort of island set in a sea of social problems —its aim to 'civilize' whole neighbourhoods. The goals of these institutions and of their personnel were unambiguously presented, without any modern rhetoric about 'treatment', 'helping', or 'therapy'. As the Whig T. S. Macaulay put it in 1847,

> I say that all are agreed that it is the sacred duty of every government to take effectual measures for securing the persons and property of the community and that the government which neglects its duty is unfit for its situation. This being once admitted, I ask, can it be denied that the education of the common people is the most effectual means of protecting persons and property? (West, 1970).

Although few of the results of mass education would seem to

justify the governmental faith in schools as a 'solution' to youthful problems, this same belief in the power of the education system to socialize the young into acceptable codes of behaviour is still in evidence in many contemporary government reports and reflects present-day government thinking. For example, the Robbins Report on Higher Education (1963) stated, 'There are, of course, also important social and political benefits of education which accrue to the population as a whole—a better informed electorate, more culturally alive neighbourhoods, a healthier and *less crime-prone population*, and so on.' (Appendix 4, Part 3, para. 54, italics supplied.) In spite of the evidence that when the school leaving age went up to 15 in 1948 the peak year for juvenile delinquency moved in step from 14 to 15 as well, the Crowther Report (1959) commented that there was nothing in the existing state of affairs to make anyone doubt the value of being at school. 'The delinquency may arise' it blandly reported, 'not because boys are at school but because they are not at school enough'. (para. 63.)

Quite apart from the attraction of the educational system as a means of social control of young people through its built-in 'hidden curriculum' of values and expectations, more cynical motives may be discerned behind continued governmental enthusiasm for schooling as the antidote to many diverse youthful problems. It is possible that enthusiasm for education may simply reflect a government desire to appear to be taking action on social problems, action which has the advantage of leaving untouched the grosser inequalities by our social and economic system. Governments may also have taken shelter in the cry of 'more education' in simple despair of any other solution. As Halsey (1972, p. 8) notes, reflecting this view,

... there has been a tendency to treat education as the waste paper basket of social policy—a repository for dealing with social problems where solutions are uncertain or where there is a disinclination to wrestle with them seriously. Such problems are prone to be dubbed educational and turned over to the schools to solve.

A further reason why many have tried to use the educational system as an agency of problem prevention is the manifest ineffectiveness of most of the current 'treatments' applied to delinquency and other criminal behaviour. Perhaps because such treatment has been applied late in the lives of offenders or perhaps because of a continuing rigid custodial philosophy, the 'success' rates of approved schools has been woefully low. The percentage of offenders who were *not* recidivist (reconvicted within three years of release) dropped steadily in the decades after the war until it reached 43 per cent by the late 1960s. (Rose, 1967, p. 86.) Rates of success in borstals have conventionally been regarded as being even worse (Rose, op. cit.) Even in spite of the advent of community homes, an increased amount of secure provision and of better assessment facilities for delinquent adolescents, there is no evidence to suggest that the effectiveness of conventional institutions has been increased. Barbara Wootton's forceful point made almost 20 years ago still holds true: 'We have to face the disagreeable paradox that experience of what are intended to be reformative institutions actually increases the probability of future lapses into criminality' (1959, p. 69). Early prevention of delinquency by the educational system can hardly be less successful than later attempts at 'curing' the problem through conventional correctionalist methods and has the further advantage of being substantially cheaper.

Furthermore, arguments that favour the use of the educational system as a form of social as well as academic training have been strengthened by the growing importance of the school in the lives of adolescents and by its growing influence over the character of their later lives. Following the decline of organized religion, the close-knit communities and the extended family networks of many working-class people, and the consequent reduction in their importance as agencies of socialization, the 'moral vacuum' created by the increasing absence of these factors has increasingly become filled by the school. As Husan (1974, p. 13) notes, 'Parallel with the schools' mission in terms of both substance and time its institutional character has become strengthened. As already indicated, it is no longer responsible merely for the inculcation of certain knowledge and skills—even though these tasks have of themselves been enlarged with the advent of new subject matter'.

Quite apart from the increased importance of the school in a modern industrial society, manipulating the formal organization of schooling to prevent problems like delinquency has the added advantage of at least being theoretically possible. Schools—as society's imposition upon children and adolescents—are changeable in a way that the families and communities of the working class are not. Since we have no real evidence that social work intervention can really stop families from behaving as their own culture and immediate environment predispose them to, the malleable, changeable institution that is the school has added attractions as an area for social engineering and for policy operation.

But the final—and most important—reason that explains why education has increasingly been given the role of 'antidote' to the problems of delinquency is the mounting evidence that children who are delinquents are also very often school failures (West, 1969, 1973). Although this association between delinquency and educational failure is supported by much research, the precise explanation for the association remains rather debatable. It could be simply that delinquents, being of lower intelligence and being initially more maladjusted, tend to end up as school failures also. In this case, the school failure merely reflects the initial predisposition of the delinquents, and the schools have little independent effect of their own. But a further—more likely—explanation is that the school failure itself is an independent influence on, and cause of, delinquency—as Rhodes and Reiss (1969, p. 13) argue,

> It would stretch the facts too far to argue that all persons react to school failure by choosing some form of deviant adaptation. It would require a further stretch of the imagination that those who make a deviant adaptation must choose a form which would result in their being apprehended and officially defined as delinquents. One can only argue that lack of success in school will provide an additional source of stress and that some persons will react to it in such a way as to increase their life chances of being labelled as a delinquent, without specifying the exact nature of the process.

Recent analysis by Little (1977, p. 66) of rates of maladjustment and scholastic failure in inner city schools also points to the same conclusion:

> On this analysis, social factors cause poor performance which in turn may generate maladjustment: further, regardless of social factors, poor educational performance is seen as a cause rather than a consequence of maladjustment.

American research evidence too supports the view that school failure can generate delinquency. To Hirschi (1969) school failure affects the commitment of the adolescent to the school and to adult institutions in general; to Frease (1972) school failure affects adolescent self image. For Stinchcombe (1964, p. 179)

... rebellious behaviour is largely a reaction to the school itself and to its promises, not a failure of the family or community ... For a large part of its population, especially the adolescent who will enter the male working class or the female candidates for early marriage, the school has nothing to offer.

Goldberg (in the President's Commission on Law Enforcement and Administration of Justice, 1967, p. 230) clearly summarizes the available American research connecting delinquency to school failure when she concludes that

Early difficulty in mastering the basic intellectual skills which the schools and thus the broader society demands leads to defeat and failure, a developing negative self image, rebellion against the increasingly defeating school experiences, a search for status outside the school together with an active resentment against the society which the school represents. The child early finds status and protection in the street and the gang which requires none of the skills which are needed in school but makes heavy use of the kinds of survival skills which he learned in his early home and street experiences.

In view of the available British and American evidence that links educational failure with the generation of delinquency, changes within the educational system to decrease its failure rates, to increase its pupils' commitment and to decrease pupil alienation, have therefore appeared a very attractive policy for the prevention of delinquency.

Some Conventional Responses

So far we have argued that, for a number of highly understandable reasons, governments have been drawn to various changes within the education system as a means of preventing juvenile delinquency and other adolescent problems. Governments—and virtually all other pressure groups from the Alcoholics Anonymous to the Jesuits—have seen the potential of the system as a 'moulder' of children. Intervention through the schools can occur early, is preventive, and therefore is an attractive, rather than patently alternative to later ineffective 'cures'. Schools are malleable and changeable, unlike the families and communities of the working class.

c

School failure, furthermore, appears an important cause of delinquency in itself.

Spurred on by the success which school-based intervention promises, policy has been of two main kinds. First, English governments have been largely concerned to give children more education by means of the raising of the school leaving age in 1973, by increasing expenditure and by reorganizing education on comprehensive lines. Second, quite apart from these general policies, specific educational reforms and innovations have been introduced within the expanded system in order to enhance its delinquency preventing potential. That these reforms represent little structural alteration to the system and that they fail to deal with those aspects of the system that have delinquency-producing potential, will become rapidly obvious.

The first example of an innovation within the educational system that is to 'prevent' juvenile delinquency is reform concerned with increasing inter-professional communication. Pupil problems like delinquency, it is argued, simply reflect the inability of either the teaching or social work professions to work together and to pool knowledge in the interest of achieving beneficial change in the character of the child. A recent Department of Health and Social Security collaborative exercise between the Education and Social Services Departments of South Glamorgan County Council provides a classic example of this type of supposed solution. Entitled *Working Together for Children and Their Families*, the exercise was introduced by the Parliamentary Under-Secretary of State for Wales, Barry Jones, who argued that

> Children in trouble, disturbed children, delinquent children ... these are a source of concern for schools and social services departments, for teachers and social workers... Difficult behaviour, lack of interest, truancy, minor offences, vandalism, drinking, drugs, violence, these are problems which may arise at home, in the classroom, and in society, and we can only tackle them by pooling our experience... It has become more and more evident that the role of teacher and social worker do and indeed should complement each other.

The final report of this unique departmental exercise is filled with suggestions as to the best way of 'helping' the truant, the delinquent and the troublesome—better communication between professionals, standardization of records, better record-keeping, common in-service training, more pre-school education, early preventive work and even the development of luncheon clubs as an arena in which informal contact between professionals may be made. But the latent assumption throughout the report is that the problem child is a problem because of personal, individual pathology in the child himself, or in his family background: he is to be 'helped' to 'adjust' to the realities of the educational system. Whether the educational system *itself* needs readjusting to help the child and whether the system may be aggravating his individual behaviour is rarely discussed.

Precisely the same problem arises with the second of our attempts to prevent delinquency by minor modification of the educational system—which is the appointment of school counsellors to an increasing number of our schools. Most presentations of counselling theory emphasize its developmental purpose—Hamblin (1974), for example, states that it should encourage (i) the growth of self-acceptance in pupils, (ii) the development of controls from inside the pupil rather than continuing his reliance upon external influences and pressures, and (iii) the learning of relevant and competent coping strategies and of problem solving techniques which are both realistic and viable for the pupils. Hamblin goes on to emphasize that school counselling as an activity is client-centred and not school-centred. However, research shows that schools do not expect client-centred counselling: they wish to resocialize their deviants and minimize their pupil wastage (Murgatroyd, 1976). The pupils see counsellors as those who check the attendance registers, report truants, find lost property and tell you how to behave (op. cit.) The counsellors themselves see their role as that of promoting agency, rather than individual, needs which may lead them merely to become agents of social control within the school.

Traditional methods of dealing with truancy provide a classic example of the use of school counsellors as part of an institutional 'soft machine'. (Soft machine is a term used in an attempt to differentiate between two possible approaches to deviant behaviour in the school. The first, more traditional approach, would be to punish the deviant behaviour in the hope of eradicating it, e.g. caning or extra work for truancy; the second is the 'soft' approach of talking the child out of the behaviour, e.g. counselling. However, both approaches accept that the school as an institution is faultless and the child deviant, and neither examine the school in order to see whether major structural changes are needed to reduce deviancy. Thus a 'soft machine' is apparently more radical and liberal but in fact has the same objectives as the traditional more punitive approach.) Although truancy may be the rational reaction of a psychologically normal child to an institution which is not using his talents (Reynolds and Murgatroyd, 1974), most counsellors tend merely to attempt to get the truants to attend, rather than attempt to see if the child is being mis-used by the institution (Murgatroyd, 1975). The theory of counselling as a client-based activity is difficult to square with its use to minimize pupil deviance within schools. It appears to be simply a school-based, school-centred attempt to solve school problems.

These are but two examples of conventional approaches to the problems of pupil deviance and delinquency which represent little change in—or worse—further reinforcement of the structure of the educational system. Other examples include the detection of 'at-risk' children who can be adjusted to fit the needs of the schools (Davie, 1975); the minor modification of the curriculum to make it more attractive to the disadvantaged (Schools Council, 1970); the development of social care teams within schools; and a large increase in the provision of educational psychologists and child guidance clinics to deal with the problems referred to them by the schools. These developments, together with the increasing use of sanctuaries, special units, schools-within-schools, and free schools, are typical of our conventional current responses to the problems of young people within the educational system.

These policies, although seemingly diverse, have one basic theme in common—they see the problems of delinquency, deviance or maladjustment as caused by pathology that is internal to the child, his family, his neighbourhood or his culture. Their aim is to fit the deviant—who is malfunctioning in some way—back into the school system that is assumed to be functioning properly. The child is seen as maladjusted to the demands of the school system. The system is not seen as maladjusted to the needs of the child.

Over the years, a vast quantity of research has accumulated that appears to support the importance of the child's own personality, family background, character and intelligence as factors that determine his delinquency and deviance. Studies of truancy (Tyerman, 1968) educational retardation and maladjustment (Davie, 1972), vandalism (Kellmer Pringle, 1973) and delinquency (Douglas, 1968), all show the importance of these home factors, yet most of this body of research has been designed to do exactly that. Working within the paradigm of conventional educational psychology, pupil problems are 'explained away' by reference to latent personality disorders, family malfunctioning or parental effects on their children's development.

Research on truancy provides a classic example of this 'individualising' in attempts to explain what may in fact be institutional problems. Although we now know from studies on this subject that low social class, low intelligence and 'school phobic' personality may put certain children at a higher risk of becoming truants, it seems reasonable to ask whether or not the organization of their schools, the quality of teacher/pupil interaction and the system of rewards and punishments that schools use can affect children's levels of truancy. On this question, existing studies of truancy can provide little information, since most of them neglect to study in any detail the schools that truants are meant to attend; a large amount of data is usually amassed on the quality of the plumbing in children's houses and on their parents' values and characters, yet little attention is paid to studying the schools from which the truants absent themselves. Since children spend much of their time in schools and since the school is the first significant area of authority relationships that the child enters outside the home, this neglect by researchers of the school situation of truant children seems frankly disturbing.

This neglect is carried to absurd lengths when researchers consider children's stated reasons for truancy; the reasons they give are not seen as valid explanations in their own right but merely as reflections of some psychological abnormality. Some of Tyerman's group of truants, for example, told him that they were truant from school because of fear of the teacher and, in some cases, fear of being given the stick. Instead of accepting that these fears may in fact be a possible cause of the boys' behaviour, Tyerman comments that 'These reasons may to some extent be valid but it is unwise to accept truants' excuses at their face value. The limits of self-deception are wide and it is easier to blame other people than oneself. Parents and children look for scapegoats and teachers are often chosen' (Tyerman, 1958).

It would seem, therefore, that the case for conventional, individual-centred strategies to minimize pupil problems and wastage is supported by a vast body of research, the great majority of which suggests that it is factors within the pupils themselves and within their home environments that cause their problems. It is generally assumed that the school is not a causal factor in itself, yet little of this research investigates whether pupil problems are institutionally —rather than individually—produced. It seems that the ideological belief that the school is not a causal factor in the generation of deviance has been responsible for the structuring of research which, concentrating as it does on investigating only the deviant's home and family backgrounds, reinforces the initial ideology that created the research in the first place and the policy measures which follow from it.

A Maladjusted System?

Three major sociological theories, however, hold that a crucial role in the generation of delinquency is played by the education systems of advanced industrial societies. The first of these theories, advanced in different forms by Cohen (1955) and by Cloward and Ohlin (1961), holds that delinquency results from blockages upon the attainment of highly valued success goals. The educational system and the teachers that staff it may, because of their middle-class assumptions as to what constitutes the 'good pupil', deny working-class pupils status within the schools because these pupils have not been socialized to fulfil the status requirements of middle-class society and its schools. Their chances of obtaining the success goals that they wish for through the schools are therefore much reduced —their delinquency may be a response to their 'status frustration'. Schools may contribute to this process—and thereby generate delinquency—by tracking certain students into lower streams, thereby increasing the likelihood that they will adopt illegitimate norms.

The second theory holds that delinquency can result from a basic lack of commitment to conventional middle-class norms and community behaviour, a theory that has been put forward by Miller (1958) in the United States and, with certain variations, by Mays (1964) in Britain. Delinquency is seen simply as a manifestation of lower-class culture—working-class adolescents have as their focal concerns trouble, toughness, excitement and smartness. Mays' classic study of Liverpool argues a similar case for seeing delinquency as the 'natural' behaviour of a large section of working-class youth— he concludes that '... delinquency is not so much a symptom of maladjustment as of adjustment to a sub-culture in conflict with the culture of the city as a whole' (op. cit.). Sugarman (1967) too notes how so-called youth culture is the culture of the non-mobile working class—many of these children accept the role of teenager which is in many ways an inversion of the official pupil role:

In place of deferred gratification it puts an emphasis on spontaneous gratification or hedonism. Similarly, it repudiates the idea of youth being subordinate to adults.... In conflict with the school is a rival view of life which is held fairly self-consciously but not very explicitly by a fair number of pupils in common.

Similar versions of this theory of 'cultural conflict' between working-class pupils and middle-class schools have been applied to the working-class child and the grammar school (Jackson & Marsden, 1962), the child and the secondary modern school (Partridge, 1968), and to the 'battle' or conflict between working-class pupils and middle-class teachers, who have been called by one proponent of this view 'the steward of the whole middle-class consciousness' (Searle, 1972).

School practices that may be responsible for the working-class child's alienation and therefore for his delinquency include a non-relevant curriculum, the middle-class ethos of the schools, teacher perceptions of working-class children as ineducable, the language differences between teacher and pupil and, of course, many of the processes of 'blocking off' legitimate opportunities to gain status within the school that the first theory also describes. According to this theory, adolescent commitment to school is low at the outset—the 'alien' world of school makes it lower and thus generates delinquency.

The third theory that locates the roots of juvenile delinquency in aspects of children's school experience concentrates on the inter-action of pupils and teachers, the treatment of pupils by teachers and the 'labelling' effect by which teacher judgments may have the effects of reinforcing and confirming delinquent and problematic pupil behaviour. In this perspective, the school is seen as having certain rules, and rule breaking is seen as deviance. If this rule breaking is followed by the imputation of the label 'deviant' to a pupil by formal or informal sanctions, the consequence may be perhaps a change in the pupil's self identity. Labelled as a within-school troublemaker, he may begin to reconstruct his identity as an outside-of-school delinquent. The deviant may then enter on a moral career in which the school punishes him, he changes his self conception, the school views him differently, he acts differently, and in which he is further confirmed in his deviance by the school's sanctions. Crucially, if the school, by its treatment of the deviant, 'blocks off' any chance of his attempting to re-enter the conventional world of the school, then it is likely to increase the chances of the deviant's adopting illegitimate values.

Research that uses this 'interactionist' viewpoint includes that of Cicourel and Kitsuse (1963) who argue that the typing of certain pupils into the category of 'problem pupil' launches the child into a certain moral career within the school, and that of Werthman (1967) who suggests that when teachers assess their pupils on what the pupils perceive as unfair grounds (like length of hair), the students refuse to recognize the school's authority. Deviance, delinquency and pupil rule-breaking can therefore be generated by the 'typing' of pupils in this way.

Although they differ in the emphasis they place on different factors, all these three theories hold that, as Hargreaves notes (1967):

> There is a real sense in which the school can be regarded as a generating factor of delinquency. Although the aims and efforts of the teachers are directed towards deleting such tendencies, the organization of the school and the influence on sub-cultural development unintentionally foster delinquent values.

Whether or not the adolescent starts school with high aspirations and finds them blocked (theory one) or starts school with already low aspirations and low commitment (theory two), the schools will tend—because of their ethos and their functions—to reject the working-class child. Faced by an irrelevant curriculum, hostile teachers, a lack of payoff from effort and the experience of failure, the child will begin to dissociate (Downes, 1966) himself from the school. Increasing stigmatization and labelling within the school and the reaction of the school organization to his increasing deviance (theory three), cut off the delinquent from obtaining status from conventional sources. He may turn instead to gaining status from within his peer group by the commitment of delinquent acts, which further reinforce his rejection of conventional values. By a process of deviancy amplification, the pupil's primary deviation is confirmed and becomes secondary deviation.

This picture of the school delinquent's moral career is derived from a synthesis of these three quite similar theories and seems, on first analysis, eminently plausible. Yet, it must be said that we have no real scientific evidence that it is correct and that the features which we have mentioned as important within the school are so in reality. As C. M. Phillipson (1971), writing on the same theme, argues: '... sociologists seem to be operating with highly abstract models of the school which rest on their intuitive hunches about what schools are really like.'

A further point, apart from the absence of rigorous empirical study of the school in these three theoretical positions, is that we are still operating with the implicit assumption that all schools of a particular type have the same effects on pupil delinquency. To quote Phillipson again,

> The idea that there may be considerable differences between overtly similar schools, that some schools may facilitate and others hinder the drift into delinquency does not seem to have occurred to writers on delinquency (op. cit.).

Thus, the links between school experience and delinquency, even though plausible, appear to rest on merely descriptive studies.

The reasons for the absence of such research are complex and are dealt with more fully elsewhere (Reynolds and Jones, 1977). In part, this reflects the belief mentioned earlier that schools only solve adolescent problems, do not generate them. The organizations that control research workers' access to the schools have, not surprisingly, viewed research into individual schools and their 'delinquency proneness' as a threat. Important work by Michael Power into differences among the delinquency rates of Tower Hamlet secondary schools was stopped by the National Union of Teachers before he could find out the reasons for the differences (Power, 1967, 1972). The theoretical framework that would permit a sociology of the school is also clearly absent. Furthermore, most educational researchers (Jencks, 1972) agree that the individual school is not a great determinant of the academic or social quality of its output of children and that the important determinants of educability lie outside the control of the educational system. In spite of the many criticisms of this body of work (for example, Dyer, 1968), most educational researchers do not believe that the educational system does anything more than *reflect* the differences that are imposed on children by other environmental factors and by the general system of social stratification.

The Delinquent School

We have so far argued that conventional approaches to the prevention of delinquency have merely involved the throwing of more resources at our schools and some minor modifications in their functioning which makes it easier to 're-socialize' the problem and delinquent pupils that they are faced with. Although the great majority of the research work reinforces the view that family background and vaguely defined 'social deprivation' are the causes of pupil problems, we have noted three theories which argue that the problem may be caused by the ethos, structure and processes of our secondary schools: in short, that the school system is maladjusted to the needs of our children. However, research which would confirm the independent effect of the school in producing delinquency and other pupil problems appears to be absent.

Only relatively recently a small body of knowledge has begun to gather which does suggest both that the school system itself may be an important influence on whether pupils drift towards delinquency and that there are identifiable factors within certain schools which actively facilitate the process.

The first of these studies was the important work of Michael Power which has been already mentioned. He showed wide variations—from 0·8 per cent to 17·0 per cent per annum—in the incidence of delinquency (defined as a guilty court appearance) in secondary modern schools. These variations among the schools could not be explained by the size of the schools or by the age of their school buildings. More importantly, they were substantially independent of the delinquency rate of the schools' catchment areas (the district or zone from which a school's population is drawn). Power's suggestion was that some schools were actively promoting— and others preventing—pupil deviance and delinquency.

Rutter's (1973) work in London primary schools also suggests that there is something within the organization of certain schools that is associated with low rates of educational attainment and high rates of behavioural deviance amongst their children, a conclusion that is echoed by Gath, who has revealed large differences among schools in their delinquency rates and child guidance referral rates (1972). These differences between schools are, furthermore, remarkably consistent over the years.

Over the past five years, work in South Wales concentrated on a group of nine secondary modern schools has revealed large differences in the delinquency rates of the nine schools, whether such a rate is the proportion of children who are *first* offenders per annum or is the total number of offences that the children at the school accumulate per annum. (See Table V.)

These differences in the delinquency rates of the schools are consistent over time. They are also closely associated with differences in the schools' attendance rate (r = −0·579) and academic

TABLE V

Delinquency rates for boys at secondary modern sc

School	First offenders per 100 boy risk years	Number of offenders 100 boy risk years
	%	%
A	10·5	13·0
B	8·6	13·2
C	8·3	9·6
D	8·1	12·0
E	7·4	8·9
F	7·2	8·8
G	5·2	6·6
H	4·5	5·8
I	3·8	4·4

Product Moment Correlation = 0·942 (significant at 1% level).

attainment rate (r=−0·526) (see Table VI). Such differences in the output of the schools are not explicable by the social class of the schools' catchment areas or by the academic quality of the pupil intake to the schools, as Table VII shows (for further details see Reynolds, 1976, 1977).

Since it appears that the schools of our area may have an independent effect in generating delinquency and other pupil problems, do we know what it is about the schools that can so dramatically affect the social and academic development of its pupils? Over the past three years, a programme of research has been undertaken in eight of the nine schools in an attempt to find out what it is about their schools that may make their children so different and deviant. Apart from the collection of routine data on the resources, rules and organization of each school, this work has included interviews with head teachers and staffs and assessments of the social climate of the schools, the system of rewards and punishments used, the quality of the teaching, and the type of pupil (and teacher) subculture to be found in each regime. Further important insights into the schools' operations have come from the observation of their day-to-day functioning conducted over two years, by the writer and by a specially trained participant observer. This observer—who was not told the relative success rates of each school—spent a considerable time in each school taking lessons, observing classroom

TABLE VI

Secondary modern school performance for boys, 1966/7 to 1972/3
(All figures as percentages)

School	Delinquency	Attendance	Academic attainment[1]
A	10·5	79·9	34·8
B	8·6	78·3	26·5
C	8·3	84·3	21·5
D	8·1	77·2	8·4
E	7·4	89·1	30·4
F	7·2	81·3	18·5
G	5·2	87·0	37·9
H	4·5	88·5	52·7
I	3·8	83·6	36·5

[1] Academic attainment for these children as defined as proceeding to the local Technical College at age 16.

TABLE VII

Overall school performance for boys and characteristics
of school input

Overall rank[1]	School	Proportion of population of catchment area in social class 4 and 5 (*per cent*)	Mean raw IQ score of 1974 intake
1	H	37·5	34·3
2	G	42·5	33·1
3	I	42·9	34·0
4	E	42·2	35·4
5	C	43·9	34·7
6	F	43·4	34·5
7	A	44·8	33·2
8	B	38·1	35·5
9	D	38·9	no information

[1] Overall rank is calculated by simply averaging each school's relative position on each of the three indicators of output.

interaction in other teachers' lessons, talking to staff and pupils and assessing the nature of each schools' educational and social ethos.

Unfortunately, analysis of this data is still in progress; we cannot say with certainty which factors within the schools appear to 'explain' their delinquency rate and, more importantly, *how* these factors appear to produce pupil delinquency and other forms of deviance. All that can be done here is to outline some of the initial hypotheses behind the work that have been suggested by other educational, social and criminological research. Whether these ideas are correct in explaining why some schools are delinquent schools will only be discovered by the testing of these hypotheses in our research schools, and in other schools elsewhere.

Some Possible Features of a Delinquent School

Rigid Streaming By Ability. Many impressionistic studies suggest that streaming by ability may inadvertently generate delinquency (se President's Commission on Law Enforcement and Administration of Justice, 1967, for a review). Hargreaves (1967), for example, found enormous differences in the attitudes, behaviour and delinquency rates of groups of boys in the upper streams and those in the lower streams of Lumley Secondary Modern School. In the upper streams, the pupils shared similar values to those of the teachers; status within the peer group was achieved by adopting the 'good pupil' role. In the lower streams the pupils had oppositional, anti-school values; status was achieved by holding values different to those of the school. Such a differentiation of many pupils into a delinquent sub-culture is produced by the streaming system, which serves progressively to demote and alienate many working-class children.

In view of this evidence, we would expect a modification of the streaming-by-ability system to be a delinquency preventive measure. Such modification may be achieved by the radical measures of complete unstreaming, or by the grouping of children by subjects, rather than by forms. More minor modifications to the streaming system, such as ensuring high mobility between streams, designating the streams other than by the obvious labels of 'A' and 'B', and trying to incorporate the lower streams into the school in the non-academic areas of leadership positions, societies and sports teams, may achieve the same ends.

Given that recent research (Barker Lunn, 1970) into the effect of unstreaming at junior school level concludes that the children in un-streamed schools held more favourable attitudes to school than those in streamed ones, and given that abolition of streaming would probably have no significant effect on educational attainments (Rutter and Madge, 1977, p. 127), modification of the streaming system within a school would seem to be a valuable delinquency preventive measure.

High Rates of Corporal Punishment. Although belief in the efficiency of physical punishment in preventing problem behaviour is still widespread, high rates of physical punishment within a school have repeatedly been suggested as a causal factor in the generation of delinquency. Clegg's work in the West Riding of Yorkshire (Clegg and Megson, 1968) suggests that behaviour was best amongst children who attended schools where caning was lightest, a finding that applied in both poor and more affluent areas. Schools with high rates of delinquency invariably had high rates of corporal punishment and although high rates of physical punishment may in part *reflect* the fact that a school has problems, it seems likely that these high rates may be a cause of problems too. The authors in fact are sufficiently convinced to comment that 'The evidence from these schools supports the commonsense view that, even in adverse circumstances, the school itself can do much to combat delinquency and juvenile crime' (op. cit., p. 124). Another study indicates that caning has in fact a weaker reformative effect than a simple 'telling off' by a teacher. Of a group of boys caned for smoking, 35 per cent apparently increased their smoking over the next year, whilst only 8 per cent of those who were simply reprimanded did likewise (Palmer, 1964). Although this study, too, is clearly open to a number of interpretations, this evidence combined with other more impressionistic surveys (Stone and Taylor, 1977) would suggest that high rates of physical punishment and the teacher attitudes that accompany them are delinquency creating.

Quite how high rates of physical punishment have this effect is unclear. The extensive use of violence by teachers may act as a model for children to imitate. It is possible that high rates of physical punishment affect children's sense of self-worth and self-esteem. Repeated hitting of children is likely to affect adversely their commitment to the school and maybe generate delinquency in this way. Whatever the precise links are between these factors, the extensive use of violence by staff who are harsh, intolerant and bad tempered, seems likely to produce similar behaviour in the children.

High Staff Turnover. Many studies have linked the educational and social problems produced by certain schools with high rates of staff turnover (Rutter, 1975). It seems likely that this turnover may function to produce a high rate of pupil delinquency by its adverse effects on the pupils' identification with the staff. Phillipson (1971, p. 247) notes:

A high staff turnover means that pupils are regularly faced with different authority figures who make different and often conflicting demands upon them: the lack of steady, stable relationships will tend to result in a confusion among pupils about how to respond in similar situations to a constant flow of different teachers. A regular turnover of teachers provides a setting for the growth of cynicism among pupils about the worth of their school: one result may be a steady decline in the evaluation by pupils both of the school and of themselves.

Given the existence of other supporting evidence about the importance of high staff turnover in promoting low inmate pride in mental hospitals (Aubert, 1965), and common-sense evidence that schools with high staff turnover are schools that lack social stability, any policy that increases staff stability is likely to be delinquency preventive.

Custodial or Authoritarian School Climate. We have always had good evidence that the social climate of schools has an effect in shaping children's political attitudes (Newcomb, 1963) and scholastic attainment. The American studies of McDill and his colleagues have shown that, other things being equal, students make better progress in schools which are rated by pupils and teachers as placing a high value on academic achievement (McDill, 1974).

But recent evidence has supported the view that the 'tone' or 'ethos' of a school can also have important effects on levels of pupil delinquency, vandalism and alienation, as well as on purely academic factors. Finlayson and Loughran (1976) show that teachers in high delinquency rate schools are perceived by their pupils as hostile and authoritarian in their dealings with their classes—

In such a cycle of events the repressive measures which the teachers are perceived to adopt could themselves be an important factor in the contribution which the high delinquency schools seem to make in inflating their delinquency problems. (op. cit. p. 144.)

American research on the pupil control orientation of teachers and the sense of alienation among students too suggests that

A high school imbued with a custodial pupil control orientation generally does not provide an atmosphere conducive to positive commitment on the part of students to their teachers and school; in fact, it seems to make such identification more difficult. (Rafalides & Hoy, 1971, p. 110.)

Other evidence shows high-vandalism schools to be schools with low pupil commitment to the teachers (Goldman, 1961) and pluralistic, democratic schools have lower levels of pupil aggression (Johnston & Krovetz, 1976). Together the research suggests that an authoritarian, repressive, or custodial attitude amongst the teaching staff of a school is likely to be delinquency creating.

We have seen so far that the general direction of policy measures that have been implemented has usually been to deal only with the pupils who have become deviants. We have attempted policy measures that seek to change the pupils themselves and their attitudes to school. None of the existing measures, such as the detection of at-risk children, or the increase in professional collaboration, involve changes in the organizations that may produce the problems. In fact, the 're-socializing' of misfit children to accept the school and the development of alternative institutions for those who still cannot accept it merely means that the institution of the school is likely to survive its problems relatively unchanged, since it is only the deviant children who are likely to change it. Just as control units in prisons serve to allow the institution of the prison to continue its normal (or maybe abnormal) functioning, the free schools, truant centres and child guidance clinics function to allow the schools to *resist* pressure for change. In the case of the prison and the school, the institution is involved in a complicated process of pattern maintenance.

Our principal conclusion is, then, that if the schools are responsible for producing problems amongst their pupils, 'common-sense and economy alike would suggest that whatever is wrong with them be put right, rather than a whole fresh layer of institutions be created to make good the deficiencies of those we already have. . . .' (Wootton, 1959.) What steps are necessary for the development of this approach, based as it is on the need to modify school regimes?

First, we need to collect information on the actual levels of performance of our schools and on the levels of the dropout and deviancy that they generate. Teachers, who must be drawn into the profession by a feeling that they do make a difference, currently receive very little routine information that enables them to assess the value of the methods that they use, or which enables them to find out the best ways to make a difference in their children's development. Many teachers do not know the attendance rate, delinquency rate and academic success rate of their own school, let alone those of the other schools around them. In the absence of such basic information on the characteristics of the children they are producing, headmasters and teachers are in no position to assess the worth of the methods they are using. We need urgently to feed back to teachers information on their own school's performance, relative to that of other schools taking similar pupils, so that schools can begin to assess whether they are performing at the levels to be expected of them. With such systems of evaluation, examples of what can be called good practice and of schools that appear to be coping well with their pupils' problems could be made generally known to other teachers in other schools, based on the sure knowledge that such information does not reflect simply changing fashions but scientific evidence of the worth of the particular methods.

It is unlikely, however, that the simple feeding back of information on schools' levels of performance will be enough to change those institutions that are not working to the advantage of their pupils. The institutions may simply ignore the evidence of failure and then externalize it by 'blaming the victim', or, in other words, explaining their failure as due to deficiencies in the nature of their children, catchment areas and community support.

Some further measures of increasing the accountability of our schools appear therefore to be a second pre-requisite of the attempt to modify certain school institutions. This could be obtained by reinforcing mechanisms of accountability up to the 'centre' of educational policy making, such as by an increase in the frequency of school inspections and encouraging of teachers' unions to root out their less competent colleagues. Alternatively, accountability may be obtained at a local level by the publishing of schools' individual results to their communities or by increasing parental choice of school, thereby encouraging a process whereby the schools with the poorer results would either change or lose pupil numbers.

All the above statements and recommendations envisage a different attitude both by society and involved professions as to the role of the school. Whether or not the child comes to the school from one social class or another, or from one way of life or another, it is still the role of the school to initiate him into adult life. If the initiation is poorly conducted, then the child will likewise produce poor

D

conduct because he will reject the school and the society that it represents. The fact that the school is simply one of many institutions that the delinquent child rejects must surely not be allowed to absolve the school from its responsibility in the rejection process and from its responsibility to change what it offers children if they continue to reject it.

The research reported in this Chapter was undertaken at the Medical Research Council Epidemiology Unit, Cardiff.

CHAPTER THREE

Diversion of Juvenile Offenders from the Criminal Justice System

ALLISON MORRIS

Diversion was not, until recently, a word much used in Great Britain, and yet it is quite clear that the ideas underlying this concept are not new, and that they have greatly influenced the development of measures for dealing with children in this country. Of course, the term 'diversion' can cover a variety of activities. It can refer to diversion from court rooms, from official programmes, from the criminal justice system or from the juvenile justice system. A recent working paper by the Law Reform Commission of Canada characterized four different kinds of diversions:

(1) community absorption. Examples of this are schools or families which deal informally and internally with their difficult children, or clinics designed to deal with specific difficulties e.g. school phobia, mental illness and so on.
(2) screening—where, for example, the police refer an incident back to the family, simply dropping the case rather than laying criminal charges.
(3) pre-trial diversion. This involves dealing with offenders who have already been charged by settlement or mediation outside the normal criminal or juvenile justice system.
(4) alternatives to institutions, for example, the increased use of community measures like restitution, probation and community service.

I shall concentrate on screening agencies and on pre-trial diversion (for the two are inter-linked), and when I refer to diversion I shall be referring to these techniques only. They are mechanisms which, in the words of Cressey and MacDermott, 'minimize penetration' into the criminal or juvenile justice system. But I shall also discuss a further type of diversion—diversion of child offenders from a criminal justice system altogether and into one of social welfare. I want to raise the question of whether this can be described as diversion at all.

Why divert?

The juvenile court, itself, was originally planned to divert children from the more formal court procedures applied to adults, and many of the arguments now presented in favour of diversion from the juvenile court derive from a feeling that the juvenile court has failed —failed to provide the sort of care envisaged by the proponents of the early courts, and failed either to stem increasing rates of juvenile crime, or to reduce recidivism. (In 1955, 41,069 children (8–17) were found guilty or cautioned for indictable offences; there were 148,865 such children (10–17) in 1975.) Now, Edwin Lemert has argued that if there is a defensible philosophy for the juvenile court, it is one of judicious non-intervention—in other words, a philosophy of diversion.

Advocates of diversion point to many possible advantages, some of which contradict each other. First, diversion is seen to provide an earlier opportunity of working with defendants than would otherwise be possible and this, in turn, provides hope that such work will be more successful. Diversion in this approach is a *gateway* to resources; the reasoning is that juvenile court only failed because treatment measures were applied too late in the child's career. Conversely, it is argued (because we have too little information about appropriate and successful ways of dealing with children who offend) that diversion can *protect* children from the consequences of these same treatment measures. The other major arguments in favour of diversion are variants of this latter view, the theoretical basis of which lies in labelling theory and differential association theory. The labelling perspective suggests that the process of arrest, trial and conviction changes the self image of the juvenile. He increasingly sees himself as delinquent, acts *as if* delinquent, and others respond to him as if he *always was* delinquent (see Lemert, 1972). Differential association theory suggests that criminal behaviour occurs when individuals have more contact with those with delinquent than non-delinquent attitudes (see Sutherland and Cressey, 1970). Diversion, it is suggested, can avoid the stigma often associated with a court appearance. There is certainly some evidence that such stigmatization can intensify a deviant self-image and lead to further acts of deviance, and that intervention may exacerbate delinquent behaviour (see, e.g. D. Farrington, 'The effect of public labelling', *B. J. Crim.*, forthcoming). Diversion, it is also argued, can avoid contamination; it can prevent naïve and early offenders from meeting with more experienced offenders. Proponents of this view commonly feel that too many minor offenders appear in our juvenile courts, that many of the acts committed by children referred to juvenile courts indicate family, educational, or welfare difficulties, or difficulties in growing up. The criminal justice system, it is felt, is too heavy handed for such offenders; the criminal law and its processes should be a last and limited resort. Finally, of course, there is the argument of costs, that diversion saves scarce resources.

But diversion also has its disadvantages. The major ones, in summary, are:

1. The loss of the possible deterrent value of a court appearance and a diminution of the symbolic importance of the court process.
2. The possible pressure on children and parents to admit guilt in order to participate in the diversion programme and to avoid an appearance before the juvenile court.
3. The possibility that diversion can involve greater interference with the offender's liberty than if he was dealt with by the juvenile court.
4. The possibility that diversion will involve discriminatory practices and discrepancies in the exercise of police and prosecutorial discretion, suggested by research (see Piliavin and Briar, 1965, Sudnow, 1965).
5. The possibility that diversion will extend, rather than limit, the network of social control. The argument here is that children who would not otherwise be a charge on the system are brought into the system and then diverted from it. A corollary of this is that diversion may involve greater interference with the liberty of those offenders still dealt with by the criminal or juvenile justice system.
6. The possibility that insufficient weight will be given to the rights of the victim.
7. The difficulty of dealing with 'failure' after the decision to

divert has taken place and whether or not this should then lead to prosecution.

In the following sections, I will outline some current diversionary practices in Great Britain and attempt to highlight their advantages and disadvantages.

The English approach

First I will briefly outline the philosophy and practice of the English juvenile court system. In the White Paper leading up to the Children and Young Persons Act 1969 (Children in Trouble, 1968) offending was seen as merely a symptom of more general underlying disorders: the child who offended had 'needs' which could be identified and met. Protecting society from his delinquency and helping his development were seen as complementary concepts. Consequently, it was proposed that children under the age of 14 should not be referred to the juvenile court solely on the ground that they had committed offences. Rather, where it could be established that such children were not receiving the care, protection and guidance which a good parent might reasonably be expected to give, it was proposed that 'care and protection' proceedings should be brought. Criminal proceedings would be possible against children between the ages of 14 and 17 who had committed offences, but only after mandatory consultations had taken place between the police and social service departments. The expectation was that such children would also, in the main, be dealt with under 'care and protection' proceedings.

These proposals, with few modifications, reached the statute book as the Children and Young Persons Act 1969. Though the formal composition and constitution of the juvenile court was left virtually unchanged by the Act, its jurisdiction was radically altered by the provisions. There was a substantial move towards voluntary agreements, and towards civil rather than criminal proceedings. The Act, therefore, introduced for 10-to-14-year-olds what has been called 'the double-barrelled test': such children would not be brought to court unless they had committed criminal offences and unless, in addition, they were in need of care and control which they were unlikely to receive unless the court made an order in respect of them. The onus of establishing this need was firmly placed on the referring agency. In the 14-to-17 age group the police or 'any qualified informant' (e.g. local authority official) could prosecute where an offence had been committed, but only if satisfied 'that it would *not be adequate* for the case to be dealt with by a parent, teacher or other person or by means of a caution or through the exercise of powers not involving court proceedings'. (Sec 5(2) Children and Young Persons Act, emphasis added.)

The overall aims of the Act were to reduce the number of children appearing before the juvenile court and to make the commission of an offence no longer a ground in itself for intervention. The juvenile court was not only to become a welfare providing agency, but was also to become an agency of last resort: referral to the juvenile court would take place only where a voluntary and informal agreement could not be reached with the child and his parents. Indeed, the Act was a mixture of social welfare and diversion. One commentator has described it as a decriminalizing Act, but this is an arguable point, for what the Act did was to *substitute* one form of social control for another. Terms rather than consequences were changed. (Section 4 prohibits criminal proceedings for offences committed by children under 14. Section 5 restricts criminal proceedings for offences committed by young persons under 17 and section 7 raises the minimum age qualification for a borstal sentence from 15 to 17 and plans the phasing out of detention centres and attendance centres as intermediate treatment facilities become available.)

In practice, however, this model has never come to fruition, and to a large extent the Act is still a non-Act. Although ideological differences between the political parties caused key sections to remain formally unimplemented (see Bottoms 1974), it is clear that the Act could have been implemented *informally*. Key agencies— for example, police and social service departments—could have consulted together more; but they did not (see House of Commons, 1975, C.Y.P.A. Report 1975). Even implemented sections have had minimal impact. Care proceedings on the commission of an offence are rare, and between 1971 and 1975 the number actually decreased: In 1971 care proceedings using the offence condition were brought on 81 occasions, whereas in 1975 such grounds were used on 19 occasions. What this reveals is the importance of *practice* rather than *policy*. This seems a fairly obvious point, but it is one which I wish to stress. New systems may be set up, but if those operating the system do not give primary allegiance to the values inherent in that system then its aims can be defeated. In England, groups who found their roles in conflict with the new philosophy were able to continue working within their traditional perspectives. I will expand on this point by looking more closely at the role of the police in

England in dealing with juveniles. The police, after all, are a critical point in any system of screening and pre-trial diversion.

Police cautioning and juvenile bureaux in England

The police in England, as in most jurisdictions, have a discretion not to prosecute. This can be exercised informally on the street, and we can never assess the extent to which this occurs. But the police can also decide to give a formal warning—oral or written—to an offender as an alternative to prosecution. The practice of cautioning was well established in some areas before 1969, and a Home Office guide, published in 1970, stated that this practice should be extended. It stressed that 'the Act does nothing to inhibit the continuance of this practice; on the contrary it leaves full scope for the use of the caution as one of the variety of available courses of action, other than court proceedings, to be used as appropriate'.

The number of cautions for all age groups for indictable and non-indictable offences rose sharply after the Act. In 1969, just over 74,000 cautions were given; this had reached about 136,400 by 1975. Almost all of this increase is attributable to increases in the number of children cautioned. For example, in 1975, 18 per cent of all detected offenders in England and Wales were cautioned; 88 per cent of these were juveniles.

Most police areas in England (26 out of 43 in January 1975) have set up juvenile bureaux since 1969 to make the decision whether or not to refer particular children to the juvenile courts. The juvenile bureau is not regarded as a specialist department and officers are accepted for an average period of four years away from normal duty. Very little formal training is given to these officers, but a special selection of volunteers is made, and certain qualities are looked for —especially an understanding of the type of problems that are likely to confront them. (Oliver, 1973)

Once a child comes to the notice of the police and it is established on the face of it that the child has committed an offence, the police officer involved in the case submits to the bureau a report setting out the facts of the offence. Bureau staff then collect information about the child from their own records, from the social service department, from the child's school and from any other relevant agencies, and usually, in addition. visit the child's home. On the basis of this information, the chief inspector in the bureau decides which course of action is the most suitable for each particular child;

to prosecute, to caution or to take no further action. The criteria for administering a caution are:

1. The police must be satisfied that an offence was committed by the juvenile, and that the available evidence would be sufficient to sustain a successful prosecution.
2. The juvenile must admit the offence and that he knew it was wrong.
3. The parent must consent to the juvenile being cautioned as an alternative to a court appearance.
4. The victim must consent to leave the matter to the police.

In most areas, where the decision is made to deal with the matter by caution, nothing else happens. The caution is usually administered in a formal way to bring home the gravity of the occasion. In a few areas, however, the police undertake follow-up supervision—they continue to visit the child and family and to offer guidance and advice. But this is felt in most police areas to stretch scarce police resources too far and to be a task which should be carried out by the social service departments. (Supervision was an integral part of the former police juvenile liaison schemes—there were 18 of these prior to 1969. But various Government Reports were critical of the liaison schemes. They felt that the police lacked the requisite skills and training (See Report on the Committee on Children & Young Persons, 1960.) Where supervision is thought appropriate most bureaux prefer to refer children to the juvenile court or to the social service departments on a voluntary basis (but the latter is rarely done because these departments themselves are under-staffed).

There is another side of the juvenile bureaux which I should mention briefly. One of the terms of reference of the bureaux is to identify and combat areas of juvenile delinquency and, to this end, a comprehensive schools programme is undertaken in many areas with a view to aiding young people to become better citizens. Bureaux officers give talks, take part in discussions and show films to young people in the hope that they will be prevented from committing delinquent acts. In 1976 the police in the Metropolitan district of London made over 4,000 visits to schools in their area.

The juvenile bureaux scheme is based on the principle of keeping child offenders out of court wherever possible, and the Annual Criminal Statistics indicate that police practice in dealing with juveniles has, to some extent, changed, particularly with respect to younger children. In 1969, 45 per cent of juveniles who admitted committing an indictable offence were cautioned; in 1975 this rose to 63 per cent. Up to 1968, far more children under 14 were being brought before the courts and found guilty than were being cautioned, but by 1973 the number of children cautioned was twice the number being found guilty. This was not so for the 14-to-17 age group. Though cautioning increased—from 22 per cent in 1969 to 33 per cent in 1975—there was also an increase in the number found guilty at court. In all, in spite of the Act's aim of reducing the number of children appearing before the juvenile court, the number of males proceeded against in the juvenile courts in 1975 *increased* by 4 per cent over the 1969 figures. This could be explained in a number of ways, e.g. by a vast increase in serious juvenile crime, but what evidence there is calls this explanation into question.

It is at least possible to suggest that the existence of juvenile bureaux has led to a *widening of the net of social control* rather than diversion from it. For example, 17 out of the 26 bureaux actively encourage schools and shopkeepers to report children to them rather than to deal informally with the children themselves. This is not an uncommon phenomenon. The general aim of youth bureaux in the United States, to which I will refer again later, was also the diversion of children from the juvenile justice system. But it appears that the police there now send children to the bureaux when formerly they would have taken them home and persuaded their families to deal with them, and that schools and other organizations refer troublesome children to the bureaux almost as a matter of course. The net was cast wider under the 'illusion that something constructive was being done for the community's children'. (Howlett, 1973.) This happened in England, too, in the former police juvenile liaison schemes. The West Ham scheme, for example, dealt with children who *in the absence of such a scheme* would probably not have been taken before the juvenile court. (Taylor, 1971.) It is possible that children who would previously have been dealt with informally are now referred to juvenile bureaux, precisely because such agencies exist, and are subsequently formally cautioned.

Can this 'inflationary' effect be demonstrated? A recent report (Ditchfield, 1976) points to two features which provide some support for this suggestion. First, taking the police forces of England and Wales as a whole, Ditchfield found a close connection between the growth of juvenile cautioning since 1968 and increases in the known offender rate for juveniles. Those areas with the greatest number of cautions also recorded the largest increases in the number of known offenders. Second, some areas with increased cautioning rates also showed large increases in the ratio of juveniles to adults in the offender population, often much larger than could reasonably have been accounted for by changes in the age structure of the population.

For example, juvenile cautions increased in the Metropolitan Police District from 207 in 1965 to 12,125 in 1973. This increased cautioning was accompanied by a significant increase in the proportion of juveniles to adults in the offender population: in 1966 there were 25 juveniles for every 100 adults in the offender population compared with 37 in 1973. However, in urban police forces which made no special arrangements for dealing with juvenile offenders, little change in the ratio of juveniles to adults in the offender population was found—the ratio of juveniles to adults in the offender population in Birmingham was 52 in 1966 and remained so in 1973. As Ditchfield stresses, it would be misleading to draw firm conclusions from these figures, but it at least raises the question of whether changes in police practices resulting from the 1969 Act have led to the official cautioning of some juveniles who would previously have been dealt with informally.

I suggested earlier that even where guidelines or criteria for diversion are set out an an official level, there can be little guarantee that these will necessarily be followed, especially where new practice directives conflict with old. The practice of police cautioning in England serves further to demonstrate what I meant by this.

The philosophy underlying the new legislation stressed the importance of identifying the child's needs and of possible underlying disorders. Phillip Priestley, in his survey of the operation of the Act in two areas of England, concluded that the police there did not take much notice of personal factors in deciding whether or not to prosecute—they looked more to the nature of the offence and to the age of the child. Priestley found that officers were reluctant to differentiate between children caught committing an offence in a group. This has changed recently in some areas but not all. He also found that it was rare to give a child more than one caution. In some areas, e.g. the Metropolitan police district in London, children may be cautioned more than once. To do otherwise, Priestley suggested, would offend values closely held by the police—values such as justice and equality. One aim of the new system, however, was to challenge these values.

Moreover, the central duties of the police are the prevention, control, and detection of crime, and the normal end product is to take the individual to court. But the job of the juvenile bureau officer is to recognize and refer to the court the child who needs skilled treatment and to keep others out of the court. This can create a conflict in the various roles to be performed by an individual officer, and can also lead to conflict with his colleagues. Bureaux officers may, as a result, experience pressures implicit in their desire to maintain good relations with their colleagues and in the demands of referring officers of certain kinds of actions. We may, therefore, in our official policy on children in trouble, put the police in a position of conflict—ask them to do jobs which they may not be equipped for, or want to do. Edwin Lemert suggested that diversion programmes in the United States often failed because of police alienation from the aims of the schemes.

The Scottish approach

The philosophy underlying the new system in Scotland is similar to that in the English Act, but Scotland chose to abolish juvenile courts and to replace them with welfare tribunals, staffed by lay people. (See Bruce and Spencer, 1976.) Children's hearings, as these are called, are concerned only with the question of what to do with the child. If the child or the parent denies the ground of referral, for example the commission of an offence, the case is referred to the sheriff court (an ordinary court presided over by a professional judge) to establish the commission of the offence by the child. If the child or parent objects to the children's hearing's decision on the appropriate disposition for the child, he may also appeal to the sheriff court. There is a complete separation, in theory, between judicial and disposition functions. The hearing can discharge the referral or place the child under the supervision of a social worker with or without conditions. It also has continuing jurisdiction until the child is eighteen.

More than 90 per cent of the children dealt with in the new system are children who have committed offences. A system of police cautioning exists in Scotland similar to that in England, though there are no police juvenile bureaux there. About one quarter of the children referred to the police each year are dealt with in this way. The police refer those whom they are unwilling to caution to the *reporter*—the key figure in the new system. Reporters are appointed by the Regional Councils and are drawn from a number of professions including lawyers, police, social workers and teachers. It is the reporter's function to decide, on the basis of records, whether the child referred to him by the police, by social work departments, or, indeed, by the child's parents, is in need of '*compulsory measures of care*' (Social Work [Scotland] Act, 1968, Sec. 39[3]). Only when he believes that this is so, is the child referred to a hearing. The reporter asks first whether action is justified and, if so, whether it is necessary.

Built into the Scottish system, therefore, is a *double* screening device. The reporters stand as independent and visible sifts between the police (and other referring agents) and the children's hearings. Their independence is such that, although employed by the local authority, their contracts of employment cannot be terminated by the local authority. Nor are reporters subject to any controlling authority. Traditionally, of course, in the Scottish legal system an independent assessor exists between the police and the adult courts, namely the procurators fiscal.

Reporters were created as a professional group only in 1970. What kind of people are they? The Kilbrandon Committee—the committee whose recommendations led to the new Scottish system—felt that the role called for 'a degree of practical knowledge and understanding of children's problems', and that a reporter 'should preferably be an officer combining a legal qualification with a period of administrative experience relating to the child welfare and educational services'. Such creatures are rare to find, and, in fact, the majority of the reporters appointed in 1970 were lawyers or social workers; indeed many of the legally qualified reporters were part-time and continued their legal practices. (Other groups were also represented—for example, former police officers and clergymen.)

The appointment of a representative both of the legal and social work professions was a common pattern throughout Scotland in those areas where more than one reporter was appointed. But why should the 'ideal' reporter have 'legal qualifications'? This is at odds with a social welfare approach, an approach dominated by social work values. It might be argued that this was an attempt to introduce legal considerations into a social welfare approach. But if it was, it was a somewhat half-hearted attempt. For although the reporter alone is responsible for the decision to refer the child to the hearing, there is no machinery for appeal against his decision, there are no criteria set out anywhere for determining whether or not compulsory measures of care are necessary, the decision is made in private and the reporter need not give reasons for his decision. (By 1976 most reporters had some form of social work training.)

A comparison of the effectiveness of the Scottish and English screening systems is of some use, I think, in attempting to answer the vital question in any discussion of diversion: who should divert? I demonstrated that in England the practice of police warnings had not reduced the number of referrals to the juvenile court and did not reflect the new emphasis in the 1969 legislation. This was so, too, of police practice in Scotland. The Kilbrandon Committee described the police as 'one of the primary sources of identification of children in need of special educational measures: as well as being part of the sifting or assessment agency'. One expected, accordingly, changes in police policy and practice, but few occurred. Current procedure in the allocation of police warnings is still in accordance with the recommendations of the Scottish Advisory Council Report of 1945—allocation is determined primarily by the type of offence committed and by whether or not the child had a previous record.

Nor have the police operated fully as a sifting mechanism. Many of the cases actually referred to the reporters by the police are not subsequently referred by them to the children's hearings for consideration of compulsory measures of care, and it is worth stressing that the number of 'no action' decisions in cases referred to the reporter by the police is considerably higher than in, for example, educational referrals: in 1975, 54 per cent of referrals from the police were given a 'no action' disposal compared with 29 per cent of those referred by educational authorities. The reason for this difference in 'no action' rates seems to be that educational referrals, unlike police referrals, usually take place after a number of other measures have been attempted. Because of this lack of change in police policy and practice, the role of the reporter in the Scottish system is a crucial one.

The major task of the reporter is to decide whether or not the particular child referred to him is in need of compulsory measures of care—in other words, whether or not the child can be diverted from the formal social control system. To do so, the reporter gathers information about the child's actions, school behaviour, social characteristics and family background, and pieces this information together so that a picture of the child emerges. The significance of the original ground of referral—for example theft—is understood by the reporter by considering the action in its wider social context. The decision taken depends on the type of picture which emerges.

The reporter begins with the report of the referring agency which is, in the majority of cases, a report from the police giving details of the offence or offences which are the reason for the referral. But it is clear from the fairly high proportion who are not referred to a children's hearing that the original ground of referral, particularly in offence referrals, is not necessarily seen in itself as indicating a need for compulsory measures of care. The reporter attempts to distinguish between the 'normal' delinquent and the 'problematic' delinquent, between the 'normal' runaway and the 'problematic' runaway. Objective criteria to determine this sort of question do not exist. Reporters, therefore, are thrown back on their individual values, attitudes, experiences and training. Consequently, considerable regional variation exists in the rate of referral to the children's hearings. In 1975 the reporters in Lothian region referred 51 per cent of the reports referred to them on to the hearings; the reporters in Borders region referred only 35 per cent. (These figures are provisional figures provided by the Social Work Group, Scotland.)

I should at this stage probably clarify the meaning of the phrase 'no action'. (The decision to take 'no action' is the reporter's alone. The victim is not consulted, and no further proceedings can be taken unless the child offends subsequently.) 'No action' may in fact mean 'no compulsory action'. The phrase 'no action' can include an interview or letter (similar to a police warning) in which the reporter usually warns the child of the consequences of his action, voluntary social work help or psychiatric care for the child, restitution (for example, the child may be required to clean walls sprayed with paint in cases of vandalism), or the child may be required to make compensation either financially or by some form of community service. Most of these actions lack legal force but have the 'consent' of the child and his parents. However, in many cases it *does* mean that *nothing* happens to the child—a clear acknowledgement that delinquency for the majority of children is a part of growing up. In 1975, only 11 per cent of children given a 'no action' disposal became involved in voluntary social work help. Furthermore, 'no action' disposals by the reporters led to a vast reduction in the number of children appearing before formal social control agencies. In 1969, 27,220 children were proceeded against in all courts in Scotland; in 1975, 13,947 reports (not children) were referred to the children's hearings (a further 2,262 were dealt with in the courts)—a reduction of 60 per cent.

It is perhaps not surprising that the police are the major critics of the new system in Scotland. The majority opinion of the Association of Police Officers was that

in some cases at least, the best interests of the child are not served by taking 'no action'. Indeed, the reverse might be the case as the most criminally minded will be likely to regard 'no action' as an inducement to commit more crime and therefore continue on a criminal career. (Assn. of Chief Police Officers, 1974.)

This highlights the clash of values mentioned in the discussion of the police role in England. The police are unlikely to become integral parts of a welfare or diversionary approach towards children in trouble—such values have a low or marginal position in the values of their profession. It seems to me that the reporters in Scotland can offer the best of both worlds. In addition to keeping a large number of children out of the system of social control, they may also reduce value conflicts within that system.

This is not to say that reporters view their sole task as the promotion of social welfare and 'helping' juveniles in need. They do not, in dealing with children who offend, ignore ideas of law enforcement and community protection. Nor do they ignore the community's expectations of appropriate behaviour for children. Reporters are required to balance conflicting claims of social welfare, law enforcement and the prevention of future offending or other problematic behaviour—such considerations are bound to arise in *any* system dealing with children who offend. There is, thus, a fairly explicit acceptance of the importance of not letting juveniles 'get away' with too many offences. The Scottish system, therefore, is just another form of social control. Indeed, social welfare is a euphemism for, and one of the most efficient modes of, social control. But the Scottish system has shown that it is possible to reduce considerably the number of children appearing before formal agencies.

The operation of the Scottish system does, however, alert us to a possible danger in diversionary schemes. Though reporters referred fewer children to the hearings than had previously been referred to the juvenile courts, once the children reached the hearings the level of intervention was greater than that in the juvenile courts—more children were placed under the supervision of a social worker and more were removed from their parents' homes in 1975 than in 1970. (In 1970, 3,529 children were placed on probation by the juvenile courts; in 1975, 5,915 reports to the hearings were made subject of supervision requirements, an increase of 68 per cent. In 1970 children were the subjects of approved school or fit person orders; in 1975 children were removed from their homes by the hearings and, in addition, were removed by the courts.) There are now about

40 per cent more children in List D schools (former approved schools) than in 1970). Indeed, Scotland refers twice as many children per capita to institutions as does England.

This greater level of intervention highlights a deficiency in Edwin Lemert's model of 'judicious non-intervention'. He suggested that referral to a court should be a measure of last resort—a sign that all else had been tried and failed. He seems to assume that the court will know better how to deal with those appearing before them, but there is no reason to suppose that this is so. For, if all else has been tried, what can courts or hearings do other than punish or attempt to deter these children? In other words, children are controlled and punished in the guise of 'care' or 'treatment'; and because action is disguised as 'treatment' the number subject to such measures increases.

Such children also continue to be stigmatized perhaps to an even greater extent than in other kinds of systems because they are, by definition, the *most* troublesome, the *most* disruptive and so on. Lemert's response to this criticism (Lemert, 1975) is that *any* system of social control is stigmatizing; but the point is that the approach categorized by him as 'ideal' may lead to increased stigmatization. He also argued that even if such children were being 'warehoused', it did not matter too much because they would pass out of the jurisdiction of the court or hearing at eighteen (or at whatever age was determined by statute). But children can come *into* such systems when quite young and can remain within it for long periods.

Diversion in America

In 1966, while Scotland and England were moving towards a policy of social welfare for dealing with children who offend, the United States President's Commission on Law Enforcement and Administration of Justice recognized, to a large extent, the failure of the American juvenile court which had been based on similar policies. One of the Commission's major recommendations aimed at remedying some of the defects of the juvenile court was the creation of a Youth Service Bureau. Agencies were to be available for:

1. Youths who had not committed criminal acts but whose problems (at home, in the school, etc.) might lead them to do so if they are not helped—i.e. potential delinquents.
2. Delinquents whose behaviour was rooted in similar problems.

E

The Commission stated in its report:

> Such an agency ideally would be located in a comprehensive community center and would serve both delinquent and non-delinquent youths. While some referrals to the Youth Services Bureau would normally originate with parents, schools, and other sources, the bulk of the referrals could be expected to come from the police and the juvenile court intake staff, the police and court referrals should have special status in that the Youth Services Bureau would be required to accept them all. ... These agencies would act as central coordinators of all community services for young people and would also provide services lacking in the community or neighbourhood, especially ones designed for less seriously delinquent juveniles (page 83).

The Commission went on to say that the 'formal sanctioning system should be used only as a last resort'.

By 1971 it was clear that many agencies with differing and conflicting rationales claimed the label of 'Youth Service Bureau', due perhaps in part to the availability of massive Government funding. Bureaux were something of a growth industry. In 1967 there were only about half a dozen bureaux; by 1971 more than 150 such organizations were in existence throughout the country.

The philosophy underlying the Youth Service Bureau is not without its critics. Howlett asks: 'Will further development of the youth service bureau broaden the umbrella of ineffective services for children?' He feels that society has already gone too far in transferring family problems and responsibilities to the public domain, that the bureaux 'will contribute to even further disintegration of the family unit'. (Howlett, 1973.) Where a youth service bureaux exist, police officers, as I mentioned earlier, appear reluctant to return children directly to their homes for informal handling. This amounts to what has been called the *overreach* of treatment. In the words of the National Institute for Mental Health, 'for much of what is now labelled as deviant, the problem is not how to treat it but how to absorb or tolerate it' (1971). Another critic (Klapmuts, 1972) raises the question of the validity of 'non-coercive' nature of the bureaux: 'If referral by the agency or bureau for services or treatment in the community is backed by the threat of referral to court, then the allegedly non-penal agency is really an adjunct of the justice system and "diversion" a verbal fiction'. It is doubtful whether even *persuasion* to accept such services can amount to anything but coercion. Indeed, it seems that bureaux, or variants of them, are in essence creating secondary probation departments, attached to the policing agency. Rather than providing an *alternative* to juvenile justice processing, the model has duplicated and further confused the already existing system. All that has happened is that old ideas have been recycled (Lemert, 1971).

Other reports are, at first sight, more encouraging. Duxbury (1973), in an evaluation of the youth service bureaux in California, claimed that delinquency was reduced in most of their service areas. She pointed to a reduction in the number of arrests after they were opened, but this is not an adequate test for her claim. A more significant finding was that only 12 per cent of all referrals in 1971-2 were from law enforcement agencies (a further 9 per cent came from probation officers) and these tended, in the main, to be of *potential* delinquents. This suggests that the bureaux were not operating as *real* alternatives to handling within the juvenile justice system.

A further possibility for diversion from American juvenile courts occurs at what is generally called the *intake* stage. The case begins with the intake investigation and interview and ends with dismissal of the case, with informal handling or with referral to the prosecutor and defence counsel. To ensure fair and uniform handling it was intended that decisions should be based on *offence* rather than social data (President's Commission, 1967). However, a national sample survey of intake procedures (Creekmore, 1976) found *no* apparent relationship between type of offence and intake decisions; other factors appeared to play an important role, such as family background, school record, etc.

Indeed, the same survey (Sarri, 1976) revealed that only 42 per cent of courts had a formally organized programme for diversion; that many courts lacked specialized intake units, with the result that probation officers functioned in that capacity; that routine processing of cases was common and that most juveniles were diverted only from formal courtroom hearings to informal handling by probation officers. Furthermore, 45 per cent of the probation officers interviewed reported that they told youths that the diversion referral was for a 'trial period' and that if they engaged in further delinquency, cases would be dealt with more severely. To the extent that this was so Sarri concluded that diversion was a sham.

A Canadian proposal

A commission of the Solicitor General of Canada has recently made a number of far-reaching proposals in the area of juvenile justice, including raising of the age of criminal responsibility from 7 to 14 and the provision of additional legal safeguards. Part of the report—'Young persons in conflict with the law'—is concerned with creating a structure for diverting children from the formal court process. Under the new proposals, the Attorney General or his representative will have the option of referring the child who has committed an offence to a screening agency as an alternative to a court hearing. The process of screening is two-fold in design. First, controls are placed on the initiation of criminal proceedings (proceedings require the authority of the Attorney General or his representative) and second, an agreement reached between the child and the screening agency or advice by the agency not to proceed with the case will act as a bar to proceedings. If the child is referred to the screening agency it has the option of reaching some agreement with the child about compensation, restitution or community service. (The child has a right to legal representation at this stage.) If an agreement cannot be reached, the case will be referred back to the Attorney General who may either send the child to the court or drop the proceedings. If the screening agency recommends that no action be taken, the Attorney General *cannot* proceed against the child. Although there are no provisions for penalties if the child breaks the agreement, the screening agency has a two-month period from the time of referral of the child from the Attorney General in which to make a recommendation. The screening agency can, therefore, defer its recommendations to allow the child the opportunity to keep to his part of, or to participate in, the agreement. If it makes *no* recommendation it is assumed to have recommended that no proceedings be taken.

A possible flaw in this approach is that the Attorney General or his delegate need not refer the child to the screening agency. The preamble to the Act, however, states that young persons should be referred to courts *only* when their acts or omissions cannot otherwise be adequately dealt with. Details of the composition and administration of screening agencies are still vague. Some concern has also been expressed over the idea of 'trial by the community'.

Currently, at the provincial level, the key diversionary figure is the probation officer. In British Columbia, for example, Section 16 of the Provincial Courts Act 1969 required probation officers to 'endeavour to solve family problems without the intervention of a judge'. In 1975 this section was replaced by Section 7 of the Corrections Act. A probation officer is now *required* to carry out a pre-court enquiry in all cases where there has been an offence by a juvenile under federal legislation and *may* do so where the offence comes under provincial statutes and municipal by-laws. The probation officer then makes a recommendation to the prosecutor as to whether formal court procedure is useful or necessary.

Diverted offenders might be offered what is called 'diversion' or short term counselling. (This accounted for 19 per cent of probation officers' caseloads in the northern, interior and island regions of British Columbia in June 1976.) Diverted juveniles are also eligible for a number of special programmes, e.g. camping or outward bound programmes, and educational or vocational programmes, and recently there has also been a rapid expansion in the use of restitution, victim-service and community service.

Diversion is still a relatively untried idea. Many of our current diversionary practices are no more than acts of faith. There is, as yet, no research evidence that they are successful; they may merely *temporarily* remove offenders from the system. Nor is there clear evidence to support the notion that diversion into formal programmes reduces the impact of labelling. It is, therefore, at least possible that offenders and their families see diversion as merely an *adjunct* to the criminal or juvenile justice system. If this is so stigma will not be reduced.

Our enthusiasm for diversion has in some cases led to the official processing of many more children than before, and has probably led to the postponement of more necessary and radical reforms (e.g. in our schools). It is now becoming widely accepted that a rehabilitative or social welfare ideology is an inadequate basis for our juvenile courts; yet that ideology is perpetuated in many pre-trial diversionary programmes. Only the recent Canadian proposals take into consideration the legal rights of the child at this stage, though intervention in the child's life can be considerable.

In short, diversion may become another method of social self-deception—terminology may be revamped without seriously altering what happens to juveniles. At the moment, all that can be said is that diversion offers a set of social controls of a *lesser* form than the official or formal social control system, whether the latter be based on principles of criminal justice or social welfare. But a system of social control it remains.

CHAPTER FOUR

Intermediate Treatment

DAVID THORPE

The term 'intermediate treatment' first appeared in a United Kingdom government White Paper in 1968 ('Children in Trouble', 1968, p. 9), and was used to define a range of services for juvenile offenders to be provided by a projected new Act of Parliament intended to alter substantially the methods used to control juvenile offenders in England and Wales. Both that White Paper and the legislation which followed it—the 1969 Children and Young Persons Act (CYPA)—offered only very vague and broad definitions of intermediate treatment, which in practice have created some difficulty in the articulation of policies and the achievement of comparability and consistency in implementation. The historical roots of intermediate treatment are not, however, difficult to discern.

The 1969 CYPA represents a further stage in the evolution of policies on juvenile delinquency. Until 1908, few legal distinctions existed between juvenile and adult offenders. Theoretically at least, everyone who was found guilty by a court was subject to the same penalties, although in practice alternatives to imprisonment had been available since the middle of the nineteenth century. The objectives of the Reform School movement established in the 1850s by Mary Carpenter and her followers were based on the need to provide young offenders with experiences which would prevent them from going to prison and thereafter following a life of crime. It was recognized by some, even at such an early stage in the history of penology, that successive contact with penal institutions had a damaging effect, and seemed to increase the incidence of repeated criminal acts.

In the century and a quarter since Mary Carpenter's time, those concerned with the reform of the penal system for juvenile offenders have succeeded in creating a system for dealing with delinquents which is almost entirely separate from that which deals with adults. Not only are the actual courts and legal procedures different, but also the community and institutional services are in large part staffed and administered by bodies separate from those which service the adult criminal population. One of the reforms brought about by the 1969 CYPA has been to provide services to both delinquent and deprived children by the same organization, with the intention that, although a legal distinction remains between delinquent and deprived children, the services provided be identical. However, just as it was recognized in the early nineteenth century that institutions for adult offenders had an adverse effect on juvenile offenders, so it gradually became apparent that even those special institutions for juvenile offenders created in the recent past seemed to produce individuals who were likely to commit further offences. In an effort to prevent youngsters from receiving institutional care, the 1963 Children and Young Persons Act authorized local authorities to spend money on whatever 'preventive' measures were deemed necessary. Such expenditures, however, remained open to a variety of interpretations, and by and large, it was the non-delinquent who received the benefits of this service.

In the 1969 CYPA, the 'preventive' policies of the 1963 CYPA were extended to, and specifically focussed on, juvenile offenders. Delinquents can now be 'sentenced' to receive 'treatment' which is intended to prevent them from reaching a stage where institutional care and control is required. As described by the White Paper 'Children in Trouble', intermediate treatment is a sentencing possibility for juvenile courts which would have the effect of removing a child from his immediate home environment for a brief period or succession of brief periods of time:

> Existing forms of treatment available to juvenile courts distinguish sharply between those which involve complete removal from home and those which do not. The juvenile courts have very difficult decisions to make in judging whether circumstances require the drastic step of taking a child away from his parents and home. The view has often been expressed that some form or forms of intermediate treatment should be available to the courts, allowing the child to remain in his own home but bringing him also into contact with a different environment. ('Children in Trouble', p. 9.)

The key definition in terms of juvenile penal policy is 'allowing the

child to remain in his own home'. This phrase firmly places intermediate treatment as a community-based service for those offenders
who would, in all probability, normally receive a sentence involving
custodial care. Intermediate treatment is thus defined as a service
which supplies care, control and treatment specifically to high-risk
juvenile delinquents within a non-custodial context.

'Children in Trouble' made a distinction between two types of
intermediate treatment:

> ... The first will involve temporary residence, attendance or
> participation, for a period or periods totalling not more than
> one month during each year of supervision. The second cate-
> gory will involve residence at a specified place for a fixed period
> of not more than three months, beginning with the first year of
> supervision. ('Children in Trouble', p. 10.)

While the first type of intermediate treatment appeared to be a form
of intensive supervision, the second resembled short-stay institutional care. 'The words "intermediate treatment" do not appear in
the 1969 CYPA, but Part I of the Act contains a section dealing
with the Supervision Order, and subsequent sections mention 'Power
to include requirements in supervision orders' (1969 CYPA Sect. 12,
1–5). These requirements have the effect of intensifying the supervision process by empowering the social worker responsible for the
order to direct the subject of the order 'to do all or any of the
following things'—

(i) to live at a place or places specified in the directions for a
period or periods so specified,

(ii) to present himself to a person or persons specified in the
directions at a place or places and on a day or days so
specified,

(iii) to participate in activities specified in the directions on a
day or days so specified; but it shall be for the supervisor
to decide whether and to what extent he exercises any
power to give directions conferred on him by virtue of the
preceding provisions of this subsection and to decide the
form of any directions. (1969 CYPA Sect. 12, 2.)

Section 19 of the 1969 CYPA stipulates that Children's Regional
Planning Committees have a 'duty' to provide facilities for which

supervisors issue directions. These facilities for intermediate treatment amount to regional schemes which require the approval of the Secretary of State before they can be used.

It can be seen, therefore, that the legislation, apart from providing a very basic legal and administrative framework for intermediate treatment, gives little information about the form of such treatment. The burden of defining the supervision process was placed squarely with supervising officers, Children's Regional Planning Committees and the Secretary of State, who would give final approval. Perhaps it was inevitable that such a broad and flexible legal obligation should lead to a good deal of confusion, and a range of interpretations which have at times appeared to bear little resemblance to each other. Some Regional Schemes saw intermediate treatment as a method of dealing with juvenile offenders by directing them to attend local youth clubs; others believed that specialized facilities which would deal almost exclusively with offenders, and not be available to non-offenders, were required.

The first government circular exclusively devoted to describing a policy for intermediate treatment tended to compound the problems of definition. 'Intermediate Treatment: a guide for the regional planning of new forms of treatment for children in trouble' was published by the Department of Health and Social Security in 1972. This guide said that the activities open to a child undergoing intermediate treatment

> ... may involve ... the development of new facilities, but they normally should be of a kind in which other children can also participate, and not confined to children under supervision through court orders. (This does not rule out the provision of facilities specially to meet the need of intermediate treatment schemes, but it will still be desirable that new facilities provided primarily—or even exclusively—for this purpose should be of a kind in which children not under supervision might share.) In this way the child will be able to continue to participate in activities which have aroused his interest beyond the time when he is formally required to do so. It will be an important aim to secure the child's acceptance of his treatment, so that he does not resent it; and this aim is unlikely to be achieved if it involves activities which appear to him to set him apart from his contemporaries (p. 14).

Social work agencies responsible for carrying out supervision processes reacted in a variety of ways. Some took a literal interpretation of the guide, and merely offered a list of youth clubs to supervising officers. Others concentrated primarily on the short-term residential type of intermediate treatment and modified children's homes, while others began to develop specialized methods of social work in which small groups of offenders were supervised in the community, and gradually phased into available youth facilities when it was considered appropriate. In no single case has a range of facilities yet been developed. Yet taken together, the types of intermediate treatment which are currently being practised do in fact offer the beginnings of a comprehensive range of community control facilities suitable for most juvenile offenders. The White Paper 'Children in Trouble' offered an original definition in terms of an alternative to institutional control by suggesting that many delinquents were sent by the courts to institutions simply because the traditional methods of supervision supplied inadequate control, and that intermediate treatment should enable this group of offenders to remain within the community. The 1969 CYPA supplies an adequately flexible legal framework for such intensive supervision.

Of course, individual juvenile offenders vary considerably, not only in terms of the frequency and nature of their criminal activities, but also in their motivations for committing offences and their developmental needs. Ryall showed that juvenile offenders committed to correctional institutions were routinely offending every fortnight prior to removal from the community (Ryall, 1974). He also suggested that the majority of such delinquents tended not to display symptoms of psychiatric disturbance, but were generally retarded educationally, under-stimulated and habituated to delinquent activity. The motivations underlying this behaviour were broadly seen as a combination of the acquisition of peer-group status (where socially acceptable, status-conferring behaviours would not normally have such a result), excitement, and to a lesser degree material gain. Such adolescents seemed to have developed a relatively powerful commitment to pursuing a delinquent career, for a non-delinquent career would not appear to offer any of the rewards obtainable by committing offences. West discovered that anti-social behaviour among a sample of 9-year-old boys correlated significantly with low intelligence scores and poor educational attainment, unpopularity with peers at school and a range of environmental factors broadly described as 'social handicap' which included inconsistent control at home, low income, poor housing and material circumstances, and large families. (West 1969.) A further study (West 1973) showed that it was this group of boys who developed delinquent careers in later adolescence.

While not all children with such disadvantaged backgrounds grow into persistent offenders, nevertheless it may be that attempts to pursue non-deviant careers during adolescence provide few, if any, of the rewards so easily gained by delinquency. In this context, however, it may be worth noting that the majority of adolescent offenders cease to commit delinquencies in early adulthood—they literally grow out of it. Some writers have recently suggested that these 'maturational' processes are brought about not by biological growth, but by a change to a life-situation in which non-delinquent behaviour does bring rewards—remuneration as a result of employment, and deeper and more meaningful relationships with both sexes. Those who have little to lose by delinquent activity while attending school suddenly find themselves with a great deal to gain by staying out of trouble as the rewards of adult life become more apparent. The relative strength and weakness of bonds to conventional social values and behaviour may constitute the single most powerful factor in determining whether or not people commit offences. Where these bonds are weakest, the greatest amount of crime will occur, and vice-versa. The child who does badly at school and cares little for what his teachers may think of him has little to lose by getting into trouble. If he comes from a poor family which supplies inconsistent or ineffective controls, then he may have slim regard for his parents' feelings. At the same time the prospect of acquiring material goods which the family may not be able to afford would be a powerful attraction. In the absence of youth clubs which give both status, interest and relationships with adults, then a delinquent career has much to offer when compared with a more conforming pattern of behaviour.

Schur sums up this view of delinquency causation: 'Because "commitment" or "attachment" deters some youths from becoming delinquent, this approach reverses the idea of constraint'. (Schur 1973.) Instead of seeing some individuals as constrained by individual or social forces to commit delinquent acts, he emphasizes the ways bonds of conventionality constrain some individuals to remain law-abiding. This implies, furthermore, a new outlook on the role of values in promoting delinquency. Whereas earlier interpretations stressed the development of special oppositional values that rush lower-class youth into delinquency, the emphasis here is on the common influence (in all classes) of dominant middle-class values. Individuals are not driven into delinquency by their frustration in achieving cultural goals; they are driven to it because their attachment to these goals has been *weakened* and *neutralized*. . . .' Intermediate treatment seems to offer opportunities of strengthening the bonds of convention among those where they are weakest. In short, the availability of interesting activities and the possibilities of caring relationships with non-parental adults supplied within the framework of a supervision order provide good reasons for staying out of trouble. The 'treatment' of intermediate treatment may very simply be seen as the provision of a non-delinquent career, rather than some esoteric psychotherapeutic experience which would in all probability be beyond the scope and skills of the average social worker. Where limited choices of behaviours were available to a child with a 'failed identity', intensive supervision in an organized programme gives much greater choice when status and excitement are needed. In this respect, the making of a supervision order with intermediate treatment conditions may have the effect of supplying a much-needed 'push' to conventionality for a child drifting into a career of delinquency.

'Control' theories of delinquency (see Hirschi, 1969, Polk and Halferty, 1972, and Matza, 1964) also explain the usual negative outcome of institutional programmes of delinquency control. When a child is removed from the community, he may be well able to adapt himself to the demands of an institution, but, on his return to the community, vital links with others of his own age, relationships with adults and a ready-made job are all too frequently missing. Attachments that existed before committal to the institution are severed, the maturing roots of relationships and employment do not develop, and only a minimum of commitment to 'going straight' exists when the youth is discharged into the community. In this context, removal from the community can be seen as the ultimate weakener and neutralizer; the bonds of activities and relationships are in the institution effective only *in that setting*. They are abruptly severed on discharge. Community-control programmes can offer most of the advantages of institutional controls, and *none* of their disadvantages.

In the United States, intermediate treatment programmes had their origins in the translation of institutional techniques for controlling delinquents into community-based projects. The evolution of a successful scheme used in a Highfields, New Jersey, programme is an example. It was a group therapy system for young male offenders in a specialized institution. (Weeks, 1958.) At the end of the 1950s, however, the increasing popularity of group methods of treatment was combined with a growing interest in community-based programmes, and discussions were opened up on the possibilities of using such techniques whilst delinquents lived at home. In 1961, the New Jersey authorities established a group rehabilitation centre in the middle of Newark, the largest city in the state. The new centre was called Essexfields—partly because the centre was in Essex County, and partly because it acknowledged that its techniques were modelled on the Highfields programme. Unlike the participants in the Highfields centre, the Essexfields boys lived at home.

Researching the Essexfields programme, Stephenson and Scarpitti (1974) described the rationale of the programme thus:

> This new approach appeared to have many theoretical merits. If juvenile delinquency is an attempt to cope with environmental and group pressures and strains, the individual should learn how to handle these problems in a conformist manner in his natural setting, where they exist. Removing him from his community and placing him in a temporary institutional environment creates an artificial setting where his real-life situation can only be simulated at best. Participating in an intensive rehabilitation program while remaining in his real world should permit him to test his new learning immediately where it counts, and to seek ongoing assistance from the program as he confronts strain-producing problems.

Attendance at Essexfields was a condition of probation (just as intermediate treatment is a condition of a supervision order) and most boys spent only four or five months at the centre. In effect, Essexfields supplied day care to its boys; the programme consisted of a mixture of group meetings and activities centred around maintenance tasks at a local mental hospital. Essexfields accepted up to twenty boys at a time, and significantly, its first intake consisted entirely of boys *discharged* from the Highfields institution. Many boys were found full-time employment during their period of treatment and were then asked to attend in the evenings, while others, not yet old enough to work, were allowed to return to their normal schools. Participation in the Essexfields programme was confined to those delinquents who would otherwise have been removed from the community and placed in a state reformatory. Selection was limited to persistent offenders whose delinquencies were normally peer-group based, and who were largely free from psychiatric disturbance.

The design of the research at Essexfields was almost identical to that used to study the Highfields institution, and Stephenson and Scarpitti found that rates of recidivism were lower from the community-based programme than from the residential programme. That is, 27 per cent of those undergoing the community-based programme reoffended within one year, whereas the percentage for those discharged from the state institution's programme was 38 per cent reoffending. Not only was the intensive supervision more successful in controlling delinquency than the institution, but, as the authors pointed out in passing, it was vastly cheaper.

One of the more interesting conclusions which Stephenson and Scarpitti drew from comparing their results with the findings of other comparable studies in the United States, was that there were few predictable differences between programme successes and failures, and that the same situation was true of the successes and failures of institutional programmes. The individuals who were more likely to be programme successes tended to be the older youths who committed multiple offences in a peer group. The programme failures tended to be the younger youths who had offended on their own. However, when research on traditional probation or supervision methods of control was examined, the differences between those offenders who succeeded on probation and those who failed, were much more marked. These American studies support the findings of Davies in the United Kingdom, who concluded that the boys who least needed probation appeared to derive the greatest benefits from it, while those from the poorest and least adequate material and familial backgrounds were much more likely to fail. (Davies 1969.) It may be, therefore, that conventional low-intensity supervision acts as a filter for high-risk juvenile offenders who have traditionally moved on to receive custodial treatment. If, however, such methods of control seem less successful than highly intensive supervision, the implications for the development of intermediate treatment programmes are very far-reaching indeed. On the basis of these limited studies, criteria for institutional treatment need to be far more clearly defined than is the case at present, and because no obvious differences exist between those who fail and those who succeed on community-based programmes, then these criteria will inevitably have to revolve around the seriousness and frequency of the offending rather than more abstract considerations of personality and social background.

Similar results to those described by Stephenson and Scarpitti were found by Empey and Rabow at Provo, Utah, where the Pinehills centre provided a programme of intensive supervision for persistent juvenile offenders (Empey & Rabow 1961). As at Essexfields, the traditional narrow 'treatment' emphasis was discarded in favour of a programme which offered structured group discussions as well as leisure and work activities—an approach to treatment which takes account of the delinquent's relationships with both the community and his peers, as opposed to the more traditional types of treatment which tend not to use group interaction as a medium for stimulating change.

A more recent example of intensive supervision as an alternative to institutional care is the Providence Educational Center (PEC) in St. Louis, Missouri. This centre has 'demonstrated notable effectiveness in treating delinquents who have a history of truancy, poor school performance, and behaviour problems. It has decreased the incidence of further offences among youngsters, increased their ability to function in schools or on the job, and strengthened their family relationships.' (Baddeley, 1975.) In many respects, PEC is a day-care programme similar to the Essexfields and Pinehills experiments, but focusses much more specifically on improving self-image. In effect, it uses an educationally-orientated programme 'aimed to providing delinquent youth with effective alternative ways of relating and functioning in the community'. There are three distinct and complementary threads to the PEC programme, one dealing with educational matters and providing a very personal and intensive remedial education curriculum by teachers, one providing a highly structured group experience by social workers; the third item, again supplied by social workers, is the programme of re-integration back into the community, either to an ordinary school or job. Staff at the Missouri Law Enforcement Assistance Council say that the delinquents who went to the Providence Educational Centre '... were less involved in crime than in the year prior to joining Providence ...,' and claim a recidivism rate of only 28 per cent as compared with a rate of 81 per cent for those sent away to an institution. Approximately 12 per cent of the children at the PEC are non-offenders, but for the majority, who are persistent high-risk delinquents, attendance at the centre is a condition of their probation. The implications for a Providence type system for intermediate treatment are spelled out by Baddeley in his summary 'Administrators, social workers and directors of community homes (in England and Wales) may be rather cynical when reading of such novel innovations as the Providence Educational Centre but in many parts of the world long-term residential rehabilitation is being quietly phased out. Today the emphasis is being placed on the proven juvenile offender staying in his home environment under the jurisdiction of a skilled caseworker and utilizing the community treatment facilities which are available in a given area—hence the new radical philosophy behind the Children and Young Persons Act, 1969, with its forward-thinking concept of intermediate treatment, which in due time will become reality and the backbone of future rehabilitation of the young offender.'

Unlike the United States, where policies on the management of juvenile offenders vary from state to state, England and Wales have one policy under the 1969 CYPA. Theoretically at least, this legislation should bring about a dramatic decrease in the number of delinquents currently in institutions. As yet, there are only a very small number of day-care centres of the Essexfields, Pinehills and Providence types, but already many agencies are either in the process of planning such facilities or have actually succeeded in setting up small experimental projects. At the moment, two types of 'alternative' facilities exist, one which uses the day-care system to help those unable to manage either employment or school, and one which concentrates on providing evening and weekend care for delinquents able to attend school or to manage a work situation.

The Islington Family Service Unit Intermediate Treatment Centre offers an illustration of a scheme which helps delinquent and pre-delinquent children to remain at home when they might otherwise be sent to an institution. The centre, located in a decaying urban area, consists of a short-life property staffed by two teachers and a social worker giving day-care to as many as fifteen children. The children are referred from a local secondary school, and by and large have demonstrated their problems by refusing to go to school. Hence they are withdrawn and socially isolated—quite different from the average delinquent—but nevertheless promising potential difficulty. Normally such children are sent away from home. The educational and social work techniques used by the centre staff concentrate on the development of creative skills using art, wood-work, needlework, gardening and many other 'non-academic' activities which have proven therapeutic value with withdrawn adolescents and children. These activities are normally scheduled for the afternoons, the mornings being spent in more formal educational pursuits in which the teachers use their remedial skills. At one stage, the centre opened as a youth club for several evenings each week, and attracted many other children who would have been otherwise 'at risk' on the streets.

The Sandiacre Intermediate Treatment Scheme in Derbyshire is also an 'alternative' facility. Indeed the prime criterion for selection is that referred children should have received a custodial sentence or 'Care Order' from the juvenile court, which normally has the effect of removing a child from his home and placing him in an institution. All the adolescents in the Sandiacre Scheme, however, need to demonstrate an ability to fit into the local schools, and the facility provides evening care through a social worker who not only does the evening groupwork with the delinquents, but also carries out the on-going casework with their families. This scheme does not have premises, but uses a local youth club and some of the volunteer youth workers to assist the social worker during the evening meetings which are held twice weekly. It is clear that the delinquents undergoing intermediate treatment are from families who are unable to offer sufficient support and control to their children during the time when they are not at school, hence the evening care with occasional residential weekends.

School can be a problem for some, but the social workers stay in close touch with the local school, and have so far been able to keep the children attending there rather than being forced to set up an 'alternative school' as was the case in Islington. Perhaps one of the most interesting innovations of the Sandiacre Project is its use of the youth club in which it is based. In view of the fact that the children in the project are in need of intensive supervision while they are not at school, the social worker actually saw his task as creating a situation where the children could be phased into this youth club rather than continue to be maintained in his special group. To this end, the local youth leader attends many of the group sessions, then personally invites the children to come into his club for the latter part of the evening. Because the children know him already, they go into the club and participate in its normal activities with the non-stigmatized adolescents who use it as part of their leisure activities. This systematic and planned progression from a specialized facility into a standard community facility provides a good illustration of the operation of the policy which was originally intended for intermediate treatment. At the stage where the children cease to receive their treatment in the special group, their Care Orders will be discharged by the juvenile court, and a Supervision Order made with a condition of attendance at the youth club.

For delinquents less immediately at risk of removal from the community, many well-developed examples already exist in

F

England and Wales. Such facilities can best be described as 'middle-range' schemes, i.e. schemes which provide intensive supervision for adjudicated offenders whose behaviour and home backgrounds are not yet considered sufficiently damaging to give rise to the question of removal from home, but nevertheless show a developing commitment to a delinquent career. As with all the schemes described in this chapter, the medium for intervention is the group, and activities are used in the group therapy programme to develop systematically more positive self-concepts, thereby increasing social adjustment, as well as providing physical supervision in the evenings and weekends when boredom and lack of supervision at home can lead to a drift into delinquent activity. Such groups are usually run by social workers and volunteers, and their objectives are to provide a more positive and intensive type of intervention than that which normally would ensue from a Supervision Order.

An example of a typical 'middle-range' scheme is the St. Helen's intermediate treatment project currently operated by the Social Services Department for St. Helen's Metropolitan Borough. It has two components, one based in the community, and one based at a residential centre. Each of the six groups meets weekly for an evening in the community and also attends the residential centre for three weekends and a full week during the year. The weekly meetings take place in the neighbourhoods from which the children are drawn; a variety of premises are used, ranging from youth clubs to specially rented rooms depending on whatever is available and appropriate in the area. During the weekly evening meetings, the social workers lead a variety of activities—formal discussions, table games, communication and drama exercises and standard leisure activities such as swimming and bowling. In this setting, relationships are established with a peer group and with the adults who supervise. The relationships with the supervising adults are the only resource provided which would not normally be available for these delinquents, most of whom are selected from families unable to supply adequate care and control. The children themselves are 'middle-range' delinquents with low self-esteem, poor educational attainment, a high degree of peer-group dependence and a record of at least one episode of delinquency which has resulted in either a formal police caution or a court appearance. The residential component of the programme takes place at Brathay Hall in the Lake District, which offers staff-led outdoor and indoor activities not normally available to the groups in their weekly meetings in the community. The social workers who attend with their groups also participate in the rock-climbing, fell-walking, canoeing, art and drama activities with their children. The programme has the effect of intensifying the group processes already established because the range of behaviours and roles open to the social workers and their clients expands as a result of having to live together rather than meet in an evening for a few hours.

This type of programme has proved more effective than traditional supervision; the in-treatment failure rate appears to be as low as 10 per cent, considerably lower than would normally be expected. At the moment, few opportunities exist for systematically phasing these children into normal community youth clubs, partly because the programme has not been running for very long, and partly because as yet the dialogue with the youth service has been rather limited. The social workers correctly see the need to maintain the delinquents in the groups for up to two years, but would prefer to see a 12-month programme followed by phasing into youth clubs. As the Islington Centre depended on disposal to ordinary schools, so the St. Helen's programme will ultimately perhaps depend on disposal to youth clubs. The need for this type of co-operation was foreseen by the government in 1968 in 'Children in Trouble', and very clearly illustrates the extent to which the poor self-image of the delinquent and the social stigma attached to his or her personality renders the child incapable of using standard schools or youth clubs. This mechanism all too often compounds the degree of social and psychological handicap, which the adolescents compensate for by developing commitments to activities which do provide status, a peer group and excitement, but also eventual incarceration.

Nevertheless, there are delinquents who are capable of using conventional youth facilities, whose families do provide adequate supervision, and whose delinquencies can effectively be prevented by means of a direct attachment to a youth group or club. These adolescents have no immediate need for the specialized groups which I have so far described under the heading of intermediate treatment. It is difficult to estimate the numbers of such delinquents placed on supervision, but they would undoubtedly be found among the ranks of those who would usually respond well to the supervision process, be able to establish a good personal relationship in the one-to-one casework context with their supervisor, yet show themselves to be in need of an extra stimulus to raise their self-esteem and check a potential drift towards membership in a peer-group with stronger anti-social tendencies than is normally acceptable. The type of intermediate treatment scheme which would be suitable for such children is illustrated by the present Regional Plans for intermediate treatment—literally lists of available youth clubs and activities. The leaders of these clubs would, under normal circumstances, have consented to accepting the occasional child referred by a social worker or probation officer responsible for the supervision order. The child would be directed to attend the club, usually after an introduction from the supervising officer, and whenever possible should have indicated an interest in club member-ship or some of the activities offered by the facility. Many delin-quents are currently benefitting from such 'allocation' types of intermediate treatment, though the actual numbers receiving this type of help are in all probability fewer than those who use the more specialized facilities such as the St. Helen's project. Attend-ance at a youth club is the least intensive form of intermediate treatment currently practised in England and Wales. Such a scheme does appear to be suitable only for the low-risk juvenile offender, although of course this type of activity is set as an objective by the social workers who run the more treatment-intensive facilities, for their clients to be phased eventually into normal community activi-ties.

The in-treatment failure rates of institutions are low compared with post-treatment failures, and in programmes which supply intensive supervision, these relative rates of failure appear to be less far apart. If, as I have already suggested, the inability to use schools and youth facilities serves to handicap a delinquent adolescent even further, then it is clear that the provision of specialized educational and recreational experiences can only provide a temporary compen-sation. The treatment works while it is being received although rates of absconding from 'open' institutions can be quite high. The critical phase seems to occur at the end of a period of institutional training or day care, and probably evening care too. It would appear therefore, that all rehabilitation programmes are at their most vulnerable when the period of treatment ends, and the child has to go back to school, or to his home or a job. In short, the disadvan-tages of residential care offer an extreme example of the disadvan-tages of all specialized social work intervention for delinquents. In this respect, the systematic and gradual phasing or 'after-care' programmes offered by the Providence Education Centre and the Sandiacre Project seem to optimize the chances of successful rehabilitation. The Providence Centre begins discussions with prospective employers and schools long before discharge, and the

Sandiacre group actually holds meetings at a youth club which form part of the treatment programme.

Consideration of this issue could lead to the formation of a coherent policy for the management of low and high risk juvenile delinquents within the community. Such a policy has been called a 'continuum of care' (Paley and Thorpe, 1974), and it is possible to construct a programme of intermediate treatment which would theoretically provide community-based supervision for virtually the full range of juvenile delinquents, leaving only those who require highly skilled attention in institutions, primarily because their behaviour is such as to constitute a serious danger to others. The following table illustrates such a policy.

If Table VIII is compared with many conventional policies for the management of juvenile delinquents, then the two items missing from the table would be the ones which conventionally occur in most agencies, that is *either* one-to-one casework supervision in the community, *or* full-time residential care in an institution. Experience tells us, and research has shown us, that those two limiting extremes are indeed extremes, for not every adolescent who receives casework or residential care benefits by such provision—hence the formulation of the concept of Intermediate Treatment, which offers the potential of maximizing the opportunities presented by conventional casework, as well as giving many of the benefits of residential care without some of its disadvantages.

Legal provision for alternatives to care already exist in England and Wales. The 'Care Order' merely commits a child to the care of the Local Authority, and it is that body which decides what form the care should take—whether it be of a residential, day-care, or evening and weekend care variety. The 'Thirty Day Order', a condition of supervision, provides the initial stimulus for weekly group meetings or attendance at a club. Whether a total of thirty days' enforced attendance is adequate is not yet known. Experience suggests that it is, although as the majority of delinquents participating in specialized group schemes either have not had this condition as part of their supervision, or have accepted continued attendance after the expiration of thirty weeks of once-weekly attendance (almost a year when holiday periods are taken into consideration). In turn, the Regional Plans for children in trouble should eventually provide comprehensive schemes such as that outlined in the Table on Intermediate Treatment Facilities.

The 'Ninety Day Order', contained in the 1969 CYPA and loosely described as intermediate treatment, amounts to a fixed short-term

TABLE VIII

Intermediate treatment facilities

Nature of facility	Intensity of supervision	Staffing	Programme components	Criteria for selection	Disposal
Day Care	Highly intensive. Some week-end care.	Teachers Social workers Craft/Trade instructors Volunteers	Remedial education Trade training Group work Programme After-care preparation	Alternative to care High-risk offender No serious danger to community. Inability to attend school or work.	To Evening Care or a weekly group. Attendance at local school or full-time employment.
Evening Care	Highly intensive. Some week-end care.	Teachers Social workers Youth workers Volunteers	Group work Programme Leisure activities Some remedial work After-care preparation	Alternative to care High-risk offender No serious danger to community. Must be able to attend school or work during day.	To Weekly Group or Youth Club.
Weekly Group	Medium intensity. Some week-end care.	Social workers Youth workers Volunteers	Group work Programme Leisure activities Programme After-care preparation	Persistent petty offender. Attends school or works. At risk of further court appearances.	To Youth Club or other group which will continue to maintain positive self-concept.
Youth Club or group	Low-medium intensity. No week-ends.	Youth workers Volunteers	Leisure activities, to be continued at termination of supervision.	One or two isolated offences, but requires stimulation. Able to form relationships relatively quickly.	Continue to attend without need for official direction.

residential order within the context of a supervision order. Strictly speaking, the 'ninety day order' is not of an intermediate treatment nature as it would not appear to be an alternative to care. In the context of the 1969 CYPA, this particular order is intended to replace the Detention Centre Order—a sentence which results normally in the removal of a delinquent from the community and placed for up to three months in a prison-type institution. The notable lack of success of Detention Centres necessitates a replacement, and this replacement has appeared within the ambit of the supervision order.

Many questions remain on alternatives to institutional care for juvenile offenders. Some will be answered by research and experience; others may not be answerable. Hitherto, most programmes for the management of delinquents in the United States and the United Kingdom have met with very limited success, and one would not expect intermediate treatment to supply any kind of 'miracle cure'. However, judging from the American experience, alternatives to institutions are at least as effective as residential programmes, and more importantly, they are much more humane. If intensive supervision should develop into the major method of social work intervention with high-risk persistent offenders, one would envisage a vastly reduced population in institutions for delinquents. The difficulty is still that of deciding who should receive residential care, thus bringing the social work profession face to face with the fundamental principle of social work with children and young people— that of 'the best interests of the child'. Because the sentencing options for delinquents in England and Wales have been relatively limited in the past, the best interests of the child, and the best interests of society have generally appeared to coincide. With the development of intermediate treatment, only a very small number of delinquents will need residential treatment, and the criteria for receiving such help are more likely to revolve around pressures for punishment and control, rather than the social and psychological needs of particular offenders. The problem will then become one of determining and defining the stage at which a particular act, or sequence of acts are considered such a serious danger to society that residential control becomes the only choice. In the meantime, the closing of institutions should release resources which will, one hopes, have the effect of improving the quality of care within the community by providing delinquents with genuine alternatives to deviant careers.

CHAPTER FIVE

The Use of Family Placements in the Treatment of Delinquency

NANCY HAZEL

Alternative systems of placement

One starting point of any strategy for coping with crime is intervention while the young offender is living in his own home. This intervention is preventive, seeking to prevent further misbehaviour which would lead to removal from home and consequent placement. Intermediate treatment schemes are an extension of these preventive measures in that periods away from home may be included. Placement away from home is normally the last resort and, for older boys and girls in England and Wales, has usually been in residential care classified by age, sex and symptom. Children in England and Wales may be prosecuted from the age of 10 years and the tariff system of sentencing in the Juvenile Courts reflects the progression from 'preventive' measures to placement, beginning with fines or supervision before resorting to care orders, detention centres or Borstal training. 'A court may sentence a young offender (15 to 21 years) to borstal training if he is convicted of an offence for which an adult offender may be sent to prison. Borstal training is a custodial sentence, the period in custody, being at least 6 months, depends on the response to training, but can not exceed two years.' On the issue of sentencing the laws of most European countries differ from England's in that children under the age of 18, or sometimes 16, generally cannot be prosecuted except for very serious offences or matters related to road traffic. In other words, in these countries, offences by juveniles tend to be construed as matters of upbringing rather than crimes against society. This probably reduces the risk of these children being labelled as anti-social, even if it does not affect their immediate placement.

Representatives of all the countries of the Council of Europe agree on the priority to be given to preventive work. This was formally stated at Nice in 1972 at a meeting of government ministers responsible for the family where it was agreed that policies should be developed to support and help families and that placement should be seen as a last resort. Most industrialized societies would support this idea. However, in all countries there is a population of children who can no longer remain in their homes with their own parents, either because their parents are unable to give them satisfactory care or because their own behaviour has become unacceptable to society. For this population of children and young persons who enter the care of public or voluntary bodies there is no agreement about the best mode of placement. In some countries virtually all children and young persons, including offenders, are retained in the community, either living with families or in some other small-scale, private arrangement. Sweden has chosen this pattern, using residential care only for specific short-term tasks of assessment and treatment, and with a small residue of 500 places (not all of which are filled), for delinquent young persons up to 21 years of age. Two national commissions have recently (1974) reported in Sweden—one on the placement of children and young persons and the other, the social commission, on broader issues. The Swedish view appears to be that research gives little support to residential care as a means of dealing with delinquency for either sex or any age group. On the other hand, new methods of social work are being developed to give more intensive help in the community. One example is called 'together at home', in which the social worker spends many hours sharing the family's life and tasks. At the same time, the National Commission on the Placement of Children and Young Persons found that foster care was successful for most children up to 15 years—only 10 per cent of those in foster care aged 7–15 years showed 'considerable' difficulties and the terminations were generally related to factors outside the child himself, such as actions by the family of origin. In only 5 per cent of the cases were the changes of home due to breakdown, that is, a decision by the foster parents not to continue. Older adolescents also live successfully in foster homes, and placement in private families has now been developed for the most difficult group of all—Stockholm adolescents with problems of drug abuse. Although not yet fully evaluated, this scheme appears very promising.

The Swedish system of foster care has evolved from the placement of pauper children on distant farms, and many foster children
are still living in substitute homes far from their area of origin. A
proportion of these represent the last generation of stigmatized
illegitimate children. However, the system offers a good basis from
which the placement of disturbed and delinquent children and
young persons can be developed in line with more modern ideas of
normalization and localization. Evidence of outcomes of the
Swedish system is hard to come by and hard to assess, but this
system is certainly humane, inexpensive and is considered preferable
to residential care.

Other countries, however, rely entirely, or almost entirely, on a
residential system of placement. Belgium, for example, has a fostering rate of about 16 per cent, with other children and adolescents
placed in residential establishments. (Kalveston, 1976.) Belgians
traditionally mistrust foster parents; it is felt that the complex and
difficult task of bringing up deprived or delinquent children or
young persons should be entrusted to experts, as ordinary people
could not be expected to have the necessary skills. There are many
small children's homes in Belgium, but delinquent adolescents are
placed in large one-sex institutions with a range of expert staff and
education on the premises. The approach involves the use of
psychiatrists, psychologists, residential care experts, teachers, social
workers, speech therapists, and remedial gymnasts. Findings are
co-ordinated at frequent case conferences. This system is extremely
expensive, there is a shortage of qualified experts, and there is no
evidence to show whether it is effective or not.

England and Wales have a 'half-and-half' system for the placement of children and adolescents in public care. Although the proportion of children under supervision at home has increased recently,
the proportion accommodated in foster homes and residential care
does not change very much. In 1975 it was 32 per cent in foster
homes, and 34 per cent in residential care (D.H.S.S., 1975). Although
a high proportion of young persons enter care at adolescence (in
Kent by far the greatest number of care orders are made for 15-year-
olds, and this trend is probably general), only a very small proportion of them are placed in foster homes, and a very low proportion
of the total population of adolescents in care live in foster homes.
For example, in 1975 in the large county of Kent (population $1\frac{1}{2}$
million), 40·9 per cent of the boys and 45·0 of the girls in the care of
the local authority were over 14. Of these only 9 per cent of the boys
and 23 per cent of the girls were in foster homes, and these almost

certainly represented the least delinquent individuals. Only 5·3 per cent of the boys and 12·2 per cent of the girls had been placed after their 14th birthdays (figures from unpublished survey of 20 per cent of children in care in Kent).

Most English fostering appears to be concerned with the short-term placement of young children and the provision of long-term substitute homes. Disturbed and delinquent older boys and girls have traditionally been considered 'unsuitable for fostering', and for children of all ages in foster care the breakdown rate is about 50 per cent—a high figure (National Children's Bureau 1973). The majority of delinquent boys are placed in one-sex community homes with education on the premises, an expensive solution with an apparently poor success rate. Cornish and Clarke compare two regimes, a conventional structured regime and a therapeutic community regime. The re-conviction rates over three years for both regimes were 67 per cent for those released on after-care and 75 per cent if all releases are included. The authors suggest that 'only for about 20 per cent of those admitted to the school could it be argued that institutional intervention had provided more than a temporary interruption of their delinquent behaviour' (Cornish and Clarke, 1975).

Other research studies also demonstrate that residential treatment for delinquent adolescents is expensive and ineffectual, but the bias of priorities continues to be towards residential care. In 1975 the amount spent on residential care was £110m., compared with £14m. on fostering (D.H.S.S., 1976). At the same time considerable resources were devoted by the Department of Health and Social Security to the Development Group, which was established in 1968 'to provide a resource for exploration of ideas and methods in conjunction with field agencies, government departments, universities, training bodies and others. Its broad aims were to build 'models' to assist development of services and produce publications to stimulate discussion and debate.' (D.H.S.S., 1976.) Unfortunately, the 'models' which were developed referred to residential care and no comparable work was undertaken to develop placements in the community.

How then can research findings be used to change social policy? So far research in foster care has been of the academic type. It has been received with approbation by an elite audience, and fed to generations of students, yet has had little or no impact on practice.

The Kent Special Family Placement Project is of a different

nature. It is a small-scale demonstration project attempting to develop a model of placement in the community, mainly based on the theories and practice of other countries.

Setting up the Kent Special Family Placement Project

In 1974 I found myself becoming increasingly aware of the vast potential for family placement of children and young persons who, in England, had previously been considered 'unfosterable', whilst, at the same time, the Department of Health and Social Security was planning to build new and costly secure units, and an increasing number of adolescents were being sent to adult prisons and remand centres. At that time statements were constantly made about the shortage of residential accommodation, whereas to me it seemed that there was far too much residential care—a point of view reinforced by the findings of Rowe and Lambert, who estimated that about 7,000 children were, on the judgement of their social workers, in need of long-term substitute homes (1973).

Nicolas Stacey, Director of Kent County Council Social Services Department, was also at that time particularly concerned with the treatment of adolescents, and Vic George, Professor of Social Work and Social Administration at the University of Kent, had a long-standing interest in foster care. Thus at a time when the treatment of delinquent adolescents was a matter of considerable public concern, the key people in the Kent scheme happened to be in the same area and interested in developing new methods.

With the backing of the Social Services Department and the University, funds were obtained from a charitable trust, the Gatsby Charitable Foundation, to set up a 5-year demonstration project, starting in January 1975. The project was to be an attempt to challenge the conventional thinking that adolescent delinquency can only be tackled by supervision at home, which has obvious limitations, or by a (preferably escape-proof) residential placement.

In the first progress report the objectives of the project were defined as follows:

> an attempt to test the long-held view that a large proportion of English children are 'unsuitable for fostering' . . . More specifically, what we want to know is: If you spend as much money on developing a family placement in the community as it costs

to use a residential place, can you obtain more effective help for the adolescent with severe problems who must, *unavoidably*, leave his home, at any rate for a short period?

Can ordinary people, in their own homes, provide *effective* help to teenagers with severe problems?
If help can be given in this way, are there some adolescents who cannot profit by it? If so, which? (Hazel and Cox, 1976.)
The project is a small semi-independent unit, with the staff salaries paid by the Gatsby Charitable Foundation, and project organizer employed as senior research fellow by the University of Kent. The project places adolescents who are in the care of the Kent Social Services Department, which pays the professional fee and all other expenses. This tri-partite structure gives the project a degree of autonomy in developing methods of work different from those traditionally used by the department. This autonomy is almost essential if traditional ways of working are to be effectively challenged. It has, however, certain drawbacks. Communications with the large Social Service Department are complicated and do not always work well. A small unit, outside the mainstream of day-to-day social work practice, may be perceived as both privileged and threatening. It therefore tends to attract hostility from the central administration, because it does not easily fit the accepted rules; from the field social workers because it is novel, specialized, and in control of substantial resources; from the residential workers because it may be seen as a criticism of their way of working; and from the traditional foster parents who may think the project families receive much larger sums of money than themselves for the same work. Care was taken at the start of the project to invite existing foster parents to join if they wished, but hardly any seemed to be attracted to this kind of work. (Similar problems have been experienced by other fostering projects. For example the province (Land) of Hessen, Germany places disturbed older children and young persons who are in the care of the local (Kreis) youth offices. Difficulties of communication can arise from time to time between the province and local offices.)
The Kent project has a life-span of five years, with the expectation that successful procedures will in the long run be incorporated into the department. The project is:

(1) Specialized, so that the objectives can be made as specific as possible.

(2) Time-limited, so that evaluation and feed-back cannot be delayed.
(3) Small, so that relatively complete descriptions of the course of events can be published at regular intervals during the life of the project.
(4) Experimental, so that its success or failure can be assessed by research.

From the outset we in the Kent project aimed to enlist the backing of the media in the belief, first, that help from local communities can be gained only if people understand what is needed, and, secondly, that if the project is an attempt to change policies, some way must be found of telling the public what is at stake, and to publicize solutions which appear to be successful. In fact the media —television, radio, the national, local and professional press—have shown consistent interest in the scheme and their reporting has been both fair to the professional staff and sensitive to the need to protect vulnerable individuals. Similarly, the degree of interest expressed by local authorities, voluntary child care organizations and the Department of Health and Social Security was unexpectedly high. This wide interest reflects to some extent the public uneasiness about the relative ineffectiveness of current forms of care. In 1976 over 2,000 copies of the first progress report were distributed. Three articles by project staff appeared in professional journals. The project staff were inundated with invitations to speak at conferences and seminars and a number of authorities and voluntary bodies have now set up similar schemes.

The Berkshire scheme for salaried foster parents, which was set up shortly before the Kent scheme, has also published an account of their work, which has been received with a similarly high degree of interest (Hartnell, 1974).

It would seem fair to say that the impact of the two small schemes in Berkshire and Kent has been to shake ideas once taken for granted—that older delinquent children, once removed from home, must almost automatically enter residential care.

Developing a 'methods package'

The Kent project is trying to develop a 'methods package' which can be transferred to other areas. The basic components of the package are:

(1) *The professional fee*—a professional fee, in addition to the maintenance payment, is paid to the project parents for the duration of the child's placement. One placement is held to be roughly the equivalent of a part-time job and two placements a full-time job. The fee maintains the freelance status of the project families.

(2) *The groups*—all applicants wishing to become project parents must obtain a vacancy in a local group. The groups usually meet fortnightly, although some well-established groups may meet at monthly intervals. They are composed of about five couples and one or two social workers. The groups are the work place of the project; they carry responsibility for selection, training, mutual support and help, and the development of policy. New entrants remain in the group until it is felt that they are ready to proceed to a placement. Once the boy or girl is placed the group provides a forum for discussion and evaluation of the placement.

(3) *The contracts*—each placement is defined by written agreements which set out the estimated duration of the placement (this can subsequently be reduced or extended), the objectives and the responsibilities of all parties to the agreement, i.e. the adolescent, the project family, the social workers and the family of origin. Agreements with the last are not always written because of practical difficulties; it is hoped this area of work will be further developed.

The placements are essentially problem-solving, that is to say, concerned with working on problems which are evident to the adolescent himself, such as school problems, stealing, running away or bad relationships with his own parents. Other problems may be recognized later in the placement and can be added to the contract.

The project workers believe that the basic theoretical framework of social work practice should be as simple as possible, so that it is easily comprehended and can be used without a lengthy preliminary training. The project aims to harness the commitment and affectionate concern which many people feel towards 'adrift' adolescents, and to utilize their intelligence, sincerity and commonsense to work on defined problems within an agreed time span without bringing in any elaborate sociological or psychological theories. The work of the project is based on four important principles which were set out by the Swedish Commission on the placement of children and young people (1974).

Normalization. The project seeks to implement the principle of 'normalization'. Given that a certain population of young people have already been separated from their own homes, to which they may or may not eventually return, the task is to equip them for successful living in 'normal' society. We believe that they can best acquire this equipment by living 'normal' lives. As most people live in families and go out to school or work, it is in this situation that they should be helped to become viable adults. They will have both the freedom and opportunities of 'normal' living and also be faced with its stresses and difficulties—but they should have constant support and help to understand and meet these challenges.

The delinquent or disturbed adolescent will be a minority of one in a 'normal' family group whose members will not themselves usually be interested in delinquent or generally unacceptable activities. In this sense a family placement is in contrast to many residential placements where, for example, delinquent boys are placed together so that delinquency is a constant topic of conversation and interest.

Similarly, in a family placement boys and girls will grow up together at home and at school or work, so that the adolescent can develop his sexual identity and standards of behaviour in an open and natural way with the help of the foster parents. Most residential placements for adolescents are in one-sex establishments where sex may become a highly charged topic.

The fostered adolescent will also attend a day school or go out to work. If he needs special educational or vocational help, this should be sought in the community, as it would be for children living with their own families.

In a sense there is of course no such thing as a 'normal' life-style. The life-style of the placement family will always differ from that of the family of origin, as no two families are alike, and, in any case the project does not seek to match by similarity. The adolescent is required to fit in with the project family's life-style during the placement, but there is no reason why he should choose to live as they do in the long run. He may choose the life-style of his family of origin or he may develop a way of life different from either of these models. It is hoped that the experience of the placement will give him the confidence, the social and vocational skills and the flexibility to develop successfully in his own way.

Individualization. The project seeks to provide adolescents separated from their own homes with one or two people who will offer them a committed individual relationship, and who will be prepared to listen carefully and to try hard to see and understand the adolescent's point of view. They will then act on his behalf in any ways which appear to be helpful to him. The adolescent will have acquired an advocate who will stand up for his rights, but who is also entitled to criticize him and to make suggestions concerning the solution of the problems for which the placement has been initiated. In residential systems, the numbers and turnover of staff and their conditions of service make such individual relationships difficult to sustain, and the interests of the group as a whole make the advocate role almost impossible. The greatest strength of a family placement is that it can provide almost unlimited listening. The family is 'on the side' of one adolescent in a way that can never be the case in a group.

The project will sometimes place two adolescents with complementary needs in one family, but never more.

Participation. This principle rests on the concept of equality of esteem and status. There are four parties to a placement:

the adolescent
the family of origin
the placement family
the social workers.

All should negotiate on equal terms to reach voluntarily agreed conclusions. All agreements should be made as explicit as possible. This principle, however, has certain limitations:

(1) Legal accountability. The adolescent is still a minor in the eyes of the law, which places certain restrictions on his freedom through the guardianship either of his own parents or the social worker acting *in loco parentis*. Conversely, the social worker is legally accountable for the adolescent's welfare, and cannot agree to courses of action which appear dangerous or otherwise unsuitable.
(2) Coercive measures. The courts may use coercive measures, such as care orders, which place the power to decide in the hands of the social worker who has then no obligation to consult the other parties.

The project believes that coercive measures are undesirable and generally avoidable, and that there should always be consultation.

Localization. People normally have their roots and social networks in one area, and placement should not deprive an adolescent

G

of this important part of his identity. Placement should therefore usually be within the home area, so that contact with family and friends is maintained. However, the placement of delinquent adolescents or others whose behaviour has become very unaccept- able to the local community may require that this principle be breached. A delinquent identity may be so firmly established in school and in the streets, that the adolescent will be blamed for every crime and expected to act out a delinquent role before his peers, so that a change of school and peer group may be an essential pre-requisite to change. Some adolescents, after a lifetime in care, have no ties with any locality, or may have positive or negative links with several places.

The project is based on the belief that people should help each other; the project families' task is to help other families in the com- munity, and to help and support each other. Now that we are reaching a second generation of placements it is the task of the boys and girls already in placement to help the newcomers. We are all in it together.

Finally, we believe, with Caplan (Caplan, 1964) that crises are not unpleasant events to be papered over or swept under the carpet. A crisis may be a nuisance, but it may also be a growing point if it is used to deepen a relationship and to explore feelings which have surfaced, or have been triggered off by the crisis situation. Our placements are concerned with growth and change, which conse- quently mean movement, and disturbance from time to time.

Relationships with the residential care system

When the project was set up it was envisaged as an extension of residential care into the community. There were a number of reasons for looking at it in this way.

The most skilled help available to adolescents in care during the 1970s was probably in most cases given by residential staff. Since the re-organization of the Social Services Departments following the Local Authority Social Services Act of 1970, fieldworkers have carried generic caseloads and few of them have received specialized training or gained long experience in work with adolescents. The project therefore hoped to make available to the newly recruited families the expertise of residential staff. From the start, the groups have met in residential establishments and welcomed the presence of residential as well as field social workers.

We have also hoped to find a treatment plan established within the 'therapeutic institution' which could be transferred to the family placement, with the residential worker, field social worker and family co-operating to ensure a smooth transition. This plan was based on the German examples described by Bonhoeffer and Widemann (1974), but has not so far proved feasible.

We also planned to rely on the assessment of a residential centre at the point of referral. In practice this has not always been necessary, as a social worker may know the boy or girl very well in his own home and his information may be a perfectly satisfactory basis for placement.

We predicted that we should need to turn to the residential system at moments of crisis and this has in fact proved to be the case. What we need are 'crisis centres', which can hold a hysterical or angry adolescent for a short period and actively talk through the present crisis. In most instances a return to the foster home or replacement in the community should follow without delay.

Finally, the concept of the residential centre as the 'hub of a wheel' (Hazel, 1975) actively promoting placements, surrounded by 'outposts' of placement families, and involved with training and supporting them, has not materialized.

The Placement Families

The project has not experienced any difficulty in recruiting families. Two ideas appear to have considerable appeal:

(1) fostering as a paid career
(2) the challenge of a difficult but worthwhile task.

Traditional fostering consisted of adding a child to a family where the mother was usually at home and provided loving care in return for a maintenance payment. The task was to give the child a substitute home.

The tasks of 'career fostering' are different and consist of dealing with problems of many kinds and developing a range of strategies of rehabilitation. Skilled work of this sort should receive suitable remuneration, equivalent to outside employment.

Such tasks might be held to require professional training. The German special placement schemes all require relevant qualifications, and in England the Berkshire scheme asks for qualifications and/or experience in working with children or adolescents.

The Kent scheme has not required qualifications and it seems that a wide variety of families are able to do this work with considerable success. It seems legitimate to pay a professional fee if families are willing to undertake 'high risk' types of foster care, and are capable of doing the work. Fostering as a career seems to fit well with certain contemporary trends in society. Families are now generally small, but many people seem to wish to live in a larger, more loose-knit group, with more physical space, yet without abandoning the concept of family life. Many families base their life-styles on the availability of two incomes in the long run, so that the wife expects to work. However, many women do not wish to *go out* to work, although they need the intellectual stimulation, the social contacts and the money which employment may provide. Working for the project seems to meet these needs quite well and is, in addition, perceived as a worthwhile and important activity. Although working for the project tends to take the place of other employment for the wife, husbands are always involved and attend the groups regularly.

The families which have been recruited are difficult to classify in social class/occupational terms, but they have one common characteristic. All the wives either have relevant professional qualifications or have held down responsible jobs in business. The husbands have a wide range of skilled or professional occupations. The families tend to be buying their own houses. More of them live in country areas and fewer in city centres or on large housing estates than is the case for the population as a whole. All ages appear equally successful. Adolescents fit well into families with very young children, but also enjoy the company of other adolescents, providing they can make friends at the start. They have also settled well into households without children, where there is no competition from other young people.

The families of origin

The most striking characteristic of the families of origin is how few of them consist of both parents of the adolescent, legally married to each other. The parents of origin tend to be older than the project families, and their families are larger, often with four or more children at home, being sometimes the children of more than one marriage. These families are more likely to live in Council property, and the occupations of the adolescent's parents are generally less skilled than those of the project families. In some of the families both parents are working, and it is only in a minority of cases that poverty is a pressing problem.

It seems that the reception into care of those teenagers who are referred to the project is more likely to be related to problems of intra-family relationships than to the stresses of poverty or single parenthood, although these may be contributing factors. Many adolescents are rejected by their parents, and delinquent or unacceptable behaviour both reflects and confirms this rejection. During placement, relationships with the family of origin tend to become more amicable, probably because the pressure of guilt is eased on both sides.

Matching

The project does not attempt to match children and foster parents by their education or social class. The families of origin appear to accept the fact that the project families are fee-earning professionals with their own life-styles, and relationships between the families have generally been rather cordial. In matching, factors of personality, interests and physical environment are obviously considered, but 'arranging a marriage' of this sort is a very intuitive business. Child placement is essentially an art, based on half conscious impressions and subjective value judgements, however much information is collected.

The placements

The first placement made by the project, in May 1975, was a 14-year-old boy who had been the subject of an 'unruly' order and had been accommodated in an adult prison and a remand centre. In December 1976 he is still in his foster home, a prefect at school and a very successful boy.

By 1 December 1976 the project had made 49 placements, 25 boys and 24 girls. Referrals are made by the Divisional social workers, the only conditions that the adolescent be 14–17 years old have 'severe' problems. Adolescents with mental or physical handicaps are outside the scope of the scheme. Apart from these young people with problems of any kind are accepted, and in retrospect their problems fall into a number of categories:

'Delinquent boys'—stealing, taking and driving away, etc.
'Beyond-control girls'—staying out, promiscuous sexual relation-
ships, drinking, etc.
Emotionally disturbed girls who are receiving psychiatric treat-
ment.
Backward boys and girls who are unable to cope with adult life.
Boys and girls who have spent many years in large children's
homes.

A number of boys and girls have records of violent behaviour.
Several boys have been to detention centres. Many have records of
absconding.

An assessment of the project by an independent research worker
is to be carried out. Meanwhile, as an interim measure, the staff of
the project have made an impressionistic study of outcomes up to
the first of December 1976.

The placements were divided into the following categories:

Completions, other than breakdowns.
A—the project workers see this placement as very positive.
B—positive elements predominate, but there are some negative
elements.
C—ambiguous situation or positive and negative elements evenly
balanced.
D—some positive elements, but negative elements predominate.
E—breakdowns.
Very recent placements—under 2 months in the foster home.

Out of a total of 49 placements over the course of the project
there were:

Completions	=	6
Established placements	=	30 (A–D)
Recent placements	=	8
Failures	=	5 (E)

Completions: 6—4 girls and 2 boys. 5 returned home; 1 to local
lodgings.

Age at
Nov. 1976
Girl   16   doing well after 14 months (4 months in placement)

Girl	16	training as nurse; believed to be doing well after 9 months	(9 months in placement)
Boy	17	doing well after 6 months (in lodgings)	(7 months in placement)
Girl	17	doing well after 2 months	(13 months in placement)
Girl	18	married, emigrated 2 months ago, receiving psychiatric treatment, but very good support from in-laws	(9 months in placement)
Boy	15	at home for 2 months	(4 months in placement)

Established placements:
A placements   15
B placements   14
C placements   1
D placements   0

Failures:
E placements   3 'long-term' breakdowns
               2 breakdowns within 8 weeks

Very recent placements: 8—2 boys and 6 girls
Girl—14 years;   girl—15 years
Girl—15 years;   boy—16 years
Girl—15 years;   girl—14 years
Girl—16 years;   boy—15 years

The study continues with greater detail on the established placements graded A–E, which excludes completions and recent placements. All ages are at placement.

A Placements—boys:
Boys aged 14–15, delinquent but no prolonged residential care   5
Boys aged 14–15, delinquent and considerable residential care   2
Non-delinquent boys aged 14–15 with long residential
experience   1

                                                                8

A Placements—girls:
Aged 15, delinquent but no prolonged residential care   1
Emotionally disturbed, 15 years, little residential experience 2

Non-delinquent, 14–15 years, with long residential experience   2
Non-delinquent, 16, with long residential experience   2

  —

   7

Thirteen of the 'A' youths had been in placement six months or more. Only two had been placed for under two months. Very few of the A placements are over age 15 at placement. Younger delinquent boys without much residential experience seem to be the most promising group.

B Placements—boys:
Aged 15, delinquent, but no prolonged residential care   1
Delinquent, and considerable residential care—
                     up to age 15 years   2
                            16 and over   2
Non-delinquent, with long residential care—   14–15 years   3

  —

   8

B Placements—girls:
Aged 15, delinquent, some residential care   1
Aged 15, emotionally disturbed, some residential care   1
Long residential care—16 and over   4

  —

   6

Eight of the 'B' youths had had placements of 6 months or longer; 6 had been in placement for under 6 months. Only one of the B placements had little or no experience of residential care. Six were over school age. In these placements the less satisfactory elements may be almost entirely the consequence of limitations or crises in the foster family (one case) or may be almost entirely due to the adolescents' own difficulties of adjustment, or may be a mixture of both sets of factors.

C Placement:
Boy, aged 14, 5 months in placement, delinquent, with a long experience of residential care. Many ups and downs in the placement so far, but may have a good outcome.

D Placements—0

E Placements: 5—4 boys and 1 girl.

Boy, 15,—7 weeks in placement. Termination caused by uni-lateral decisions by Divisional Social Worker and failure of foster family to integrate boy with local peer group.

Girl, 15,—placement terminated after 6 weeks due to dangerous behaviour with younger children.

Boy, 15. In placement for 11 months. No problems in the foster home, but constant complaints by neighbours for anti-social behaviour and consistent failure to work. Too little control by foster parents, who seldom attended the group. Exit from foster home finally precipitated by a violent row. Wished to live in lodgings and this was agreed.

Boy, 15, fostered by family who already knew him in closed ward of hospital for mentally handicapped. Placement terminated after 7 months due to illness of foster mother. Project has not yet succeeded in re-placing, and ought not to have accepted a mentally handicapped case.

Boy, 15, 4 months in first foster home, 3 months in second foster home. Delinquent and affectionless. Sentenced to Borstal training following a series of offences. No rejection by either foster home, although a move onwards was inevitable due to constant diffi-culties. The boy liked being fostered.

The last two breakdowns seem to represent the kinds of failures which could be anticipated. Both were deprived boys with long residential experience and vivid fantasies about the pleasures of an expensive 'Ted' or 'motor cyclist' life-style. Both were tall and considered themselves adult. Neither was able to show considera-tion for other people.

Within this list of placements 4 transfers have taken place. Two were because of external circumstances which meant that the foster family had to move, but the boy and girl chose to remain in Kent. The other two were because the boy and girl did not settle happily into the first family to which they were introduced. All four trans-ferred easily to other families, where they settled down well.

It seems that the adolescents gain a sense of security from the groups of families they have come to know. They feel that the project provides a network within which they can be transferred and that they will not be moved into a residential establishment against their wishes.

The success of these transfers has led the project to speculate about the use of a series of foster homes as 'stepping stones' in a treatment programme for adolescents with very severe problems. It seems possible to envisage a situation where the first placement can achieve some progress, but at the cost of considerable exhaustion on the side of both the project family and the adolescent. A move onwards means that the boy or girl could leave his mistakes and failures behind and make a fresh start, consolidating at least some of the gains. The issues are quite different from those which arise in the placement of young children in substitute homes, where it is essential to be right first time.

What the outcomes suggest so far

The results so far are distinctly encouraging. In particular, although the numbers are so small, the results suggest that the placement in foster care of 14–15-year-old boys straight from the juvenile court could be an effective strategy. Placement is made at the point where removal from home is unavoidable, but before a delinquent identity has been consolidated. These boys tend to settle easily into family life and do not show the problems of boredom experienced by those who have lived a long time in residential care and are unused to creating their own pursuits.

The project placements appear to work for delinquents, in that so far many of them appear to settle happily into family life, do well at work and school and appear to lose interest in delinquent activities. Emotionally disturbed, backward or institutionalized adolescents also do well. Except for a few brief sorties, no-one has run away. The families of origin appear to like family placements, and contact by the boys and girls with their own homes usually leads either to an improvement in family relationships or to the adolescent's choosing the independence of a young adult.

The foster families report high job satisfaction and in the first two years of the scheme only one family dropped out. The reasons for this job satisfaction seem to have something to do with the current changes in family roles. The wives, who have usually worked until the arrival of the first child, no longer sees themselves as fully occupied in the long run by the tasks of child care and home-making. Many women need the social and intellectual rewards of work more than the financial gain—although this is very important, and families with a mortgage to pay off may plan this in the expectation of two incomes.

It seems that the project offers a career which is attractive to intelligent married women who welcome the challenge of a difficult task and the intellectual challenge of defining and evaluating their work. Most of the husbands are as involved as their wives in the project, but are usually in full-time employment of an unrelated kind.

The project also offers a whole new social network of interested professionals and families engaged in similar tasks. Without the groups the work would be both more difficult and less attractive. Attendance at groups has seldom been a problem and the discussion of ideals and methods produces a sense of cohesion and common purpose. At the same time, comments or criticisms are more easily accepted from others involved in the same work than from any outsider. This is particularly relevant during the selection/training period and when difficulties arise during a placement. Our use of the media is also important as the families feel that the value of what they are trying to do is acknowledged and appreciated.

In the future it would seem desirable that boys and girls who appear before the juvenile courts at the point where they have embarked on a delinquent or 'beyond control' career, and where it is felt that only removal from home can check this career, should normally proceed direct to a family placement rather than entering the residential care system. Enough information should be gathered in advance to enable an appropriate match to be made and, if necessary, residential care can be used as a brief holding operation to complete the assessment. Time-limited treatment placements seem to be a promising form of intervention leading to reconciliation with the family of origin. Family placement is also appropriate for the 'casualties of the system' for whom 'everything has been tried', but, for the rootless products of a lifetime in care, treatment homes must be willing to allow themselves to become true substitute homes.

Family placement for adolescents with severe problems is a promising strategy requiring modest financial resources and no major legislative changes. However, it would be facilitated if several limited changes could be made.

(1) Clearer recognition should be given to the need to support families who care for an adolescent who is unable to become fully independent by the age of 18. Such support can be given under Section 20 of the Children Act 1948 and Section 58 of the Children and Young Persons Act 1963, as well as under the mental health legislation for adults, but the age between 18 and 21 is a confusing area where either legislation for the

protection of young persons or that concerned with vulnerable adults may offer the best means of support.

(2) Consultation between the police and social services departments should be mandatory, so that foster parents can always be fully informed of the likelihood of prosecutions.

(3) There should be some limitation of the time lag between the commission of an offence and the appearance in court. It would be helpful if all cases which have been in abeyance for 6 months could be dropped, as a juvenile cannot be expected to settle down in the shadow of a pending prosecution.

(4) That specialists' skills should be encouraged and an inspectorate created in order to check the development of delinquency and institutionalization among children and young persons in public care.

CHAPTER SIX

Decarceration of Young Offenders in Massachusetts: The Events and Their Aftermath

ANDREW RUTHERFORD

In 1969 facilities and programs for juvenile offenders in Massachusetts were little different from those existing today throughout most of the United States and Western Europe. The nineteenth-century heritage of rurally isolated youth institutions still dominated the official response, and the few community programs offered little more than a mediocre level of supervision. These youth institutions, which are roughly the equivalent of Borstals and community homes, are generally known as training schools. In some states they have been given a more sophisticated image by being labelled youth development centers. Despite the pretensions made that these institutions provide treatment and training experiences they have in recent years become severely discredited. The work of investigative journalists and a series of lawsuits against the official departments responsible for the institutions have led to a greater public appreciation that these settings are primarily characterized by deprivation, dependency, boredom, loneliness, loss of privacy and continual fear of violence. (Key Federal court cases include: *Morales v. Turman*, 383 F. Supp. 53, E.D. Tex 1974; *Nelson v. Heyne*, 355 F. Supp. 451, N.D. Ind. 1974; *Inmates of Boy's Training School v. Affleck*, 346 F. Supp. 1354, D.R.I. 1972.) (See also Wooden, 1976; Polsky, 1962; Bartollas *et al.*, 1976.) Not only have these institutions for youth failed in most instances to be of positive assistance to their inmates, they have also been unable to provide the basic level of care required for normal growth and development. By 1973 these conclusions had become part of the establishment view, with the National Advisory Commission on Criminal Justice Standards and Goals recommending that within a five-year period states should phase out existing juvenile institutions. However, only in the state of Massachusetts has the rhetoric of decarceration been taken really seriously, and the dramatic steps taken in Massachusetts during the early 1970s comprise one of the more significant and hopeful events in the bleak history of penology. As a consequence of rejecting rather than attempting to reform the traditional institutions it was possible to develop a wide range of options for youth in trouble. The abrupt dissolution of the state and county training schools seized the attention of many persons throughout the United States and beyond. The developments in Massachusetts have continued to be of considerable interest, as the emerging processes are as significant as the termination of the old.

The events in Massachusetts are divided into two phases. The first phase, 1969–72, coincides with the term of office of Dr. Jerome Miller, who was the first commissioner of the State Department of Youth Services. (Chapter 838 of the 1969 Acts transformed the Division of Youth Services and the Youth Services Board into a Department of Youth Services, to be directed by a commissioner. The Department was placed within a newly created super agency, the Department of Human Services.) The second phase, 1973–6, covers the terms of office of Joseph Leavey and the present commissioner, John Calhoun.

Revolutionary Change: The Dissolution of the Training Schools

In retrospect, the events which occurred during this phase might appropriately be termed revolutionary (see Rutherford, 1974). They represented a rare example of the rapid replacement of an old set of organizational arrangements with a structure different in both shape and purpose. The unusual nature of the events had attracted attention outside the areas of juvenile justice and corrections (Benn, 1976). The political conditions for this revolutionary change were generally favourable. Throughout the 1960s the Division for Youth Services had been subjected to much adverse criticism. Several state and federal inquiries had reported widescale abuses and had recommended major changes. These demands for reform were supported by much of the media, in particular the influential *Boston Globe*. In January 1969, Francis Sargent became Governor, and within two months had secured the resignation of the long-term director of the Division for Youth Services, Dr. John Coughlin. In August legislation which in previous years had been stalled was enacted which created a new organizational structure with considerable authority invested in the commissioner. Sargent appointed a blue ribbon committee to undertake a nationwide search for commissioner. After considering some fifty applicants, the new committee recommended that the Governor appoint Dr. Jerome G. Miller. Miller became the first commissioner of the newly constituted Department of Youth Services on October 28, 1969.

Jerome Miller was born and raised in Fergus Falls, a small community in northeastern Minnesota. At the age of 18 he entered a Maryknoll Seminary, and underwent training for the priesthood for the next five years. On leaving the order, where he gained a master's degree in social work, he was drafted into the United States Air Force and for the next ten years worked as an official social worker latterly in England with the children of airforce personnel. During his five years in England he was impressed by pioneering work around the concept of the therapeutic community, and in particular by the residential settings developed by Maxwell Jones, George Lyward and R. D. Laing. On leaving the Air Force in 1968, he returned to the United States and after a very brief appointment with the Department of Youth Services in Maryland he joined the faculty of the Social Work Department at Ohio State University.

During his first year as commissioner, Miller's principal goal was to humanize the training schools, and if possible to move them in the direction of being therapeutic communities. He became one of the sharpest critics of the existing arrangements, believing it was necessary to rebuke publicly his own agency and, by implication, many of its personnel. He built on the constituencies for change which existed at the time of his arrival in Massachusetts, and showed considerable ingenuity in dealing with the media. He was, for example, able to present dramatically his message that existing institutions were destructive places. He regularly took part in television and radio shows, and spoke at meetings throughout the state. On some of these occasions he was accompanied by youth who echoed his dismay at the existing institutional arrangements. The presence of these often articulate and persuasive youths served to support Miller's purposes of modifying the public image of the juvenile delinquent, and of demonstrating the havoc and destruction inflicted by institutions on the lives of countless juveniles over the years.

Miller established some allies in the leadership of the state legislature, and although he had a number of persistent political enemies
he was often able to use that opposition to polarize the issues in a
manner that gained him support from other groups. In what became
a moral crusade for children in trouble he had the backing of such
varied groups as the League of Women Voters and the Lifers' Group
at Walpole Prison. The support from these and other lay groups
was, in fact, more consistent than that of professional social work
and the established penal reform organizations, many of which
maintained a somewhat ambiguous stance throughout Miller's
commissionership.

Miller and his key aides set out to humanize the training schools
in a forceful and direct manner. (Miller was joined in Boston by
several former colleagues from the Air Force and from Columbus,
Ohio. Several of these persons were to later work with him in
Illinois and Pennsylvania.) He developed open lines of communication between his office and the juveniles in the institutions. Attempts
were made to train personnel in new techniques, and to provide
them with a broader understanding as to the needs of youths in their
care. These efforts included sessions in group techniques and the
therapeutic community, and among the training consultants at such
sessions was Dr. Maxwell Jones, a leading British psychiatrist who
was an early proponent of therapeutic communities. Miller became
increasingly aware of the difficulties in upgrading the quality of
personnel, and became disillusioned about the prospect for real
institutional changes. The personnel, on the whole, remained hostile
to these initiatives, and on occasion sabotaged the reform efforts by
encouraging runaways and other devices. It required enormous
effort to maintain the momentum for change and Miller became
increasingly impressed by the tendency of the institutions to resume
a deadening routine. He recognized the ease with which a future
administration would be able to undo progress that had been made,
and that the humanization of the institutions at best could provide
little more than short-term relief. As some of the group techniques
began to take hold in the training schools Miller and his colleagues
became impressed by the possibilities of extending them to community settings, residential and otherwise, and removed from the
largely negative context of the institutional milieu.

The process of decarceration in Massachusetts did not follow a
preconceived plan, but was the culmination of a series of events and
developments. The first institution to be closed was the maximum
security facility used by the Department at Bridgewater Correctional

Institution, the state facility for the criminally insane, jointly administered by the Departments of Correction and Mental Health, and the setting for the Fred Wiseman documentary film, *Titticut Follies*. Miller was appalled by the conditions at this eighty-bed unit, officially designated the Institute for Juvenile Guidance. On one occasion he visited the institution with Mrs. Francis Sargent, wife of the Governor, and they together witnessed an episode of staff brutality and later observed the obstacles in disciplining the personnel involved. Miller was convinced that there was no way in which this institution could provide humane care, and in October 1970 it was closed.

During his early period of office he was able to make overall reductions in the training school populations by shortening the length of stay. As commissioner he had the authority to parole juveniles from the schools, and to transfer them to alternative programmes. He did not have the authority actually to close the institutions, or to dismiss the personnel. Despite these limitations on his official power, however, he showed considerable ingenuity in gaining the initiative. For example, although he was not able to fire training school superintendents, he was authorized to order leaves of absence. By ordering the superintendent of the Shirley Industrial School to take sick leave the *de facto* control of the school was placed with one of his key aides, Paul de Muro, who had taught medieval English literature at Ohio State University, and who was appointed as janitor to the institution. He later worked with Miller in Chicago and in Pennsylvania, where in 1976 he became, in effect, director of the state juvenile corrections agency. By speeding up the parole processes attempts were made during 1971 to phase out the Shirley school population, but these efforts were continually thwarted by staff resistance. By the end of that year Miller was certain that gradual decarceration was not going to be successful. He was also confident that it would be politically feasible to abruptly transfer the youth remaining in the training schools to alternative programmes. The main effort to transfer youth from the training schools took place in January 1972, through an original and effective device. About one hundred youths (including some girls from the Lancaster Training School) participated in a one-month residential conference on deinstitutionalization held on the campus of the University of Massachusetts at Amherst. Joint student-youth groups had the goal of developing alternative placement plans for the youths so that it would not be necessary for them to return to the training schools. The 'conference' was run in a rather informal

H

manner, with one research team commenting: 'Advocates and "their kids" did their own thing and for the most part this appeared to work out rather well' (Coates, Miller & Ohlin, 1973). The conference was timed to coincide with a university recess, and it also occurred at a time when the state legislature was not in session. The day before the conference one of Miller's assistants briefed a senior aide of the Governor as to what had been planned, and it was arranged that the Governor should visit Amherst to participate in part of the proceedings.

The last training school to be closed was the Lancaster School for Girls, abandoned in 1975. The fact that the institution for girls was the most difficult to close probably reflects both a neglect by the agency of the need to develop alternative placements for girls, and much resistance to the efforts to phasing out the institution. The Department of Youth Services then began to develop a new organizational structure reflecting the priority given to the purchase of services from the private sector as opposed to direct provision by the state agency, and the establishment of regional offices with wide responsibilities. This new organizational structure is outlined in greater detail below, but it should be noted at this stage that during the final stage of Miller's commissionership and for much of Leavey's tenure very severe strains were placed on the formal bureaucratic processes as attempts were made to adapt to the new situation. A critical problem arose from the fact that both the old and the new structures had to be paid for from the Department's budget. Although the juveniles had been removed from the training schools the institutions continued to be funded through the legislature's line item appropriations. During this time the agency was attempting to expand massively its purchase of services account so as to pay the increasing number of private vendors. The fiscal mechanisms (in part located with government agencies outside the Department of Youth Services such as the state Rate Setting Board) did not adapt at the same pace as the structural changes which were taking place. The severe strain was, in part, relieved by the utilization of national funds made available through the active cooperation of the Governor's Committee on Law Enforcement and the Administration of Criminal Justice, the agency in Massachusetts responsible for the allocation of the block grant to the state by the Law Enforcement Assistance Administration of the National Justice Department. Miller sought to develop a wide range of program options so that placements by the agency might meet the different needs of youth, with the flexibility to provide for simultaneous and sequential combinations. He was aware of the danger that the developing arrangements might merely involve a shift from penal to medical definitions, and he wrote at this time:

> In terms of ideology, the question of correctional reform is not whether we can break out of previous definitions to more up-to-date definitions. It is whether we can (i) effectively break the vicious circle of definitions calling for institutional arrangements which, in turn, revalidate the definitions and (ii) build into new definitions (since they will come) enough categories that show the social and psychological strengths and lifespan of those defined as delinquent or criminal (Miller, 1973).

Miller resigned as commissioner in January 1973 in order to take up the directorship of the Illinois Department of Children and Family Services, where he remained as director until August 1974. It had been his understanding on appointment that youth corrections would be transferred from the Corrections Department to his agency. This never happened and a decline in political support culminated in his transfer to a position in the Governor's Office. In January 1975 he joined the staff of Governor Milton Shapp of Pennsylvania (as director of community-based programmes), and in May of that year became Commissioner of the Office of Children and Youth with the Department of Public Welfare. Despite rumour to the contrary there was no pressure on him to go from either Governor Francis Sargent or the Secretary for Human Services, Peter Goldmark. In fact, both these officials attempted to persuade him to stay on longer. Although there were several unresolved issues Miller felt that his deputy, Joseph Leavey, would be in a better position to consolidate on the work that had been accomplished.

Phase 2: Counter Attack and Attempts at Consolidation

Joseph Leavey, the deputy commissioner of the Department of Youth Services was named as acting director. Leavey was from South Boston and prior to joining the Department had been with the Department of Welfare. Miller was convinced that Leavey would be in a better position both to oversee the needed bureaucratic adaptations and to reach agreement with those interest groups, such as the juvenile court judges, who had been largely opposed to the changes. During his two years as commissioner, Leavey made some progress in consolidating the new arrangements and gave particular attention to problems associated with the provision of secure placements. Much of his energy, however, was absorbed in dealing with a series of counter attacks upon the agency's credibility and effectiveness by segments of the legislature, the courts and the media. His position was somewhat weakened as a result of the failure by Michael Dukakis, who succeeded Francis Sargent as Governor in January 1975, to seek his reconfirmation as commissioner by the council.

These counter-attacks did not have the effect of reversing the changes, but they were responsible for slowing Leavey's attempts at consolidation. Many of the attacks arose from the aftermath of the Miller administration. The main legislative assault, for example, was the publication of the report of the Joint Committee on Post-Audit and Oversight in April 1974. This report focused primarily on the chaos which characterized some of the new administrative and fiscal procedures during the period of organizational transformation. Numerous charges, some of a very exaggerated nature, were made by the committee, but despite these allegations the Post Audit committee attracted little attention within the state. Ironically, the report was probably more widely circulated outside than within Massachusetts. Copies were mailed to the media and to legislators 1,000 miles away in Illinois, and subsequently in Pennsylvania by detractors of Miller.

During the latter part of 1975 the Department of Youth Services was subjected to a barrage of criticism from some segments of the media. The most concerted of these attacks was launched by a Boston television network during September. In a series of editorials, each screened several times a day, and continuing throughout a two-week period, WCVB called for Leavey's resignation. Much of the criticism in these editorials centred on the question of secure facilities for serious juvenile offenders. In the last of these editorials WCVB reiterated its demand that Leavey be fired and that the number of secure beds be increased, commenting: 'A great deal of today's violent crime is committed by juveniles. Massachusetts simply cannot afford a Department of Youth Services which is so demonstrably incompetent.'

In response to the criticism on this issue Leavey stated: 'We are attempting to establish small secure units that will provide security and treatment, yet will not repeat the abuses of jail-like settings.' The pressure on Leavey continued to mount and in December 1975 he resigned.

Shortly after Leavey's resignation John Calhoun, a low-key administrator who was director of the Justice Resource Institute in Boston, an agency responsible for a variety of experimental programmes in criminal justice, was named as commissioner and quickly confirmed by the Council. In his first twelve months of office Calhoun has been determined to speed up the process of consolidation. In particular he has stressed the need for administrative and programme standards as well as the capacity to monitor effectively the quality of services provided for youth. He had also given early attention to the question of secure facilities, which is discussed in greater detail below. During 1976 the state legislature considered a proposal to merge the agency with other government departments with responsibilities for young persons. Although this effort to create a more coordinated approach, which was initiated by the Governor, was not immediately successful, it is being resumed.

Key Issues Concerning Young Offenders in Massachusetts

The significance of these events in Massachusetts can be further explored within the context of five key issues:

Adaptability of the Department's organizational structure. During this period of rapid change the Department had made some progress in adapting its organizational structure to meet the new tasks with which it is confronted. The critical policy decision after the closure of the training schools was that, wherever possible, programmes and services would be purchased from the private sector rather than being provided directly by the Department. Programme placement of youth was to be carried out largely by the seven new regional offices, with the central office taking responsibility for contract making, standard setting, monitoring and closed settings. For two years there existed two parallel structures as a consequence of the legislature's continuing to appropriate funds for the abandoned training school facilities. During this period the size of the purchase of service account expanded to 50 per cent of the total budget, greatly increasing the Department's flexibility. By late 1976 the Department had contracts with 160 different private vendors of services, mostly non-profit making organizations. These structural changes have placed the Department more in the role of a broker than of a provider and important implications result for the roles of agency personnel who are now less likely to be directly involved with youth.

The development of a variety of programme options. A wide range of programmes currently exists for youth committed to the Department of Youth Services. This is in part a consequence of the reliance on the private sector for the provision of most programmes, and in particular due to the policy of contracting with new as well as with established agencies. Young people, for example, not necessarily with professional qualifications, have been encouraged to plan creatively for the needs of youth in trouble. These new groups have varied in their ability to survive, but the principle of seeking out new initiatives and not becoming dependent on the larger established private agencies is still adhered to by the Department. Furthermore, no particular treatment or intervention theory or technique has been favoured, although the more intrusive techniques have been increasingly discouraged. Research findings are showing that the youth are less impressed by the particular type of method used than by the overall level of care shown by programme personnel.

The range of programmes can be broadly categorized according to three types of settings. There are a few very small secure residential settings which place a strong emphasis on developing a normal environment. Non-secure residential settings include hostels (known usually as group homes), placement in boarding schools and foster care. These settings often serve youth who are directly placed by their parents or by other state agencies, and the Department has shown considerable interest in locating resources which have traditionally been available only to non-delinquent youth. Especially innovative work has characterized several of the non-residential programmes. Traditional forms of probation and parole supervision have largely been replaced by approaches which vary from alternative schools, very intensive interaction between youth and staff (one example is an ice-cream business) to matching youth with adult 'advocates'. The Proctor programme is a good example of this type of programme. Young adults, often students, are paired with youths and provided with the means to undertake an extensive bus tour, perhaps coast to coast. This programme recognizes that travel can be an appropriate response to a crisis situation, and makes available to the children of the poor an option sometimes used by their wealthier contemporaries. As noted below, more than one type of programme may be provided for a youth at the same time, and much flexibility is shown by the Department in responding to the changing needs of youth during the period of committal.

Programme networking. The array of community-based programmes in Massachusetts might be said to represent a network model. The model has two main components:

(a) High level of flexibility. The model assumes that the needs of youth are not static, or assessable in a highly prescriptive manner. A dynamic approach that recognizes the need for the provision of programmes and services on both sequential and simultaneous bases is more appropriate. The agency, in its brokerage function, is therefore involved in the complex task of coordination and monitoring. The model also assumes the active involvement by the individual youth in the selection of services and programmes.

(b) The network of programmes as an alternative to incarceration. At a broader level the model provides a useful perspective for approaching the task of developing alternatives to incarceration. Instead of regarding an individual programme as an alternative to incarceration it is perhaps more useful to think in terms of a network of programmes serving this purpose. Useful conceptual work in this area has been done at the Harvard Center for Criminal Justice, where a distinction is made between programme sets, programme strategies and individual programmes. A programme set is the total of all programmes designed to fulfil a given function; a programme strategy is the specific plans which define goals at an operational level together with the means for achieving these goals; individual programmes are the means for implementing these strategies. The Harvard team is especially interested in the research implications of this perspective. They comment: 'Because of the rapid turnover of specific programmes in a changing correctional system, the different strategies become the principal focus for evaluation with the individual programmes (strategy components) becoming secondary' (Coates & Miller, 1975). If a major policy goal is to develop and sustain alternatives to incarceration the operational task for the Department is to put together the appropriate network of programmes.

A different perspective on the network model with its emerging brokerage role for the agency is to view it as being similar to the strategies used by wealthy parents who discover that their children are in serious trouble. In seeking to ensure that their children are not incarcerated in public institutions such parents often obtain whatever appears to be most promising, within their financial means.

The fact that the budget of the Department increased rather than decreased following this policy of decarceration should be considered in this context. In fiscal year 1969 the agency budget was $7·2 million (4·2 million pounds sterling), in fiscal year 1974 it was $16·3 million (9·5 million pounds sterling. The expected budget for fiscal year 1978 is, however, likely to be well below that requested by the agency and will probably be around $17 million (10 million pounds sterling) which represents a significant decrease in real terms since 1974. The brokerage role for state agencies has been further developed by Miller and some of his colleagues in both Illinois and Pennsylvania. In Chicago a federally funded programme, Unified Delinquency Intervention Services (U.D.I.S.), provides an array of programmes for inner city youth as an alternative to placement in state training schools. In Pennsylvania federal funds are also being used with regard to the Camp Hill Project, which has developed a network of programmes to replace incarceration of some 400 juveniles in an adult state prison (McGillis & Spangenberg, 1976).

Standard setting and monitoring. The new pattern of mainly privately provided programmes for delinquent youth in Massachusetts poses many problems in terms of ensuring programme accountability. In several states there has been much controversy and often major scandal surrounding the quality of care provided by private agencies, especially when these are profit-making concerns (Wooden, 1976). The Department of Youth Service has taken some important steps toward identifying and addressing these problems of establishing quality control procedures. Monitoring teams, working out of the central office, made programme site visits and developed a strong focus on the quality of relationships within the programme. This monitoring, however, was handicapped by the absence of clearly articulated programme standards. The Department has recently established a task force on monitoring, and is also attempting to develop written programme standards. If the monitoring of programmes is to be taken seriously, there is an inevitable level of tension between the monitoring group, the agency and the private programmes. This has certainly been the case in Massachusetts, where the monitoring team has perhaps remained the strongest voice for youth advocacy in the agency (Anderson, 1976). Although very considerable progress remains to be made, Massachusetts is ahead of most other states in its efforts to grapple with these quality control and accountability issues.

The availability of secure settings. The most volatile issue has continued to be the provision of secure settings for certain groups of juveniles, especially those adjudicated for the most serious offences. The development of a wide variety of programmes in the community has demonstrated that these are appropriate even for certain juveniles involved in serious offences. Some non-residential programmes have provided a high level of surveillance, such as the 'tracking' programme in Worcester, where very regular contact is maintained between streetworkers and youth. A central rationale behind the developments in Massachusetts is that incarceration can largely be explained in terms of the lack of available options. Much controversy, however, has remained as to whether enough secure settings are being provided, and as discussed above, it was largely as a consequence of active criticism on this issue by segments of the media that Commissioner Leavey resigned in December 1975. Dr. Miller had taken the view that such concepts as dangerousness are not determined in a static manner but are negotiable by the various interest groups. His approach to the problem was to limit strictly the number placed in secure settings by establishing a low capacity ceiling, and to restrict placement by regional offices to a pre-determined quota. In effect, he decided how many 'dangerous' youth there were in the state. He believed that there would always be disagreement about what that number should be, and that the resulting tension between the different interest groups involved was not resolvable in any final sense.

Under Massachusetts law, the juvenile court has authority to commit youth to the Department of Youth Services, but it is not able to direct that the youth be placed in any particular setting. The authority for programme placement, including decisions around secure settings, resides with the Department. Prior to 1972 commital to the Department almost always resulted in placement within one of the training schools. There is an inevitable conflict between the court and the agency around placement questions regardless of who has the authority to make these decisions. In some states the juvenile court has authority to determine the actual placement. Under draft standards recently approved by the National Juvenile Standards Project it would be the court's responsibility to determine the level of security required, although the state agency would make placement decisions within that category (Institute of Judicial Administration American Bar Association, 1976). It is hardly surprising that this tension has been especially heightened in Massachusetts since 1972, and it has surfaced in a number of forms. Commissioners of the Department have been called into juvenile court to explain placement decisions; judges have threatened to 'bind over' juveniles to the adult court if an understanding is not reached that a secure placement will be made. While it does not follow that youth who are bound over to the adult court will be sentenced to prison, the threat of bind over is taken seriously by the Department, which is aware that bind-over status may mean months in secure detention awaiting disposition. Certain judges have also been active in publicly criticizing the Department and in keeping the issue of secure settings in the public domain.

The number of youth actually being held in secure settings fluctuated throughout this period, and by the end of 1975 there were about forty-six adjudicated youth in small secure settings directly administered by the Department, and a further seventy youth placed in privately run programmes, which due to their design or physical isolation, could also be described as secure. One of the first actions taken by John Calhoun on becoming commissioner in January 1976 was to establish a task force to examine the issue in some depth. By including some of the severest critics of the Department on the task force, which was chaired by an assistant attorney general, Calhoun was able to take some of the political heat out of the issue. The task force recommended that the number of youth in secure settings, given the current level of commitments to the Department, be within the range of 129–160 beds, of which 30–40 should be administered by the Department of Mental Health. Opinions as to what the number of beds should be have ranged from about 45 to 400, and the task force's figure underlines its overall recommendation that the commitment of the Commonwealth and D.Y.S. to de-institutionalized community based care and treatment of juvenile offenders must be preserved and strengthened (Dept. of Youth Service).

The research efforts of the Harvard Center for Criminal Justice

The Department's research capacity has remained very limited, and even in terms of systematic information-keeping little progress has been achieved. It is especially fortunate that a major research study of many facets of the events in Massachusetts commenced in 1970 under the direction of Professor Lloyd Ohlin of the Center for Criminal Justice at Harvard Law School. The major findings of this seven-year federally funded study are expected to be published during 1977–8, although some findings have been reported in journal articles or made available to interested persons through mimeographed reports. The question as to recidivism is as yet not fully answered. A preliminary analysis, based upon incomplete data, found that in comparing the period with training schools with the alternative approach developed after 1972, recidivism could not be shown to have either increased or decreased. Quite dramatic contrasts in both directions were found if regional comparisons were made, which may be related to the network of available programmes within a particular region. (Coates, Miller and Ohlin, 1975.) The Harvard research has demonstrated the significance of early decisions as to pre-adjudication detention in terms of the determination of programme placement after committal to the Department (Coates, Miller and Ohlin, 1975). It should be noted that the Department is administratively responsible for youth placed in detention status by the courts, and that along with closing the training schools, it greatly reduced the number of youth held in secure detention. Important work is also underway concerning social climates within programmes, and on the quality of linkages between programmes and the community. Following some conceptual exploration by Robert Coates which stressed a focus on the community *linkages* of programmes rather than simply location, some interesting findings in terms of frequency, duration and quality of the relationship between the programme and the community have been reported (Coates, 1974). Substantial differences were found within the category of non-residential programmes, the category of group homes and within other programme categories (Coates, Miller and Ohlin, 1976).

The events in Massachusetts have attracted attention throughout the United States and beyond among persons interested in juvenile justice issues. It should, however, be noted that by the end of 1976 no other state had followed Massachusetts' example, although at least one national commission had recommended such a policy, 'The Commission believes that states should follow the example of Massachusetts, which has closed down all statewide institutions for juveniles' (The National Advisory Commission on Criminal Justice Standards and Goals, 1973).

Three issues concerning the problems involved in replicating the Massachusetts' experience are reviewed. First, the experience has been of a very threatening nature to many persons in the American corrections industry who remain strongly opposed to institutional closures in their own states. It is probably for this reason that accounts of what took place in Massachusetts have often been greatly distorted. There have been, for example, many rumours that the former training schools have been re-opened. This rumour took on a new variation when the director of an agency responsible for the administration of juvenile institutions (he was known to be generally sympathetic to the events in Massachusetts) received a letter from a university researcher which stated 'We have just received information that the new Governor has requested the building of two three-hundred-bed juvenile institutions'. This information had no validity. It probably arose from some remarks made at a meeting by the new head of public safety in Massachusetts. This official was, however, simply expressing his own views and in no way stating the Governor's policy or that of the Secretary for Human Services. Clearly, a major impediment to replication elsewhere in the United States is the lack of support by administrators who wish to continue to administer institutions. Dr. Miller is an unusual example of an agency director who places the need for reform ahead of his concern for bureaucratic consequences. Given that replication is most likely to occur with the initiative of top administrators the outlook for following the Massachusetts example in many states is not very promising.

Secondly, it has to be asked whether Massachusetts was somehow unique in the conditions that led up to the institutional closures. A recent report by the Harvard research group concluded that the social, economic and political conditions existing in Massachusetts at that time did not differ significantly from those in other parts of the United States. The report states:

What we have established is that Massachusetts, unique in its correctional reform, is far from unique in its general character. There are two implications. First, what could happen in Massachusetts probably could happen elsewhere, and second, the critical factors in making it happen are probably the vagaries of internal politics, not demographic profiles. (Harvard Center for Criminal Justice, 1975.)

The third consideration affecting replication is that of tactics. The Massachusetts strategy of decarceration may have had two crucial ingredients: (i) it was done speedily, and before opposed vested interest groups could effectively organize; (ii) it was an example of a 'deep end' strategy, in that it first addressed the issue in the context of those juveniles located at the deepest end of the correctional process. The more conventional approach to reform in this area is to develop alternative placements for youth at the 'shallow end' of the process. This latter approach may be politically safer, but it may also serve to widen rather than to reduce the official net, as some studies of diversion have shown. Programmes described as alternatives to incarceration may be supplementing, rather than replacing, traditional institutions. Shallow-end strategies do not appear to be very effective, as the oscillations of public and political opinion concerning criminal and juvenile justice may easily overtake gradual steps forward. Once the training schools were closed in Massachusetts the event itself soon ceased to be a political issue. Since that time there has been no serious political interest in reopening the institutions. The complex issues that have emerged are critical in terms of the task of developing a more just and humane approach to juvenile justice, and these are being more directly addressed because they are not being obscured by out-dated institutional arrangements.

CHAPTER SEVEN

The Canadian Experience: The System of Crime Control in Saskatchewan

OTTO DRIEDGER

When one considers alternative strategies for coping with crime, there is considerable logic in examining the situation in Saskatchewan as a case study in Canada. In Canada, a division of responsibility for most of the human services exists between federal and provincial jurisdictions. In the administration of justice, federal government has responsibility for legislation, enforcement on national and international matters, administration and appointments to higher courts, institutions for persons sentenced for two years or more, and parole. All other matters are under provincial jurisdiction. (*The Criminal in Canadian Society—A Perspective on Corrections.*)

In Saskatchewan, a government with a socialist orientation— Cooperative Commonwealth Federation (C.C.F.) and later New Democratic Party (N.D.P.)—has been in power since 1944, with the exception of seven years (1964–71). Shortly after coming to power, the C.C.F. government established a Penal Commission (*Report of the Saskatchewan Penal Commission 1946*) in which a basic change in orientation for services was recommended. Those recommendations of the Commission that were acted upon have had extensive influence on correctional service in this province.

The report of the Saskatchewan Penal Commission, 1946, stated the general policy as follows:

That the Government of Saskatchewan adopt a preventative and remedial policy for the control of crime and delinquency and that the programme thereof include:

120

(a) a comprehensive plan for the prevention of criminal and delinquent behaviour;
(b) a full probation service for the placing of certain prisoners under the training supervisors in lieu of a sentence to an institution;
(c) a programme of treatment in penal or correctional institutions using scientific procedures for the rehabilitation of offenders;
(d) more extensive use of parole as a stepping-stone to adjustment in a life of full freedom;
(e) an adequate system of after-care of discharged prisoners with a view to their re-establishment in the normal life of society.

It further established a basic policy related to prevention of crime and delinquency as follows:

That the Government undertake through the Division of Corrections a comprehensive programme for the prevention of crime and delinquency; that crime and delinquency be viewed as a manifestation of emotional disturbance and social ill health growing out of social conditions in which boys and girls and men and women live in the home, school and community such as inadequate housing, congested areas, unemployment, inadequate training for parenthood, inadequate school training, harmful community influences, poor recreational facilities, inadequate services for children, clients, etc.

As a result of the basic recommendations in this commission's report, the correctional institutions, as well as community services such as probation, were transferred to the department at that time called the Department of Social Welfare and Rehabilitation. Correctional services have remained in that Department.

Juvenile Services

The major shift in services for youth under age sixteen did not occur until thirteen years later. Prior to 1959, juvenile delinquents were dealt with under the Federal Juvenile Delinquent Act, and these services were considered to be under the Criminal Justice System.

Major impetus for a shift in philosophy and approach was due to the thinking of Miss Mildred Battel, the Director of Child Welfare from 1952 to 1965. She contended that children under the age of sixteen should be dealt with under Family and Child Welfare Services. She argued that the family and the social context in which children developed had a very significant impact on the development of children, and therefore, the total process should be removed from the Criminal Justice System. Implementation of this concept would mean the introduction of legislation and the development of a new delivery system for services to juveniles. Major amendments to the Child Welfare Act were introduced. The definition of neglect under the Child Welfare Act expanded to include a child 'who has been found guilty of a delinquency and is likely to develop further delinquent tendencies'. (*An Act Respecting the Welfare of Children*, 1959, Province of Saskatchewan. Replaced by the Family Services Act, 1973.) The Act outlined procedures for dealing with children who were apprehended because of an alleged delinquency. The alternatives for the judge in disposition were the same as for other children who were found to be neglected, which meant that the judge could adjourn the case with supervision by a child welfare worker, order that the child be committed to the Minister of Social Welfare for a period of up to one year, or he could order that the child be committed permanently to the Minister of Social Welfare. If the child was made a ward of the Minister, either temporarily or permanently, then the resources of the Child Welfare Branch and its Regional Offices would be available to the delinquent child and his family. The Saskatchewan Boys' School, which had been an industrial school under the Juvenile Delinquents Act up to this point, now became a resource for children under the Child Welfare Act. It became a diagnostic and treatment centre rather than a custodial institution. As a result of this legislation, hearings of the juvenile court were held under the Child Welfare Act. This shift meant a transfer of provision of services and policy formation from the Corrections Branch to the Child Welfare Branch.

This major shift in policy and service profoundly affected the juvenile delinquents and their families, various segments of the criminal justice system, and society at large.

The police continued to exercise their discretion regarding which children should be warned, but if a child was apprehended, the police immediately contacted the child welfare worker, who would interview the child. If the child was considered to need temporary detention, he would be taken by a social worker to the holding facility. In the majority of cases, the social worker returned the child to his home and discussed the matter with the parents. The social worker would explore the situation thoroughly with the family and the community. If both the police and the social worker felt that there should be informal supervision and service to the family, no charges would be laid. If an information was to be laid, it would be submitted to the judge, and the child and his family would come before the judge within three weeks. The police would present evidence in terms of the offence or offences, and the social worker would provide information with regard to the family and social context in which the child lived. If the judge found the child guilty of a delinquency, he then could order that the child be under the supervision of the child welfare worker, or be committed temporarily or permanently to the Minister of Social Welfare. If the offence was serious, such as murder, the prosecutor could request a transfer to adult court. In most instances, however, a request for transfer would be opposed by Child Welfare Services, and in the majority of cases, even serious offences were dealt with under the Child Welfare Act.

If a child was made either a temporary or a permanent ward of the Minister, he could remain in his home under supervision, but would most likely be provided for in a foster home. All the foster homes of the Child Welfare Services in the province were available to the child and attempts would then be made for the child to be placed appropriately. The foster home resource became the backbone of services to delinquent children.

During the implementation of this programme, it became increasingly apparent that the more difficult teenagers were hard to place in foster homes. If a child stayed in a foster home, in some instances, the family was disrupted, and foster parents would ask that the child be moved, or the child himself would say that he could not stay or would run away from the home. The difficulty of some children in adjusting to foster homes caused the development of group homes in 1964, and several years later, a specialized foster home programme was initiated. The specialized foster homes provided support services of professionals such as psychiatrists and psychologists and additional relief for the parents, enabling them to get away from home occasionally. A social worker on call twenty-four hours a day for these specialized homes provided immediate availability of additional social work support.

The group homes generally housed six to ten children. The house parents were hired, and the agency, rather than the parents, owned

I

the home. Relief parents and other support services were available to the home. Treatment services for children were very limited in the province, and further developments in that field occurred from 1966 to 1970. One additional treatment centre for boys and one treatment centre for girls were developed.

By the early 1970s, a fairly broad spectrum of services was available to children in this province. The services included supervision in their own homes, foster homes, specialized foster homes, group homes, and treatment services (see Table IX). In addition, emergency detention services were used mainly for children needing temporary holding or for children from other provinces who had been involved in delinquency in this province.

Some experimentation had been made in the province during the sixties with specific communities with a high level of delinquency. For example, a great deal of vandalism, particularly in the spring and summer, prevailed at Carlyle, a community in Southern Saskatchewan. Analysis revealed that when the youths returned from school and had little to do in the summer time, they turned to vandalism of cottages at a lake in the vicinity. However, delinquent behaviour decreased sharply with the development of youth services and recreational opportunities for the teenagers. Development of this type greatly increased in the seventies so that local communities, with the help of either private agencies or provincial social services, have been developing youth centres in the communities or areas of cities with high rates of delinquency. Special services such as wilderness camps have also been developed to afford youth an opportunity to develop teamwork and an identity and confidence for themselves.

Out-patient treatment services for emotionally disturbed youth are available through the Psychiatric Services Branch of the Saskatchewan Department of Health. Services were established in Saskatoon in 1953, in Regina in 1969, and in the other Health Regions since 1972.

Problems with the Community-based Approach

Several basic concerns and problems have developed with this community-based approach to juveniles. It often frustrates the police to have the juvenile back in the community immediately after apprehension, where he may again cause trouble. This approach to services often gives the impression that 'nothing is being done'. To

TABLE IX

Facility	Own home	Foster home	Specialized foster home	Group home	Treatment centres
Services	Social work supervision/ support	Social work supervision/ support	Social work support Training programme Psychologist/ psychiatric services Emergency relief staff	Social work support Training Psychologist/ psychiatric services Regular relief staff	Social work counselling Psychologist/ psychiatric services Supervision/care 24 hours per day Group work Academic, vocational and trade education in the centre
Organizational structure		Home owned by foster parents Home life pattern set by foster parent life-style	Home owned by foster parents Home life pattern set by foster parent life-style, but modified by needs of youth	Home owned by agency Home life pattern set by needs of youth, group home parents' life-style and agency policy	Owned by agency or separate agency Life-style and treatment programme set by agency policy and needs of youth

date, not enough ways of responding to delinquent behaviour have been developed in the community. Since dealing with delinquency within the community, rather than removing the youth to an institution, is relatively new, finding ways of coping within the community is slow and difficult. It appears that the work being done in the community with the youth is marginally adequate so that the backlash of return to an institutional approach to services will not develop. However, some elements in the community continually press to have the children removed.

The judges often feel dissatisfied as well. Since the only alternatives available to the judge are to order supervision or make the child a permanent or temporary ward, he becomes frustrated when children are brought before him on numerous occasions in which he actually has no alternatives left to deal with the situation. He cannot order a child to the Boys' School since the institution is a resource to the child welfare agency, not an institution to which he can sentence anyone. Some judges have challenged the right of the province to deal with juveniles under the Family Service Act and have said that since crime and delinquency are federal responsibilities, the Family Services Act is *ultra vires*. Some judges handle cases under the Juvenile Delinquents Act rather than under the Family Services Act, and have a wider range of dispositions available to them. However, a sentence to the Saskatchewan Boys' School does not produce the effect of the child's actual spending of time there. The Saskatchewan Boys' School has not been designated as an industrial school under the Juvenile Delinquents Act, and the Family Services Act interprets such an order as a temporary committal to the Minister of Social Services.

A further concern of the judiciary and others in the community is for the rights of children. Since the Family Services Court is informal, they argue that protection of the rights of children is not as great as that for adults. This is a valid issue which needs further consideration, and development of safeguards is needed for the rights of children and their families.

Advantages

However, significant advantages have resulted from the Saskatchewan approach to coping with delinquency. There has been considerable decriminalization of the process. A good example that this decriminalization has extended into the communities' thinking is the experience of the Saskatchewan Boys' School. When the Saskatchewan Boys' School first became a resource to the Child Welfare Branch, headlines would appear in the papers when a youth 'escaped' from the Boys' School. By the late 1960s, however, runaways from the school were no longer treated as escaped criminals, but were considered runaways from treatment centres or other community service facilities. Information in the newspaper might appear if a car had been stolen, but no headlines would imply or state an 'escape' from the juvenile facility.

Table X shows that the number of juvenile delinquents per hundred thousand population for Saskatchewan is substantially lower than that for any other province. Although the population of Manitoba is very similar to that of Saskatchewan and is also significantly rural, the annual average of juvenile delinquency is almost four times higher in Manitoba. The same comparison can be made between Alberta and Saskatchewan.

TABLE X

Provincial comparison of rates of persons convicted of indictable offences and juvenile delinquency, 1961–66, and crime index rates, 1973. (Rank-order in brackets)

	Indictable offenders* 1961–66	Juvenile delinquents† 1961–66	Crime index rates‡ 1973
British Columbia	508(1)	766(1)	5,248(1)
Alberta	490(2)	533(3)	4,431(2)
Manitoba	393(3)	477(6)	4,065(3)
Ontario	330(4)	705(2)	3,419(4)
New Brunswick	317(5)	344(7)	2,068(9)
Saskatchewan	312(6)	131(10)	3,296(5)
Nova Scotia	304(7)	484(5)	2,171(8)
Newfoundland	300(8)	487(4)	2,369(7)
Quebec	253(9)	268(8)	2,920(6)
Prince Edward Island	129(10)	224(9)	1,507(10)

* Average annual rate 1961–66 per 100,000 population 16 years and older.
† Average annual rate 1961–66 per 100,000 population 7–15 years of age.
‡ Crimes known to police (founded) per 100,000 total population.

('Statistics Canada Service Bulletin,' May 1975)

Similarly, the rates of persons convicted of juvenile delinquency show a difference of approximately four to one (see Table XI).

TABLE XI

Sex of juvenile delinquents for Canada and Provinces:
annual average 1961–66
(per 100,000 population 7–15 years of age)

	Boys	Girls	Ratio
Canada (excluding Yukon and N.W.T.)	854	121	7/1
Newfoundland	894	62	14/1
Prince Edward Island	423	19	22/1
Nova Scotia	868	80	11/1
New Brunswick	633	42	15/1
Quebec	476	52	9/1
Ontario	1,189	196	6/1
Manitoba	801	139	6/1
Saskatchewan	238	19	13/1
Alberta	911	136	7/1
British Columbia	1,357	184	7/1

(McGrath, p. 98.)

Dealing with the situation in the context of the family and the community has prevented a large number of children from going into institutions where they have an opportunity for negative learning as well as a reaction to stringent controls. Three communities in Saskatchewan (Saskatoon, Prince Albert, and Regina) have a capacity for a sum total of thirty-two juveniles in secure holding facilities. (Kilburn Hall, 14; Saskatchewan Boys' School, 10; Dale's House, 6; Prince Albert, 2.) Saskatchewan has a population of one million. All other provinces have much higher rates per hundred thousand of both detention facilities and usage. Other factors may contribute to the low usage and small number of detention units; however, a significant factor is the approach to juvenile delinquent services in this province.

The Federal Government has been making proposals for a new Act which is to replace the Juvenile Delinquents Act. These proposals are available in a discussion paper entitled *Young Persons in Conflict with the Law* (Communication Division, Ministry of the Solicitor General).

The introduction and passing of the proposed legislation would mean significant improvement and a move towards decriminalization of services in other provinces. But since the legislation is intended to be mandatory, it could well have a negative effect on services in Saskatchewan, in that Saskatchewan has moved beyond the proposed Act in developing a community approach to services for children and youth. Presentations which raise these concerns have been made from Saskatchewan to the Federal Agency. It is difficult to know whether the proposals will, in fact, be translated into new Federal legislation.

The difference between the approach used in Saskatchewan and the approach used in Massachusetts is interesting, Saskatchewan reflecting the more traditional evolutionary approach to social policy, in which change is brought about by painstaking consultation and small but steady progressive steps in the required direction. Massachusetts, however, represents a radical revolutionary approach in which action is taken rapidly to avoid the build-up of opposition and a rapid leap is made from one policy or approach to the required new position. Saskatchewan's attempt at using a process approach to make a major shift in philosophy, values, and delivery of services in the field of juvenile delinquency has been, in my view, relatively effective and far-reaching. Actually, the total system was changed, and although institutional services were retained, their objectives were changed, and use of institutional services was and is extremely limited.

Adult Services

Development of alternative strategies for coping with crime in the adult sphere have differed considerably from the approach used in the juvenile field, although the basic philosophy behind development of services since the mid-forties has been similar.

The developments in correctional services in the late forties and fifties centred on the development of basic probation services and development of treatment and rehabilitative services in the Provincial Correctional Centres. During this period, the wardens of the prisons (subsequently called the directors of the correctional centres) had professional education. In the Prince Albert Correctional Centre, all directors of the correctional centre for men had their Master's degrees or diplomas in Social Work, and in the Regina centre, directors had their Master's degrees in Psychology or Social

Work. Treatment and counselling units were set up, and vocational and educational services were expanded. Work camps in either resort or lumbering areas were developed for inmates who did not need secure custody. In the corrections branch during the 1960s, awareness increased of the facts that treatment and rehabilitative services in institutions and probation services were not adequate responses to the need for coping with crime. During the last ten years, extensive experimentation with alternative strategies has been undertaken at several points in the criminal justice process.

In addition to such processes as probation, absolute or conditional discharge, the use of fines, the suspended sentence, and intermittent sentencing, experimenters have endeavoured to find additional community alternatives to incarceration.

Alternative Strategies—Preventative and Enforcement Field

The work of a peace officer focuses on dealing with violence, much of which is not necessarily of a criminal nature. Police are involved with family disputes, suicide attempts, bar-room brawls, and hundreds of other situations in which social relations erupt into violence or conflict. Good police work centres on diffusing the violence, calming the crisis, and assisting those involved to come to terms with each other. Frequently, referrals to other social agencies and support services are necessary. In 1974 in the City of Regina, a mobile family service unit was established which operates under a community board and is a crisis unit which has police and social workers working together. When crises occur, the mobile unit of this agency goes into action, with both police and social workers involved. The objective is to diffuse the crisis and make appropriate referrals or arrangements for the parties involved, hopefully without laying charges. In many instances, situations can be resolved without resorting to the laying of charges, since the basic cause of the disruption or crisis was social or interpersonal rather than criminal, even though criminal acts may have been involved. Dealing with the crisis through the mobile family service unit means that the crisis can be seen in its context rather than be focused on the criminal act alone.

In Saskatchewan, the concept of diversion before a situation comes into the criminal justice system is seriously considered.

... in Canada diversion is based on the principle advanced by the Law Reform Commission that too many forms of socially problematic behaviour have been handled by the criminal justice system. Diversion is meant to reverse this trend through teaching the community to take responsibility for some of that behaviour. (*Liaison*, Nov. 1976.)

The John Howard Society of Saskatchewan has received a substantial grant from the Donner Foundation of Canada for development of an experimental diversion programme in Regina and Moose Jaw. One method will be mediation between the offender and the victim to determine if appropriate restitution and resolution of the problem can occur. A three-year experimental project which began in 1977. Other experimentation on diversion is taking place in British Columbia, Ontario, Nova Scotia, and the Province of Quebec (*ibid.*).

Providing the services of a peace officer has been difficult in some communities which are entirely or predominantly Indian or Metis. The Royal Canadian Mounted Police have had a long-standing programme in which native peace officers are appointed to serve as peace officers in Indian and Metis communities. Indian bands on the reserves use this concept to develop their own peace officers so that service can be provided in the cultural context which is appropriate to the community.

The Law, Courts, and the Judicial Process

The Canadian Law Reform Commission is thoroughly and extensively reviewing criminal law. The Commission has published a number of working papers on subjects such as diversion, imprisonment and release, sentencing, the meaning of guilt, the limits of criminal law, discovery, the principles of sentencing and dispositions, restitution, compensation, and fines. These working papers attempt to create stimulating national discussion of issues with a view to criminal law reform. Significant amendments to the criminal code have been made, and additional amendments are intended. Saskatchewan also appointed a Law Reform Commission which supplements some of the work being done by the Federal Commission, but it focuses on provincial issues. The Commissions are seriously considering ways of amending criminal law to decriminalize behaviour that has a social or moral base rather than a criminal base. In the long run, therefore, it is intended that behaviour which is not against a person or property would be removed from the criminal code.

Concern exists that many of the present laws militate against the poor and the socially or psychologically handicapped person. Orders such as 'thirty dollars fine or thirty days in jail' mean that a person who cannot afford the thirty dollars might end up in prison. Persons who cannot afford adequate legal advice might not be able to defend their rights as effectively as persons with sufficient resources.

A number of programmes are developing to respond to some of these situations. Legal Aid Clinics have developed extensively across the Province of Saskatchewan, and regional offices now exist throughout the Province with a sum total of forty-six lawyers plus an equal number of paralegal staff to assist persons in legal matters.

A Fine Option Programme has been developed in the Province so that persons who are ordered to pay a fine have the alternative of donating time by working in a community voluntary agency. A current formula determines how much time they must donate in order to work off a particular sum of money. This option means that persons who are unable to pay the fine do not need to be imprisoned since they can use this alternate method of repayment. The programme has been well-accepted in some quarters; however, when new programmes are developed, some difficulties always arise in creating appropriate opportunities for work and adequate supervision of the persons who work off their fines. The implementation of this programme has been criticized somewhat in certain parts of the Province; however, the basic principle has been accepted very well. In some jurisdictions, due to some of the developmental problems, clerks of the court and judges hesitate to use this option.

Limited experimentation has occurred with community service orders in Saskatchewan and British Columbia. In Northern Saskatchewan, the judge has used community service orders where neither a fine nor incarceration seemed to be most appropriate (Francis, 1973). Several pilot projects have also been initiated in British Columbia. (Information and Public Programs Office, 1975.)

As in the policing process, judicial services to the Indian and Metis communities were found to be inappropriate or ineffective. Judges of the Magistrate's Court generally hold court hearings in the larger centres in the rural areas, and persons charged in those districts must come to town for their court appearances. Persons from Indian Reserves or Indian Communities frequently had difficulty understanding the total court procedure and were intimidated by the formal setting. Indian Justices of the Peace have been appointed in several communities to experiment with ways of relating the judicial process more effectively to the context and needs of the Indian people.

Alternative Strategies in Corrections

A large number of chronic alcoholics have been involved with the criminal justice system for a long time. Concerns expressed in 'Drain the Drunk Tank' (Canadian Criminology and Corrections Association, 1970) and *Habitual Drunken Offenders* (Probation and After-Care Department, 1971) are applicable in Saskatchewan. The Prince Albert Council on Alcoholism and Drug Abuse, a community-based organization, began in 1973. It is responsible for forming a pool of a large number of agencies, organizations, and major employers which have designated staff and staff time to offer a co-ordinated approach to services to the alcoholic. This approach recognizes that alcoholism cannot be effectively dealt with by any one organization, and its intention is to deal with the chronic alcoholic through the various community services rather than have him move through the criminal justice system.

The same Prince Albert Council organized a united approach to the development of a Driving While Impaired (DWI) programme in Saskatchewan. This idea was initiated in Phoenix, Arizona, and it has found its way into most Canadian provinces. The delivery system of the DWI programme in Saskatchewan is different from the private one in Phoenix in that the programme in Saskatchewan is financed by the Department of Education and is under the direction of local community boards. It depends upon community resource persons and offers a programme to offenders. Basically, the offender is put on probation and ordered to attend a series of lectures and group sessions on the implications of driving while impaired. The Prince Albert Council has not moved into a pattern of compulsory community service for this group.

'Halfway Houses' have been established in many countries, including Canada. Saskatchewan began this approach in 1970 and has organized five Halfway Houses to date. Also, the Federal Penitentiary Service has established several Halfway Houses in this province. Experimentation has been done in developing Halfway Houses or group home settings for young probationers who need some supervision. An experiment with a probation employment programme in Prince Albert has been done in which young adult probationers do repair work to homes of low-income families.

The Special Offender Groups

During the 1950s and 1960s, care for the mentally retarded has shifted dramatically from mental hospitals to community-based service through mental health clinics. As a result, the population of mental hospitals has been reduced from 3,583 in 1956 to 335 in 1976. Institutions for the mentally retarded are also experiencing a reduction. With this change of philosophy in services to the mentally disordered, services to those persons who are amenable to treatment have received focus. Some persons do not respond to treatment, and are therefore discharged into the community and frequently become involved with criminal activity. It appears that an increasing number of retarded persons also find their way into prison. Some of the retarded are unable to cope with the community after release from institutions for the mentally retarded. Hence, often they get into difficulty with the law. More research and detailed analysis is needed in this area.

Similar problems result with chronic alcoholics who are unresponsive to rehabilitative services through the Saskatchewan Commission on Alcoholism or groups such as Alcoholics Anonymous. Again, these persons are frequently apprehended and receive short sentences.

With the shift from hospitals to community services for many of the persons with chronic mental disorders, many individuals find their way into the criminal justice system which provides custody and control. It does not appear that mental health services in Saskatchewan will provide for persons who are unamenable to treatment and rehabilitation, and, therefore, the corrections programme will likely need to continue to cope with the problem. The interrelationship of large systems, such as criminal justice and mental health, and the effects one has on the other, have not been resolved satisfactorily. The United States National Advisory Commission on Criminal Justice Standards and Goals points out that

the propensity for outlawing private behaviour that is fairly common in our society simply because it is objectionable to private society has resulted in over-criminalization. The effect has been a two-sided track, the criminal justice system from its mission of protecting society against crime to the uneasy role of policing private morality. The Criminal Justice System must embrace a philosophy of diversion that effectively excludes persons who behave in ways that may be counter to prevailing social norms but are of doubtful criminality. (1973.)

A philosophic issue arises when the focus of major human service systems centres exclusively on treatment and rehabilitation without a strong commitment to the concepts of 'helping' and 'caring' as discussed by Titmuss (Titmuss, R.M., 1974).

The concepts of treatment and rehabilitation can lead to the primacy of success and a rejection of persons who do not respond to treatment and rehabilitative efforts. I am reminded of the principles of the 'deserving' and 'undeserving' poor which became issues in dealing with poverty under the Poor Laws.

The person with a 'character disorder', the psychopath or sociopath, the chronic alcoholic, and the marginally retarded who do not respond to 'normalization' cannot receive 'help' and 'care' in the mental health or alcoholism related services. Frequently, persons with these chronic conditions become involved in criminal behaviour and are then dealt with by the Criminal Justice System. It appears that we have the 'deserving' client, who is responsive to treatment or rehabilitation, and the 'undeserving' client, who is unresponsive. We are close to saying that it is a crime not to respond to the treatment and rehabilitative services available. We refuse to accept failure; and we imply that it is a crime to be a failure. The management of failure through systems other than the Criminal Justice System needs development, but before such development can occur, professionals in human services and society at large must come to terms with failure. How can we develop opportunities for response, rehabilitation, and treatment, and also respond to the unresponsive person? (Two draft papers discuss these issues in more detail: S. Skinner and O. H. Driedger, 'Perspectives on Rehabilitation', and O. H. Driedger, 'The Deserving and Undeserving Client').

Another special group, the Indian-Metis group, also has difficulty coping with society. The 1971 Saskatchewan Corrections Report identifies that:

The problem with the Indian-Metis group is a very disproportionately large number of persons being sentenced to prison. Although they are estimated at forming approximately 8 per

cent of the total population of Saskatchewan, they form upwards of 50 per cent of the prison population. (Saskatchewan
Corrections Committee, 1971.)

Creation of the native peace officer, court worker, and probation
officer positions are attempting to develop services in the native
context. The causes for such a disproportionate number of Indians
and Metis in prison are complex. Cultural, religious, economic, and
social issues are involved and cannot be dealt with here.

What are the results of the experimentation with alternative
strategies for coping with crime in Saskatchewan society? It appears
that sensitivity to the issues and problems related to crime and its
control in this province is considerable. Issues related to the administration of justice have been uppermost in the minds of Canadian
and Saskatchewan citizens for the last four years. This concern has
led to major debates on capital punishment (which was abolished in
1976), riots in Federal Penitentiaries, legalization of abortion,
legislation related to drugs, a major law and security bill, and an
extensive debate on the extent to which parole services are used.
Also, provincial law reform commissions as well as a Canadian
Law Reform Commission have been publishing working papers for
public discussion. University-level educational opportunities in the
field of criminal justice have been offered in Ottawa, Montreal, and
Toronto for the last five to ten years and are now being developed
in British Columbia, Saskatchewan, and Manitoba. Service delivery
systems are also undergoing change.
  Sensitivity to the problems and issues involved and some willingness on the part of Canadian and Saskatchewan society are apparent,
but there is also considerable community hesitation at becoming
more extensively involved. An underlying fear of being victimized
prevails, and many believe that repressive measures rather than
changes in social conditions or development of positive options can
more effectively control crime. This fear and hostility is delicately
balanced with the feelings of the need for positive social action and
humane treatment of offenders. The temptation to believe in a
simple solution to crime, if only we could find it, is strong. Activity
in the criminal justice field is moving our society towards an understanding that crime will always be with us, but that we must develop
a *host* of strategies for coping with crime. In Saskatchewan the
shift to a community-based service has been accomplished in the
juvenile field; however, the adult system is still institution-based.

CHAPTER EIGHT

Another Try: An Account of a New Careers Project for Borstal Trainees

SPENCER MILLHAM—ROGER BULLOCK—
KENNETH HOSIE

This chapter discusses the early history of a hostel. At first glance, two terraced houses in northern Bristol, England, appear much like any other residential home, but in this conventional setting, a project of considerable significance was initiated. Here was an attempt to apply the 'New Careers' concept of self-help copied from extensive schemes in the United States. In the Bristol Project, these ideas were applied to a group of young men who would have otherwise been in Borstal, the majority in secure institutions. It was an experiment which not only explored new methods of social intervention but also provided the central authorities with an alternative approach for young offenders, a group whose lives had hitherto been characterized by a lack of opportunity and conflicts with the law.

The concept of New Careers developed in the United States during the 1960s in an atmosphere of concern at the persistence of widespread poverty alongside growing wealth. There was an increasing awareness that general economic affluence was insufficient to eliminate poverty. Between 1947 and 1963, for example, the gross national product in the United States increased by 75 per cent, but unemployment also grew by 67 per cent to 2·4 million—or put another way, an additional 150,000 workers each year experienced long spells of unemployment. During this period there was also growing political agitation from organized and militant civil rights groups but these movements could do little to provide new career opportunities for deprived people. Eventually, in 1964, Congress passed the Economic Opportunity Act calling for the development of community action programmes supported by federal funds.

These developments became known as 'New Careers' when Pearl and Riessman published in 1965 *New Careers for the Poor: the Non-Professional in Human Service*, a book describing the provision of socially useful careers for talented people who had been unskilled and without regular work. 'New Careers' was a radical concept which necessitated structural changes from the education, health and social services which employed the students. In addition, new demands were made on educational institutions which offered training. It was clear that educational patterns of entry to these services would have to be replaced by an open system of recruitment, training would have to take place alongside employment and promotion would have to be based more on experience than on qualifications. 'New Careers' was not, therefore, a system of providing professionals with aides or ancillaries; the trainees were to enter the professions as full practitioners. Consequently, many existing practices were challenged.

New Careers was a long-term programme. It was not seen as a stop-gap solution, but one which would lead to the complete reorganization of structures and institutions central to society. It provided an alternative to the relegation of large numbers of people to permanent unemployment, and gave them the chance to perform useful functions in society. Indeed, in the cynical seventies, reading the evangelical tracts of the mid-sixties provided by New Careers is rather like a guilty glimpse of an old Sunday School prize. The complex goals of the new movement included: providing a sufficient number of jobs for those without work and ensuring that jobs were designed and distributed so as to be available for the unskilled and uneducated. The schemes intended to make work and training simultaneous, providing permanent jobs that offered long-term career prospects. Opportunities were to be given to the talented and motivated poor so that they could advance from low-skill jobs to any station available to the more favoured members of society. The deprived were to contribute to the programme from the outset since it was suggested that the poor have a unique personal knowledge of the problems being tackled. Finally, the schemes envisaged that the work provided would contribute to the well-being of society.

It is impossible to generalize about the various projects that were implemented to pursue 'New Careers' ideals. Joan and Douglas Grant in their paper, *Evaluations of New Careers Programmes*, mention a range of programmes, each with differing aims, recruitment and standards of entry. A project in Boston, for example, listed as necessary criteria for admission: interest in mental health and training, sensitivity to minority groups, employment or volunteer experience in the community service area and interest in advancing themselves through training. However, in Mendocini, the organizers were looking for high school drop-outs, people of minority status who were under- or unemployed or who had prior mental health problems such as drug abuse or alcoholism and who had no continuous work history or marketable skills. Nevertheless, Dennie Briggs writes (1975) that by 1972, $1\frac{1}{2}$ million formerly disadvantaged people had been thus gainfully employed, mostly by various government agencies, and one in five of these is an ex-prisoner. The 'New Careers' concept also flourished alongside other trends in social work, particularly a reduction in levels of institutional provision. John Flackett, for example, explains, 'The New Careers movement has developed alongside the community treatment model and there is now considerable overlap both in the actual operation and fundamental philosophy' (Flackett, 1973).

More significant to the Bristol scheme was the application of the 'New Careers' principle to offenders in American custodial institutions. There was a growing belief, fanned by popularist interactionist sociology, that offenders have something unique to offer other offenders. Labelled and stigmatized, they know what it is like to feel criminal and so can give forms of support which cannot be provided by social workers who have not themselves been personally involved in crime. These ideas, combined with the New Careers concept, were clearly attractive to the Departments of Corrections who were responsible for the increasingly overcrowded and expensive prisons. Larry Dye, a university lecturer and successful 'New Careerist', writes in the proceedings of the 1968 seminar, *Offenders as a Correctional Manpower Resource*,

Here are men, women and youth whose backgrounds enable them to serve fellow offenders effectively. Many of them can be trained to provide services for which correction now lacks professionally trained personnel. And their period of training can contribute to their own rehabilitation.

Particularly influential in this field were the projects of Joan and Douglas Grant in California. Professor Grant had worked with deviants for many years as a clinical psychologist at a U.S. Navy

K

Training Command and he subsequently initiated New Careers programmes to selected inmates from state prisons. Two members of his team at Vacaville, Nancy Hodgkin and Dennie Briggs, were later to become a formative influence on the Bristol project.

It was probably Dennie Briggs and Nancy Hodgkin who were foremost in bringing the 'New Careers' model to the attention of the Home Office and those interested in penal reform. Particular interest was displayed by the National Association for the Care and Resettlement of Offenders (N.A.C.R.O.), which is an independent pressure group seeking to bring about changes within the penal system and to initiate experiments. N.A.C.R.O.'s obvious interest was in projects concerned with the prevention or treatment of delinquency rather than general programmes of relieving poverty. After discussions with the Home Office, it was decided that the older teenage offenders in Borstals would provide the most suitable group to use for this project, particularly as it echoed some of the Community Service Order's ideas which were to prove a success in the hands of the Probation Service and which foreshadowed the thinking of the Younger Report.

The Home Office had good reason to be concerned about the Borstal system. Increasing numbers of admissions (these were over 7,000 in 1975) were putting pressure on places, and the length of trainees' stays had shortened. Also, an increasing number of younger offenders were being admitted. In 1975, 1,150 receptions were under seventeen. The increasing public demands for security had also made it difficult for senior staff in the Borstals to initiate experiments. Morale was not helped by the high reconviction rates of boys released from Borstals. 63 per cent of trainees released in 1972 were reconvicted within two years, and for boys under seventeen on reception, this figure was even more depressing: 79 per cent were recommitted (H.M.S.O., 1975). Costs, too, were rising fast— £3,570 per trainee in 1974–5. The Home Office had every reason, therefore, to favour the new strategies proposed by N.A.C.R.O.

Senior staff in local Prison Department establishments were also well disposed to the scheme. They were even more clearly aware than the reformers of the disadvantages of residential experiences for older boys. Even if they were initially doubtful, they offered support. As one Governor told us,

My attitude to N.A.C.R.O. has changed about 180 degrees. Before, I'd thought they viewed the Prison Service as having no integrity. I thought they were well-meaning but impractical.

This project must succeed. This is a highly realistic scheme.
We need adventurous schemes to prod us, kick us in the pants.
It will force staff to look outwards. Few thinking people in the
Service would oppose such a scheme to keep people out of
prison. No jobs are threatened. I wish they'd take some girls—
they really are difficult. They take 80 per cent of my time.

Even the initial suspicions of the Prison Officers lifted. 'We reckoned
they were just another bunch of long-haired, denim-draped Com-
munists. But, they certainly took some tough customers. If they
want them, good luck, we've got enough to do. They must have
some success because not many of the boys have been back through
here.'

It was, therefore, a combination of factors that transformed the
idea of a 'New Careers' project into a scheme in Bristol for boys
likely to be sentenced at Crown Court to Borstal training.
N.A.C.R.O. found that one of their independent regional groups—
the Bristol Association for the Care and Resettlement of Offenders
—had a suitable property, a terraced house which had been previously used as a voluntary after-care hostel for adolescent offenders.
This was an attractive location because the local community had
grown to accept the hostel, and the existing designation of the
premises as residential accommodation made a public enquiry un-
necessary. Indeed, one of the major hurdles in any new project
involving delinquents is the inevitable hostility of the neighbourhood. Frequently, those faced with the task of engendering some
community consciousness in faded suburbs cannot resist the unify-
ing banner offered by a threatening hostel and their agitation often
leads to the curious situation of one group of liberal reformers
bellowing at another.

The Home Office were understandably a little cautious about the
original idea of twelve offenders, fresh from Court and largely
predestined for detention in maximum security, living a relatively
unsupervised life in a residential hostel. However, N.A.C.R.O. were
successful in getting the Home Office to accept their radical proposal, and it was agreed that the management committee would
have to be local. The responsibility for the scheme, therefore, passed
to B.A.C.R.O., the Bristol section of the National Association. The
Home Office also persuaded N.A.C.R.O. to select students for the
project from offenders who were likely to receive a Borstal sentence,
hence, some of the most criminal and institutionalized of young
people. N.A.C.R.O. would have preferred an older group of

offenders, but they accepted this system mainly because of the economic stability it offered. The Home Office were obliged to look after those sentenced either to Borstal training or residence in a Probation home, and their financial contributions would give the project a sound financial base. N.A.C.R.O. were seeking intelligent, articulate, extroverted and aggressive young men for the project, just the sort of criminal that had been successful at Vacaville (the new careers project centre in California). But there were, even at this stage, doubts in the minds of some about whether such types could readily be found among the Borstal population.

Eventually, it seemed, all was ready. The hostel, incorporating the original home and the house next door, was converted to take twelve boys, the Administrator and her deputy and three resident assistant wardens, called linkers, and the project took off early in May 1973.

Much hard work had to be undertaken in Bristol to sell the scheme to others working with young offenders. It was here that the enthusiasm and youth of N.A.C.R.O. workers were a disadvantage. Considerable skill is required to sell alternatives to established organizations because to justify the need for experiment, deficiencies have to be highlighted in penal practice. Public Relations exercises had to be undertaken to explain the scheme to the judiciary, the local probation services and the police, as well as the staff of the feeding prisons and Remand Centre. It is perhaps significant that almost every person we interviewed claimed that they had not been fully informed about the project and found themselves accepting a *fait accompli*. This situation partly reflects the haste with which the scheme had to be organized, but it is equally symbolic of the threat that the 'New Careers' concept posed to established professional groups. Despite the considerable efforts of the Project Administrators and several committee members to explain the scheme to the social work agencies, it seems that all innovatory schemes create hostility even when their aims are clearly expressed and the threat to existing systems is minimal. After all, selecting twelve boys for an experiment from among 7,000 is hardly a challenge to the well-established custodial traditions of the Prison Department! But the suggestion of an alternative strategy for helping offenders raises the conflicts between rehabilitation and retribution, between welfare and prisoners' rights, which busy people choose to ignore. The Remand Centre Governor, for example, reflected this insecurity when he commented, 'N.A.C.R.O. approached the Prison Department who then contacted the South West Region. But the first I knew was when the Committee Chairman approached me and I was suddenly presented with the papers on my desk. I threw them down in a fit of rage but after our meeting, I got more enthusiastic.' This is despite the fact that N.A.C.R.O. clearly had no alternative other than to first prepare the way by consultation with the Prison Department. The views expressed by some Probation Officers also reflect this situation and, 'We were only told of the scheme when it was here,' was a typical comment.

People in more practical situations, however, such as prison officers and heads of placements where the students were to work, seemed less concerned with protocol and tended to view the scheme as a welcome addition to overstretched resources and a new approach to an old problem. Hence, their views were more favourable and the senior prison officers, in particular, offered some pertinent but positive observations about the project, such as whether there would be difficulties in recruiting suitable lads from the South West where articulate and aggressive young offenders are less common than elsewhere. One officer commented, 'If they'd put the project at Risley, there'd be lots more to choose from and they chose some very difficult boys without much reference to us.' So, there were mixed feelings about the project even in the initial stages. For many, the idea of 'New Careers' was a challenge to professional practice, others saw practical problems and some welcomed a radical injection into a tired system. But the overall situation was still favourable, particularly as the hostel building was accepted by the local people as a place for delinquent boys. The hostel did indeed open and soon filled with young offenders who, thanks to an application of labelling theory, were graced with the title 'students'. If nothing else had been achieved, this by any standards was a remarkable event.

The aims of the project were extremely complex, and consequently everyone had different interpretations of its intentions. Each group firmly believed that the project would demonstrate the validity of its own particular philosophy. With the exception of the Home Office, whose hopes were modest, few others seemed to entertain the notion that boys might fail. N.A.C.R.O.'s hopes were for a success of national significance—it was an experiment to point the way, to demonstrate the potential and creativity within every young offender. To the Bristol Committee, it was yet one more lively contribution to a local, creative social work fringe. The Project Administrators, cherishing social work ideals, hastened towards an experiment in caring for vulnerable lads. It was a chance to help in an unusually free context; there was a nest to be built. To the project innovators, it was yet another try at a therapeutic Nirvana—community meetings occupied hours of the original time-table. To the trainees, at least it was a different experience from Borstal. To the linkers—former offenders hired to form a bridge between students and administration—it was a chance to change their image. In their early 20's, the romance of offending was diminishing and they knew that they were worth more than the guarded smile of the rejecting employer. The Remand Centre, local Probation and Social Service Departments sat on a fence from which the view of the hostel was rather obscure. They were not invited in, they did not hope for much, but at least, they would give it a try.

In theory, the American 'New Careers' concept was to be applied to a group of offenders aged $17\frac{1}{2}$–21 who would otherwise have been in custody. Dennie Briggs, who was a part-time adviser to the scheme, was confident that the American ideas could be transferred to Britain and suggested that the cultural differences between the two countries had been exaggerated. It was intended that twelve offenders who had been specially selected for the project would spend twelve months living in the hostel, during which time they would be trained in social and community work by other more mature New Careerists, the Project Administrators, placement supervisors and visiting experts. The resident linkers, who were crucial to the scheme, were employed by N.A.C.R.O. and had themselves spent time in penal institutions.

Apart from regular group work and education which were incorporated in the hostel life, it was intended that the students would also take part in a long-term training programme. Initially, this was to be a four-month introductory period, during which time the students would undertake a series of observational placements at a subnormality hospital, adventure playgrounds, youth clubs and various community schemes and would prepare their own projects on selected topics. The remaining two thirds of the training were to be spent on a longer practical placement in which the students could take up a clear ancillary position. The young men had originally been given a two-year Probation Order with a twelve-month condition of residence at the hostel. It was hoped that by the end of the year, the experiences they had gained would be accepted as a preparation, perhaps in lieu of academic qualifications, for entrance into professional positions in social work or to courses offering the necessary training.

This training was intended to provide an alternative to a spell in a custodial institution, an experience which has little positive influence, in the long-term, on a boy's propensity to offend. The project placed boys in a setting where there was group support, where there was much encouragement for them to change their behaviour and to channel their interests into community service. It was envisaged that the students would have every encouragement to develop their own ideas and the organizational structure of the hostel delegated some of the responsibility for the training programme to the three resident linkers. In theory, it was reminiscent of the nineteenth century pupil-teacher developments, where the seniors taught the novices and the project was to be continuously fed by those who had completed their training and then returned part-time to help others.

The project rejected the explicit controlling role of the probation hostel, but in fact used the regulation governing the breach of probation when lads were continuously disruptive. N.A.C.R.O. hoped that the outcome of 'New Careers' would have radical effects on social work practice. It was suggested that a new breed of radical social worker with perspectives sharpened would be born of knowing the receiving end of treatment. These in turn would train others to follow. Inevitably, this would challenge existing career structures in social work and threaten jealously nurtured professional roles. The hopes of a radical injection into social work practice was the major ethical justification for the project and differentiated it from reforms taking place within the Borstal system.

Throughout the project, there has been much discussion about the types of offenders that would benefit from the scheme and, to this day, the selection process has been the main issue of conflict. We noted that the scheme was initially intended for articulate, aggressive boys whose criminality was theoretically situational, due to blocked opportunities and poor education. It was thought likely that they would be able to get projects off the ground, to explain problems to clients and to tackle the authorities confidently. There was even support for this idea from many prison staff who, in the light of their practical experience, felt that extroverted, aggressive offenders needed greater stimulation than could be offered in prison, where they tended to cause trouble and consume resources. Several senior officers commented that this type of offender was often quite successful at coping with the responsibilities of living in an open community or working out, provided that the boys' energies were directed to areas that were socially acceptable.

Dennie Briggs, however, saw the scheme less as an alternative to

Borstal. In an interview, he stressed the value of the experience for a much wider group of people—those under thirty, capable of communicating ideas to others but who had been unsuccessful in the educational race. He stressed the need to select students whose ideas were flexible and who had a real interest in new ideas and relations with clients. He wanted students to feel valued for their potential rather than acting as a spearhead for change in the social services. These ideas in a sense were more radical. The boys were not only casualties of the system but also had a unique contribution to make.

One of the problems of the scheme has constantly been the recruitment of suitable students. Unlike U.S. social services system, which is a well developed complex of 'alternative' social services to facilitate the 'New Careerists's' entry into social work, Britain's social services are dominated by the state and protective professional bodies. They have proved inflexible and unresponsive to the idea of an ex-criminal workforce. It soon became clear, as many prison officers had predicted, that the numbers of suitable lads in the Borstal system was small. One principal officer commented, 'They might find more in a Detention Centre but I'm afraid that most of our lads are inarticulate, dim and passive'. Selection problems, in fact, seemed to illustrate the many conflicting perspectives of participants in the scheme. Those interested in the 'New Careers' concept became frustrated by the dearth of promising material. Anyone bright and disadvantaged could benefit but persistent criminality was a drawback. However, any widening of the criteria of entry would, in the eyes of N.A.C.R.O., question the significance of the project as an alternative to Borstal; and naturally, the Home Office interest centred on offenders.

These conflicts are reflected in the range of views that people held about what the project should be achieving. An influential member of the committee spoke of 'offering these lads choice, not a university course'. He claimed that, 'you need a project like this in order to give them opportunities for choice so that even if they reject the experience, this is not failure'. Another committee member said that the project was 'educational rather than therapeutic'. Dennie Briggs, on the other hand, was not only more sympathetic to the 'New Careers' concept, but stressed the importance of the residential experience in 'fostering a group culture of thinking and learning young people'. The Home Office, in contrast, seemed more concerned about the administrative and legal problems that could arise if the scheme expelled a student—such as whether it was possible to transfer an unresponsive student from the scheme to an institution, particularly when Borstal training was not the original sentence. They were also concerned about confidentiality, and whether 'New Careerists' should be allowed access to the files of the clients in the social services and Probation departments in which it was hoped they would be working.

Senior staff at the Remand Centre were less moved by the radical implications of 'New Careers' and saw this project as one scheme among many. They were, nevertheless, sympathetic to the provision of a new experience which might break the cycle of recidivism, or at least allow offenders to see life differently. The Regional Controller of Prisons, however, was less optimistic, and frankly thought the scheme insufficiently organized. He was concerned that the therapeutic regime planned for the hostel was too doctrinaire, relentless and unrealistic. He was particularly concerned about the failure or organizers to ensure that a career structure existed for those students who did show promise in social work. He was afraid that boys' aspiriations would be raised only to be dashed when faced with diploma-demanding employers or hostile staff running training courses—a fear which has been amply justified since.

The staff at the hostel were deeply committed to all aspects of the project, particularly to the 'New Careers' concept. The Project Administrator stressed the need to develop a successful rehabilitation programme which included reducing delinquent behaviour. She was also anxious to create a training programme which would offer delinquents a future and which would influence their self-perceptions, actions and achievements. The first linkers wrote in November 1973,

> Our basic aim is to provide an alternative type of treatment for offenders. . . . It will be our policy to help students to negotiate their own jobs only within agencies that offer career opportunities and realistic salaries. We think it would do the students a grave injustice to let them do menial jobs for little pay within agencies, voluntary or professional, as we believe they have plenty to offer professionals. (N.A.C.R.O., 1973.)

The first student also wrote,

> I have got no O levels or any qualifications as I was always playing truant from school, this is one more system that I kicked in the face. The kind of work I have been doing is with

kids of all ages, such as Stoke Park Hospital which is for physically and mentally handicapped children. We almost do the same work as staff, which is for example, cleaning, washing, feeding, dressing, playing and most of all, teaching the kids to do small things for themselves. I would never have had the chance to do this kind of work that holds a future if it were not for New Careers. (NACRO, 1973, p. 3.)

The opening months of the project went off well. The Grants were able to fly over from California to add their support and Dennie Briggs visited Bristol one day each week to counsel staff, advise on the training programmes and group living experience, direct educational training programmes for staff and students and link the project to other schemes and training courses. Two full-time, non-residential project administrators, both in their mid-twenties, were also appointed in January 1973. They were Cathy Mordue, a Probation officer, and Jim Dickie, who had experienced a 'New Careers' project when he was assistant governor at Ever-thorpe Borstal. Dennie Briggs had wanted qualified social workers for these posts as he felt they had much to offer in the initial stages of setting up the training programme. However, the intention was, in the long term, for linkers to be sufficiently skilled to direct the project without much external help.

The role of the administrators was to recruit and select staff and students, to manage the hostel and to undertake public relations work, while Jim Dickie also took particular responsibility for co-ordinating the educational content of the training, that is, leading seminars, discussing projects and helping students develop ideas from their experiences. A project secretary was also appointed, and she in fact became a most important person in the project, a central administrative aide and counsellor to staff and students as well as being a key figure in public relations.

The first two linkers both lived in the hostel and were paid an initial salary of about £1,300, but this was soon increased and by July 1974 had risen to £2,124 per annum. They were each to take responsibility for four students with whom they worked as a group. This was strenuous employment. Only two evenings each week were free, and alternate weekends were spent on duty. The linkers not only formed a bridge between the students and other adults, such as the placement heads or project administrators, but also fulfilled leadership functions. They were expected to provide a clear role model for the students, that of the reformed offender, and the residential living experience, especially the evening living group meeting, was to be consciously used to help the students learn a number of tasks. Before a placement, the linkers had to spend time preparing the ground and identifying problems the student might face and during the training. It was also the linkers' task to keep a close watch on the student's progress. Linkers were 'New Careerists' themselves and with the skills they developed in their work, it was hoped that they would enter full-time social work.

The daily routine for students was to be rigorous. The initial four-month period consisted of five 12-hour days (9.00 a.m. to 9.00 p.m.) with weekend work. Saturday evening was the only free time when lads could spend some of their wages of £15.00 per week (less board). Students were expected to partake in educational courses led by distinguished outside visitors, and in simulation and group exercises to develop their skills as 'New Careerists', as well as to record their experiences in detail and contribute to the daily 'group living' discussions. In the first four months, there was to be a series of placements and exercises, with about three days per week in the community working and the rest of the time in team meetings, living groups, planning, study and cultural experiences. The hostel had no television, and entertainment was at a minimum. In phase 2, weeks 9–28, an extended placement (a nineteen-week placement, virtually full-time in one post) took up much time but the student was still expected to do community service work, evening classes, remedial courses and private study in his area of interest. In the final five months, the student was expected to enter a long job placement in an agency likely to offer employment. In addition, studies were to be undertaken at an advanced level, for example 'A' level sociology, which would improve the students' chances of being accepted for professional training. On completing the course, the New Careerist should be ready for employment. The following diagram illustrates the complete training programme.

The whole project was directed by a management committee of six people representing a wide range of interests. The Chairman, Chris Holtom, directed a social work training course at Bristol University; the Secretary, Nigel Whiskin, was Regional Organizer for N.A.C.R.O. The other members represented a range of professional and 'New Careers' interests and at their monthly meetings, the Project Administrator, linkers and secretary were all represented. There was also a liaison probation officer from the local Avon office.

It was with high expectations that the first three students arrived

TABLE XII

Training programme

	Weeks 1–8	Weeks 9–28	Weeks 29–52	After leaving hostel
	Observation Placement			
	Observation Placement			
	Observation Placement	Personal Research Project		
	Observation Placement	Extended Placement		
	Observation Placement			
			Final Practical Work Placement for an Agency likely to offer employment	→ Full time employment ↑
			More Advanced courses in social work and Administration run by statutory and voluntary agencies	
	Remedial Education Leading to Examinations			
	Seminar Service on Subjects related to the Training			
	Community Service Work			
	Evening Classes			
	↑ Assessment	↑ Assessment	↑ Assessment	↑ ↑ Discharge Follow up support

in June 1973. Unfortunately, two of these absconded quickly, somewhat discouraged by the demands made on them by the project. This was a setback, but during the autumn more lads were recruited, and by the end of December there were ten resident trainees and three linkers.

It is not easy in so short a paper to assess whether since that time the project has succeeded or failed in its objectives. It would, in any case, be somewhat naïve to talk so rigidly about such a complex history of human relationships and such a diversity of expectations. The project has most certainly failed to fulfil many of the early hopes, yet in other respects, much has been achieved and learned. It must be recalled that this was no grandiose scheme to solve delinquency but a small residential hostel and, like all small institutions, the project has had its good and bad patches. The project embarked on that turbulent voyage well known to those who stand wisely watching on the margins of innovation. At times, the atmosphere has been calm and relaxed but on other occasions, there has been disarray and conflict. It is not sufficient, therefore, to speak in terms of straightforward success or failure, although we will attempt some evaluations in our conclusions. But in the meantime we intend more to describe the development of the project and to discuss the lessons of these experiences for more general processes of innovation for young offenders.

The Autumn months of 1973 went well. It was a very encouraging experience to visit the hostel and attend group living meetings during this period. Despite the external suspicion and cynicism, here were ten young men, who would otherwise have been in a secure Borstal, living in an open community and displaying deep commitment, perhaps for the first time, to a very demanding training programme. They were relaxed, welcoming and anxious for acceptance. These boys were by no means an easy intake, for despite their ability to talk fluently and intelligently, in terms of social deprivation and criminal history they were very typical of the Borstal population. Their offences included violation of property, taking and driving away and drug offences, and many had been through Detention Centre and a number of approved schools. Indeed, we had met four of the first eight boys in our previous researches into approved schools in the region and it was a bit like an old boys' reunion except that our and their life chances seemed to differ. These four students had already accumulated twenty-six years of residential experience among them. If nothing else, N.A.C.R.O. had shown that the hostel was a possible alternative, and this must be acknowledged as a major achievement, one that still leaves us full of admiration and surprise.

But, not surprisingly, problems began to emerge. First, it was one or two individuals whose behaviour disrupted the training programme. One example was the depression and grief of a student whose girl friend died in a road accident. Over time, however, the pattern of problems became more consistent.

The first difficulty was recruiting suitable students. The observations of the prison officers seemed to be correct; there were just not many bright, aggressive and extroverted offenders coming into West of England Borstals. The cultural differences between young offenders in American and British prisons were significant. In Britain, there is little evidence of large, underprivileged ethnic groups militated against by a prejudiced judiciary and police force. Black youth dominates the young offenders' scene in the United States. These are mostly boys who have had less-than-adequate educational and social opportunities and whose criminality reflects frustration with social injustice, blocked opportunities and racial prejudice rather than personal inadequacy. This is not to suggest that unequal distributions of resources, education and opportunity do not exist in Britain. Far from it, but it is more a question of the degree and pervasiveness of the injustice and the size of the groups affected.

The students selected for the project seemed either too immature, institutionalized or too disturbed to cope with the pressures of the training, and there were endless arguments about sources of recruitment, age ranges and geographical areas to be served. Some wished to abandon the concept of an alternative to Borstal altogether and, by admitting older, less criminal young men, move towards the 'New Careers' principle for those who had been deprived of opportunity. The committee and administrators, on the other hand, felt misled by the experience in America, where it appears there are more situational delinquents in institutions who, despite their social and educational deprivations, are emotionally stable. In contrast to this situation, many of our offenders have enduring psychological problems. The debates over selection raged simply because they symbolized so much of the personal investment of the various parties involved in the project, but little was achieved, and during 1974, numbers dropped.

In such an inbred environment, it was not surprising that personal vendettas also flourished. One of the project administrators became somewhat disillusioned and began to see the management committee as indifferent and remote, yet felt threatened by any intrusion into professional autonomy. Project administrators' feelings were fanned by discoveries of anomalies in the salary scales and a general lack of support. They also began to see the management committee as indifferent and remote yet felt threatened by any intrusion into their autonomy. Briggs, too, became dissatisfied with the speed at which the project was developing. Some of the committee members criticized the project administrators for failing to delegate authority sufficiently. The administrators argued back that the linkers were not experienced enough to handle the many intricacies of the hostel situation. All was not well on the committee, either, and two members felt that another member was sowing seeds of discontent amongst the management group. All gathered to criticize Briggs's group living philosophy and the therapeutic and training aims of the scheme seemed irreconcilable. Inevitably, the air of discontent rubbed off on the students, some of whom began to find the relentless zeal of a 'New Careers' project somewhat boring, especially when they realized that they had to compete in an open market for job opportunities with social services or probation departments. The students introduced a television set and demanded more leisure time. Everyone involved with the project manipulated this roundabout of frustration and projected their hostilities onto others, not least the lads. But the project battled on.

Conflict, of course, can be highly creative, and in the early stages, this was probably the case. Eventually, however, things did come to a head and, after the first review in May 1974, Cathy Mordue decided that she no longer wished to continue working on the project and Jim Dickie took over the administration.

Despite these traumas, it must not be assumed that the students' training programmes were damaged. Many young men made remarkable headway during this period such as the student who left the project after an eight month stay in June 1974, anxious to become a nurse in a subnormality hospital. He took a labouring job until a vacancy arose in March 1975. Another lad also accepted a post in an old people's home, and one of the other students left in September to work for six months in an after-care hostel for long-term prisoners before moving to become a linker on an alcoholics recovery project, so achieving the career steps from student to linker envisaged in the 'New Careers' philosophy. Of the first twelve students admitted to the scheme, two soon absconded from the hostel but, by June 1975, only four had been convicted within a year of leaving. Three had social work jobs, one was seeking this type of work and one was living at home, but clear of trouble. The linkers too, made good progress and one of them was able to move to a post on a project which rehabilitated drug users.

The first year of the project, however, began to raise deep questions about the original aims of the scheme. First of all, there were many practical problems in the hostel. After a quiet period of settling in, many disturbed boys upset the hostel routine simply because their aggression and swings of mood were so public and consequently affected everyone else. Questions were raised about whether very disturbed boys could actually be helped in such an inward looking, crowded ambience. The hostel was also noisy, and minor living problems became centres of controversy. Petty pilfering was a common difficulty and the endless argument in group meetings about thefts from petty cash and plans for its overnight security symbolized wider conflicts between the levels of independence that could be safely granted to boys and the controls necessary to prevent the flourishing of private tensions.

The performance and selection of linkers also caused more concern than was originally envisaged. Some had been out of prison for only a very short period, and on occasions, their own personal problems and difficulties of adjustment dominated hostel life. At such times, they demanded as much supervision and help as the students. The linkers' position of power in the hostel also made it easy for one or two of them to manipulate the work schedule in order to minimize their own involvement, and the problems posed by this group caused as much concern as difficulties with students. But, again, individual responses varied, and some linkers gained enormous benefits from their experiences and moved into social work positions. In 1974, Jim Dickie suggested that the scheme was perhaps more successful with linkers than with students. The selection of linkers has subsequently changed. Candidates now have to have been out of trouble for a longer period, and preferably to have participated in some previous social or community work.

More serious, however, were the doubts in the minds of staff and students about the original New Careers philosophy. It soon became clear that boys' training experiences would not be sufficient to gain an inroad into either social work or training courses. The social work professions and Polytechnic courses seemed far more inflexible than had been expected. The training concept, too, appeared something of a fairy story, for it assumed too readily that linkers would be skilled in group work and that they would be able to influence swings in the commitment of students. General interest in the project also wore off, and those charismatic innovators who had originally rushed in to organize the scheme seemed less anxious to offer the continuous administration which is necessary to keep it going. They tended to drift away and to express little interest in the day-to-day practical problems. By this time, the Remand Centre and some home probation officers had themselves become disenchanted with the aggressive and simplistic attitudes towards delinquency adopted by a few of the linkers and students. The administrators had difficulty in preserving even a façade of unity.

By the summer of 1974, there was a growing disillusionment with the idea of students' ever becoming a radical force in social work. Between June 1974 and January 1975, the project was at a very low ebb. The management committee decided that continuous publicity was adversely affecting students' work and the cameramen and journalists no longer visited the project house at Filton Road. In October, Dickie, the administrator, left to work on an Intermediate Treatment project in Greenock, and Briggs became preoccupied with projects elsewhere. The present administrator, Martin Seddon, did not arrive until December 1974, leaving a gap during which grave problems arose. The instability of this interregnum was reflected in the boys' behaviour, and during this period, six of the eight boys either absconded or quickly returned to Borstal and prison. There was damage to the property, the routine of cooking, and cleaning disintegrated and the hostel became both dirty and infested. During one of our visits, a linker who was valiantly holding the fort single-handed received a phone call from a colleague who wished to extend his weekend leave. In desperation, he turned to us and said, 'You see, even the linkers are absconding.' There could be no clearer example of the ways in which the institutional climate affects the behaviour of students.

But still most of the students did not lose heart. They may have responded violently and committed offences, but in general, their commitment remained high. Indeed, a remarkable feature of the scheme was the deep involvement expressed by the students, including those who caused most trouble. Unlike most penal establishments, where inmates come and go and few questions are asked, all the 'New Careers' students seem to keep in close contact with each other and the unit. They attend party nights with their girl friends, rather like an old boys' social. We have never encountered this before among persistent, institutionalized delinquents.

It is hard to believe that any project could go through such a low point and survive. But thanks to the considerable resilience of

L

several committee members and linkers, and to the constant support of Home Office personnel, who, although they asked difficult
questions, never faltered in their encouragement, things kept going.
Since that time the project has stabilized and is able to endure the
inevitable cycles of elation and depression. By August 1975 there
were nine students in residence again, and things seemed reasonably
calm.

It is not our function in this review of the early days to continue
the history beyond 1975 except to say that the further development
of the project has been assisted by continuity of staffing. The
present administrator and deputy have been in post for over two
years and an increasing number of ex-offenders with experience
and proven ability are applying for linker vacancies. This continuity and strengthening of the staff team has meant that lessons
have been learned and the conclusions preserved in the important
areas of criteria for student selection and the balancing of the
various components of training. Relationships with the Prison
Service, Probation and Social Service Departments have been
stabilized, and the Committee has been reorganized so that the
longer-serving members could move more towards an advisory and
consultative role.

The concept of ex-offenders' making a positive contribution to
social work also seems to be gaining wider acceptance. Although
the agencies had to take this on trust in the early days of the project,
New Careers can point increasingly to its track record. A growing
number of ex-offenders are working their way up career ladders in
hostels and other projects and three are currently on professional
training courses. To date their work has been concentrated in the
'twilight' areas of social work, but in the near future, the accept-
ability of the students to the professions will be more directly
challenged. In 1977, the project still continues and seems to be a
permanent part of provision for young offenders. The existing
structure may be markedly different from the original conceptions,
but the scheme still provides an alternative strategy for trainees
who would otherwise be in Borstal.

By January 1976, twenty-three students had been through the
project and six of these have gone on to social work jobs. Eight left
on completion of training and the other fifteen left early, either to
be transferred voluntarily to another work situation or to have
their probation orders breached and return to Borstal. Sixteen of
the twenty-three have subsequently gone back into custodial institutions: four after absconding from the hostel and twelve after leaving

the project—four to Borstal and eight to Prison or Detention Centre. Seven out of the twenty-three students stayed on the project for over nine months but, on the other hand, eight participated for less than thirteen weeks. The average length of students' stay has been six months.

It would be unwise to offer many comments about the effectiveness of the project from a sample of twenty-three. But, even if results appear disappointing—17 per cent of admissions absconded and 63 per cent of those released have gone back into custody— these figures do not compare unfavourably with the overall success rates of Borstals where, as we saw earlier, 63 per cent of trainees released in 1972 were reconvicted within two years, a figure which rises to 79 per cent for boys aged under seventeen on reception. Although the 'New Careers' students were carefully selected for ability, their previous criminal behaviour was fairly typical of the general Borstal population. In 1975, for example, seven students were accepted for the project but were refused permission to participate by the judge at their trial and were sentenced to considerable terms in custody. Five of these were given prison sentences, one was directed to Borstal, and the other recalled to Borstal, indicating clearly the sorts of experience for which the 'New Careers' project was offering an alternative. Clearly, there is no evidence to suggest that in terms of reconvictions, the open hostel has been any less successful than the secure institutions for which the students were otherwise destined, and the 'New Career' benefits gained by at least a quarter of the lads demonstrate the enormous advances made by some of the participants.

It is unfortunate that we do not have more time to give a fuller account of the history and development of the project, but lack of space must restrict our exposition. All we can do here is to draw lessons from this experiment for social work practice and make some general comments about its success.

The first clear observation we can draw from the New Careers experience concerns the problems of running hostels for young offenders. Social workers frequently stress the value of hostels as opposed to large institutions, but there is every indication that they are extremely difficult places to run. Three major studies of this type of establishment—Sinclair's (1971) survey of probation hostels, Griffith's (1969) history of an after-care hostel for adult offenders, and Hayes's (1976) account of the exercise to increase effectiveness, all emphasize the instability of these institutions and the stresses they place on staff. We saw that the atmosphere at the 'New Careers' hostel was extremely cyclical. Weeks passed when all was well, but suddenly problems would accumulate and morale would plunge. Hostels lack the inertia and the many associated personal involvements of larger institutions.

The difficulty seems to arise from the tendency within the small group for an individual's problems to affect everyone else. Hostels are normative organizations, and as such, are highly vulnerable to personal conflicts. Disturbed behaviour among clients is infectious, and overnight an explosive climate can develop. In a large Borstal, the recalcitrant inmate can be taken out of circulation or counselled in private, but in a small community, every display is public and the staff have to be seen to be effective without violating the close relationships that have been developed.

The importance of staff-student relations was stressed by Sinclair as an important factor in determining the effectiveness of hostels, and the Bristol experience confirms that the tensions between participants can lead students to display aggression and abscond. In theory, it was envisaged that the group at the hostel would be therapeutic by offering support and might also be controlling, and, for much of the time, this seemed to be the case. But when tension mounts, somebody disintegrates and everyone else is immediately anxious.

It seems also that domestic chores added to the problems. Difficulties in relating to others and accepting responsibility will arise without the added burden of organizing cooking, laundry and cleaning. Such domestic matters exacerbate the considerable strains imposed by the training programme and living situation. Unfortunately, there was an assumption that the free and easy domestic arrangements would reflect boys' own homes, so easing the culture clash inherent in the project. But, in fact, for the students, the hostel situation was far removed from the life style of the working-class adolescent, who rarely lifts a finger to assist his mother with the daily cooking, cleaning and ironing.

Both the administrators suffered much worry. One actually commented, 'At home, I would wake up in the night sweating, imagining I'd just heard the phone give that short ring as the caller hangs up. I would then lie awake worrying—is the hostel O.K.?' It is inevitable that pressures will be considerable in a situation where fifteen people, each with their own views on the aims of the project, work together seven days a week in a scheme which is scrutinized by other professionals and which has radical implications.

In large institutions, staff are protected from stress by colleagues but in the hostel, the administrators had only the encouragement of each other. To expect administrators to function without sufficient support, therefore, is unrealistic, particularly as some of them are young and not without personal problems of their own. Had the hostel had an older director, control and administration might have been less problematic. Unfortunately, progressives seem to believe that creativity and sensitivity cease at twenty-five and that understanding can exist only when client and social worker are indivisible in age, looks and dress. More often, the reverse is the case—as Sinclair found in his survey of probation hostels. When older people are in charge, elements of competition and immaturity are frequently removed.

The management committee, therefore, reconsidered its function during 1974 and had to move from a steering to an operational role. The model of management provided by governors of a school or a probation hostel seemed hardly suited to this project, and the committee began to take a more practical interest with everyday problems. Although voluntary committees have the advantages of flexibility, they can be fragile bodies and the experiences of the 'New Careers' project confirms the importance of professional guidance which they provide. The quality of this support should perhaps override more democratic concerns about representing a range of professional interests on the committee.

The lessons, then, for the management of hostels are clear. We have to accept the cyclical nature of life in these places and to devise support systems that relieve the inherent isolation and paranoia of radical experiments. At the same time, it is necessary to offer practical help and to provide the stability that is necessary to guide the project through crises. The Home Office, with its wide experience of such schemes, provided valuable administrative support throughout but it was found that the need was for support at a more individual, practical level.

The project also offers lessons about innovation. At the beginning, there are always many unknowns. It has been learned from experience that the 'New Careers' model applies best to older offenders in their twenties rather than to teenage delinquents, and it is also clear that the value of the concept varies for individuals so that even those who leave without entering social work can be enriched. However, these were issues that should have been foreseen. The superior attitudes of certain linkers to the established Borstal and probation system forfeited the sympathy and support that would have been forthcoming when difficulties arose. The difficulties of achieving a clear outlet in social work for trainees were greater than expected. On the one hand it proved insufficient to say, 'Careers will come but we can't guarantee anything', especially when boys' aspirations had been raised and on the other hand a turndown in the economy and boys' resistance to moving closed many suitable job openings. The collapse of morale during the Spring of 1974 was partly due to these factors. With hindsight, it might have been better to begin the project by a more realistic appraisal of careers which boys could achieve instead of rushing ahead to demonstrate how to cope with difficult clients.

The 'New Careers' project also aids our understanding of the actual process of initiating changes in social work practice. The scheme was a welcome experiment in an area haunted by institutional traditions. The aims, training and living situations, were in every sense a radical departure from the institutional philosophies that place nearly a quarter of a million adolescents and thousands of adults in traditional residential settings. The living situation was probably unique in that the administrators lived away from the hostel and the community was completely egalitarian. Each student was responsible for his own lifestyle. Paradoxically, this residential innovation probably stemmed from the concern of the project with wider 'New Careers' issues and a lack of interest in the residential experience as an enriching environment. Dickie, for example, once suggested that students should live out and use the hostel as a work base. It was the training experience rather than the residential structure that was sacrosanct. And yet, the training procedure told us less than had been expected, while the residential experiment has been highly creative.

Another clear feature of innovatory schemes is the charismatic nature of the leadership they attract. The 'New Careers' project has provided an arena which highlights the benefits and deficiencies of charismatic leadership. The project innovators were remarkably successful at setting things moving but seemed less interested in mundane aspects of day-to-day maintenance. Charisma holds the place together and directs the project in the early stages, but seems to resist the development of a necessary bureaucracy and a clear delegation of power that must replace it. Consequently, in all innovatory schemes there tends to be a succession crisis when the initial euphoria fades. Frequently, great initiators build into their schemes the seeds of destruction, unable to bear the prospect of others bringing their schemes to fruition. Subsequent problems assure charismatics of their inimitable gifts. Bureaucrats, on the other hand, fashion organizational structures, exorcising charisma; they see as an ideal an extensive pyramid governed by an empty in-tray. It seems to be a pattern of many radical projects that there has to be a period of soul searching once the initial excitement is over. Problems increase and are fuelled by the lack of any stable structure to maintaining the scheme. A more stable administration is usually established following a revision of aims and methods to incorporate the more practical constraints of the project. The 'New Careers' project offers a good example of this process.

It is because of this charisma and the quasi-religious involvement of staff in the early months that innovatory projects so often fail to learn from elsewhere. Ideas from California may be very relevant but is there nothing to be learnt from Sinclair's research, the Home Office Inspectorate or the Warden of the local after-care hostel? Innovatory schemes, therefore, are often in danger of seeming pretentious, obscurantist and paranoic. It is this religious stance and the evangelical, missionary zeal with which innovators approach more orthodox institutions that does so much to irritate ordinary social workers. This conviction may get the project going, but it can also antagonize people who are eventually necessary for the wellbeing of the scheme.

A further important feature of innovatory schemes is their failure to demonstrate the effectiveness of their changes. When evaluation or bitter experience reveals deficiencies in an experiment, there is a tendency for staff to change their goals to something different or to offer the experience to a population with a more favourable prognosis. For example, concepts of happy or adjusted criminals are frequently raised when the ineffectiveness of new schemes of treating offenders are demonstrated. Such clichés as, 'After all, what is success?', are on everyone's lips. Indeed, when faced by inescapable failures, such as a spate of further offences, absconding or violence, there is a tendency for liberals to become highly retributive, demanding an immediate transfer of the deviant to those very institutions whose inadequacies motivated the original innovation.

Another feature of many radical experiments is their frequent failure to acknowledge the contributions made by institutions which shelter those difficult cases which the projects cannot or will not treat. A stance that all would be well if only others followed their example may be good for morale but such attitudes alienate staff in orthodox establishments. Few 'dust-bin' locations, that is those institutions that repeatedly take back the failures from elsewhere and which cannot pass their difficult inmates on to others, get the credit they deserve. They are reproached as insensitive, although imaginative experiments, such as 'New Careers' can flourish only because these dustbins exist.

Paradoxically, one is forced to the conclusion that many innovatory approaches become highly functional for the orthodox system. Experiments can flower and wither while other humbler folk get on with the work of looking after the unloved majority. Innovatory schemes attract the attention and vociferous support of frothy radicals, draw towards them deviant staff and direct the media away from more traditional approaches. Thus, in the end, experiments not only fail to threaten orthodox practice but also have a tendency to reinforce it.

We have devoted considerable time to the discussions on innovation because the 'New Careers' project illustrates so many of the features that have been noted elsewhere, and it is only by studying the wider processes of change that we can make reforms more effective. But in raising these issues, it must not be assumed that we are dismissing the contribution of the Bristol project. On the contrary, we have tried to draw lessons from this scheme for the implementation of innovation. We certainly believe that the 'New Careers' experience has much to add to discussions about the residential treatment of offenders.

Residential institutions are facing many crises and the Bristol experience has much to offer the development of new ideas. Escalating costs have forced us to question the role of all residential provision and led us to consider methods of care in the community. The Filton Road hostel certainly illustrates one model of community care which could be far cheaper than running large institutions. During the first year of operation, the project cost just over £30,000. Economic comparisons between 'New Careers' and other forms of care can, of course, be manipulated, depending on whether average or marginal costs are compared. The marginal cost of a new admission at New Careers is very large compared with a Borstal institution, but if the scheme continues to operate at full capacity the average costs would be about 15 per cent below that of training a Borstal boy.

In another key area, the contribution of the New Careers experience is even more significant. There is a growing awareness of the client's perspective on the social interventions we offer and there is an increasing need to involve the client in what we do, to accept his viewpoint and offer him choice. This is a very different matter from the accommodation of discordant behaviour. It means that major structural changes are necessary in the care system if the services we provide are to meet the emotional and educational aspirations of young offenders. For all its faults, the 'New Careers' project does illustrate one way of approaching this and the techniques employed to gain boys' self-respect and commitment could profitably be copied elsewhere.

The project also teaches us about the mechanisms of initiating and organizing radical schemes and the pressures that staff working in such contexts will face. At a more practical level, there is much else that is encouraging. We know now, for example, that it *is* possible to place some Borstal boys in a relaxed, open situation and give them community work experience. Despite all our reservations, N.A.C.R.O. have indicated that this can be done.

The failure of many students to gain entry into social work careers and training courses, on the other hand, tells us what perhaps we try to deny. Our services are clearly viewed as part of the 'establishment' by our clients. It is also clear that our educational system is more closed than we would care to imagine, and that it can operate to exclude potential rather than encourage it. The 'New Careers' experience confirms that our professional structures are rigid and hierarchical, serving largely to protect us rather than the client.

Neither can we escape something much more unpalatable. The project has shown that bright, underachieving offenders, such as linkers and students at 'New Careers', still face an uphill struggle even when they make every effort to help themselves.

The 'New Careers' concept and the Filton Road hostel model now need to be applied to other groups of deprived people, perhaps older and less delinquent individuals than the students at Bristol, for example with the persistently unemployed. It is only by trying experiments such as this that we shall ever question the institutional tradition in this country. But this and other experiments confirm that it is only when the self images and identities of offenders are favourably influenced that we can ever hope for any improvement in their anti-social behaviour. N.A.C.R.O. have, at least, shown the way.

The Development of Community Service: its application and relevance to the Criminal Justice System

JOHN HARDING

The task of this chapter is to examine the development of Community Service by offenders over the past few years and to assess its impact on the community, the courts, the Probation Service and, not least, the programme participants. Whilst much emphasis will be placed on the effectiveness of the community service orders as a non-custodial measure, discussion will also focus on some of the less publicized schemes involving the use of offenders in giving community service. These schemes include the introduction of community service as part of the training programme for youngsters in residential homes or institutions, as a special project for children in the care of the local authority and, finally, as an alternative to monetary restitution in some of the pioneer restitution experiments recently set up in the United States.

Community Service Orders

Community Service orders were first introduced to the magistrates and Crown Courts in England and Wales under the 1972 Criminal Justice Act, later superseded by the Powers of Criminal Court Act 1973. Briefly Community Service Orders (C.S.O.'s) are a punishment of the court whereby the offender surrenders his leisure time to perform service with a community organization. The Home Secre-

tary gave authority to six Probation areas—Inner London, Nottinghamshire, Durham, Kent, S.W. Lancashire and Shropshire with
effect from 1 January 1973. Each of the six areas was properly
monitored from the start by the Home Office Research team in
Manchester, who were asked to evaluate the work of the community
service sections over a two-year period. The evaluation report
published in 1974, indicated that much was still unknown, including
the most suitable type of offender and the most desirable work
placement for different individuals, but showed that the scheme was
viable. Orders were made and completed in approximately 75 per
cent of all cases, sometimes evidently to the benefit of the offenders
concerned. The researchers ended their report on a note of cautious
optimism: 'At best, community service is an exciting departure
from traditional penal treatment' (Community Service Orders, 1975).
The Home Secretary subsequently announced the national extension
of Community Service schemes to all Magistrates and Crown Courts
in England and Wales. Probation areas outside the experimental
projects were given approval to commence their own community
service schemes from 1 April 1975. To date, all but three of the
probation areas in England and Wales have partial or complete
schemes in their areas. Although recent restrictions in government
spending threaten to prolong the complete extension of community
service to all courts for the next three years, the integration of community service orders into an accepted place in the range of non-
custodial sentences has been remarkably swift, considering the idea
was first raised in the 'Report on Non-custodial and Semi-custodial
Penalties', known as the Wootton Report, in 1970.

The Report itself was written against a background of a rising
prison population and a limited range of alternatives to custody.
The recommendations of the Wootton Report, with some amendments, were finally incorporated in Sections 15–19 of the Criminal
Justice Act of 1972. The main provisions are as follows:

(1) A person aged 17 years or over, convicted of an imprisonable
offence, may be ordered with his consent to undertake unpaid
work for any total number of hours between 40 and 240, within
a period of one year.
(2) A court cannot make an order unless (i) arrangements for
community service have been made in the petty sessions area
where the offender will reside; (ii) the court is satisfied, after
considering a probation officer's report about the offender and
his circumstances, that he is a suitable person to perform work

under such an order; and (iii) the court is also satisfied that provision can be made for him to do so.

(3) Community Service work arrangements should, so far as is possible, not conflict with the offender's work, educational or religious commitments.

(4) If the offender fails to comply with the community service order he may be fined up to £50 without prejudice to the continuance of the order, or the court may revoke it and deal with the original offence.

(5) The Act also outlines the provisions for the appointment of a Community Service Sub-Committee of a Probation and After-Care Committee. The Sub-Committee acts as a policy controller for the organization of community service in a probation area. The committee is made up of lay magistrates and certain ex-officio members whose experience in community affairs is thought relevant to the administration of the scheme.

The Organization of the Service

Each of the six experimental areas brought a fresh perspective to the development of the scheme. Some experienced problems of high unemployment amongst participants, some rural areas had problems of transport, some had well developed voluntary organizations in the community, whilst others had to stimulate the growth of community groups who would be responsive to offenders on community service. These project variations are now reflected on a national scale so that there might be within neighbouring county boundaries a considerable variation in approach in the practical application of the scheme. Clearly, common features are detectable.

Each scheme involves allocating offenders to work which may be provided by voluntary agencies, statutory authorities, community groups or by the Probation Service itself. Offenders on community service are supervised either by members of the work-providing agency or by sessionally paid probation staff. Supervision may be continuous, intermittent or nominal, depending on the nature of the task and the behaviour of the offender.

A community service team of probation officers and project workers is usually headed by a Senior Probation Officer. He is responsible, along with his colleagues, for locating tasks in the community, matching and allocating offenders to agencies, for acting as liaison with those agencies, sentencers and probation officers, following up unreliable workers and initiating breach proceedings in the courts when necessary. As with any specialist unit, it is essential that good links are maintained with colleagues in area teams so that the running of community service is seen as part of integrated practice rather than isolated specialism.

The pattern of communication includes the pre-trial consultation, the regular provision of progress reports to the officer who recommended an order, and, in those instances where two forms of involvement with an offender exist, as close a liaison as possible between the two officers involved.

Once an offender is made the subject of an order, careful consideration is given to the matching of that person to an available task before the first work allocation. Some areas have augmented basic interviewing procedures with the use of the Mooney Problem Check List to help the offender identify his areas of interest and concern. The offender's experience in that first work task confirms his suitability or unsuitability for that type of work; if he is unsuitable other work placements are tried. As a guideline an offender usually remains with one agency throughout his order, if the work continues to be available and he responds well.

Most of the contact with offenders on order is maintained by supervisors, either the sessional staff employed by the Probation Service or members of voluntary agency co-operating in the scheme. Contact with the community service is limited to initial interviews and review sessions at periodic points in the order. There are, of course, many exceptions to this pattern and it is common to find people on orders call in at the office to discuss their experiences on placement, look for re-inforcement and support and discuss problems of a personal nature in the absence of a strong relationship with another probation officer.

Supervisors, whether sessional or voluntary, are drawn from many different quarters; some are tradesmen or craftsmen, some are well motivated students, some already linked with a self-help organization for the homeless and some are ex-offenders who have graduated through the community service scheme to the point where they are assessed as suitable for the leadership role. Their task is to work alongside the client and carry out the intentions of the court in relation to the offender. Beyond this bare statement of accountability lies the underlying essence of community service, for the supervisor conveys not only the expectations of the community to the offender, but also places a valuation on the work that is performed. The attitude of the supervisor to his charge is, arguably, the key to success or failure of a community service placement. Such research and reports that have been published on offenders' and supervisors' attitudes to their relationship reinforce the point (Flegg, 1976; Harding, 1974). Flegg sums up the point in six items about the supervisor relationship which repeatedly emerged from the consumer survey on offenders' views in Nottinghamshire:

  (i) a negative experience with a supervisor could offset an offender's attitude to the whole of his community service order.
 (ii) conversely, a positive relationship, and in particular one which reinforced an offender's confidence in himself and in the job he was doing, could stimulate re-appraisal of self and others.
(iii) the extent to which the supervisor was able to interpret for the offenders affected how some tasks were seen.
 (iv) the supervisor acted as a model for some offenders, especially in his use of authority, and especially for those who were tentatively testing themselves out in new roles.
  (v) similarly, the reliability, the workmanship and skills of the supervisor were used as an indicator of how the task (and by inference the offender) was valued.
 (vi) finally, supervisors could be an important source of personal assistance as noted above.

Part of the success of the Supervisor may also rest in his non-professionalism; his ability to represent the community rather than his tenuous association with the criminal justice system. Nonetheless, whilst the Supervisor develops these community ties with offenders on shared tasks, it is important that the former is well supported by the Community Service team in this role. Regular contact is maintained with Supervisors either by written or spoken word. Each week a supervisor returns a work sheet, detailing a worker's attendance and quality of performance. Such communication is re-inforced by periodic visits to the agency or community group to obtain more detailed observations.

Many areas also hold quarterly meetings of supervisors so that common problems can be discussed and shared. Occasionally, there may be a need for specialist groups where supervisors involved in youth work, organizations for the handicapped or small work parties can look at the learning points in each of their separate settings.

In the event of breakdown through poor attendance or performance, the non-professional supervisor is not expected to attend court for the breach action. It is the usual case for an offender to be returned to a work party supervised by a probation ancillary. If he further offends in this group, then evidence is given to the court by the probation staff member.

Rationale and Purpose

From the outset community service attracted proponents of different varieties of penal philosophy. To some it appeared as a constructive alternative to short sentences of imprisonment. Others were encouraged by the notion of the offender's paying back his debt to society. Whilst others saw an intrinsic value in linking the offender with other members of the community who were in need of help and support.

Ministers of State, who guided the Community Service Section of the Criminal Justice Bill through the House of Commons were in little doubt about its purpose. They saw the measure as a means of reducing prison overcrowding and an alternative to the custodial sentence. The Probation Service, however, was left with the task of the practical implementation of the Act and, given the variety of conflicting views surrounding community service, it was not surprising that areas interpreted the measure in different ways. In three of the six experimental areas the Chief Probation Officers or working groups set up by them tended to view community service as primarily only an alternative to custody. The remaining three areas regarded community service as having a wider use, and in one of these the position is defended by the argument that, if community service were primarily an alternative to custody, the probation officer writing a social inquiry report must expect that the court would consider making a custodial sentence before he would be in a position to recommend the alternative of community service. (Community Service Orders, 1975.)

Despite the variation in approach taken by the experimental areas, the three areas regarding community service as an alternative to custody did not, taken together, have a statistically significantly higher proportion of custodial sentences passed when a community service recommendation was not taken up than did those three areas who saw community service as having a wider use. Even when courts initiated consideration of community service and then did not make an order, a non-custodial sentence was passed instead, in the significant majority of cases. The Home Office Research Unit concluded, based on the evidence available, that sentencers in many cases regard community service as an alternative to non-custodial sentences as least as much as, and possibly more than, an alternative 'custodial' sentence.

> One could argue that the experience of community service makes one pessimistic about the chances of making a planned displacement from prison actually work in the bulk of cases dealt with, and in the circumstances surrounding the community service experiment. However it may be the case that the general impression of community service communicated to the public, including sentencers, which stressed heavily its role as an alternative to custody, may have produced displacement from custody in the extent it occurred. (Peace, 1975.)

In spite of the difficulties in proving community service as a displacement measure, research has shown that offenders made the subject of orders had, on average, four previous criminal offences and, in 42 per cent of cases in the experimental areas, a previous custodial experience. For such a risk population community service appeared to offer a number of benefits either directly or indirectly associated with the programme.

(1) In most terms community service is a cheaper alternative to custodial training. An average length order of 120 hours takes approximately six months to complete and costs approximately £170. This has to be compared with the costs of imprisonment, currently approximately £80 per week.
(2) Community service also allows offender to live in the community and support his dependants by his normal work.
(3) It avoids some of the negative effects of incarceration over-dependence, loss of status, loss of decision making and loss of responsibility.
(4) It offers an offender an opportunity to contribute in some form to the community, and thereby gain status and approval for his actions.

The last assumption, whereby the offender is afforded an opportunity to re-appraise his own self image, represents the kernel of the community service philosophy. The notion of using the offender as a community resource was not in itself novel, since scattered experiments have been taking place in Britain and the United States in the sixties and early seventies. In the United States, the Kennedy/ Johnson era had seen the launching of the ambitious community development programmes in large urban areas like New York, where the ghetto resident faced environmental deprivation on a multiple scale. Community workers within these projects began hiring local residents from disadvantaged areas as organizers and social work aides, often with great effect. The New Careers Movement spread in the United States to include employment schemes for ex-offenders, ghetto residents, and the poor. Similar approaches were adopted in Britain at the start of the seventies. Five Borstals working in conjunction with the Community Service Volunteer Organization in London sent a number of trainees during their sentence to work in homes for old people or centres for the handicapped (see Chap. 8). The Community Service by Offenders scheme shared a similar philosophy to those other projects in encouraging people to dispense a service rather than become recipients of help.

Having looked briefly at the organization and purpose of community service orders it is worthwhile to examine what impact the scheme has had on those groups and on organizations most closely associated with it.

The Courts

One of the first tasks confronting any Community Service Organizer has been setting up talks with those who administer the criminal justice system—judges, magistrates, and clerks to the justices—so that some agreement can be reached on the legal interpretation of the Act and its practical implementation. Whilst sentencers invariably differed on the overall aims of community service and on whether it was a substitute for imprisonment, they did seek some clarification on the number of hours that might be given for particular offences. With a sentencing policy using such a flexible instrument no firm guidelines could be given. A useful suggestion emerged from the community service team in Nottinghamshire, which suggested that the court assess hours in terms of (1) the gravity of offence and previous record of conviction, and such other matters as would normally be weighed in passing sentence; (2) the capacity of the offender to take some regular responsibility for his attendance over an extended period; and (3) the extent of his work and domestic

M

responsibilities and other pressures he may be facing. Sentencers, for example, have been discouraged by probation staff from making long orders—upwards of 200 hours—on young offenders whose ability to work through such an order was found to be limited. The same tendency can be discerned in the recidivist with long institutional experience. Once these and other concerns about the possible effects of the length of an order have been identified, it became the practice to encourage probation officers to offer details to courts on the suitable length of an order in their reports. The response of courts in areas which have adopted this practice has been encouragingly positive, and it has become clear that the imposition of maximum orders (which may present particular difficulty simply because they are the maximum) has been reduced considerably, and that those that are made without reference to the offender's capacity to undertake them are made now only in the absence of specific advice from the reporting probation officer. It is felt that the willingness of courts to adopt the advice of the Probation Service in this instance can by extension be taken to demonstrate their general confidence in the content of Social Inquiry Reports. Findings of the Home Office Research Unit further reinforces this point in that, taking all the data available from the six experimental areas over an eighteen month period, the court acted on probation officer recommendations for community service in 74 per cent of cases. Only 18 per cent of orders were made against the recommendation of the probation officer or where he had expressed no opinion about community service.

Much early discussion was also centred on the nature of the community service task. There were some objections to a task which brought offenders into direct personal contact with the young, handicapped or elderly. Some voiced criticism that helping in a club for the handicapped was a soft option alongside the more practical task of digging a garden or wiping graffiti off a wall. There is an assumption in these comments that punishment in the form of deprivation of leisure is not enough; punishment must also extend to the task itself. The view was by no means uniform and many sentencers in conference discussions were quick to point out to those who saw community service in solely punitive terms that working with the handicapped or the very young, for example, could make mental and emotional demands on an offender which were far from soft or easy in terms of commitment.

On the whole, magistrates and judges lent their support to community service schemes, but support could have faded quickly if preparations were not made to supply magistrates with a flow of information about the progress of the scheme. Reports, progress sheets, video films, and seminars involving representatives from user organizations and community service offenders have all helped to encourage sentencers to see community service as a realistic and acceptable measure. Clearly, a system of delegated responsibility whereby the Probation Service passed over practical work supervision of the offender to a community organization cast doubts in the minds of many sentencers who questioned whether this scheme was an acceptable risk. Community Service Organizers have been able to demonstrate to courts that the scheme is viable with a low failure rate of those who failed to complete their community service orders.

The Probation Service

There was some scepticism in the Probation Service, both locally and nationally, when the legislative details of the community service were first announced. Officers questioned the assumption behind the measure. The essence of voluntary work in the community is a service freely given without any element of compulsion. Were not community service orders therefore a contradiction in terms? How could one compel an offender to give up his leisure time to some form of service? In addition, anxieties were raised about the type of task which should be made available to the offender.

All these questions laid on the organizer the onus of spending much of his time with local teams exploring and discussing the measure in some depth. In most probation areas, working parties of community staff and probation officers have been set up. The task of these groups has been to examine policy and to share information about the scheme. The organizer's next task was to help probation officers to look at the selection of suitable offenders for the scheme. The probation officer's skill in assessment was an essential feature in starting a new sentencing venture. The difference in focus, however, between a recommendation for a probation order and one for a community service order demanded that the probation officer switch emphasis in his diagnostic thinking. For, traditionally, probation officers assess problems rather than identify positive qualities which can be used in a helping role.

The change in emphasis was difficult for probation officers to accept, particularly, for example, where one had felt a failure with a difficult client over a number of years only to find in a matter of months that he was regarded as a success in terms of his response to an identified task by colleagues in the community service section. It has become important, therefore, to keep fellow probation officers in touch with the potential of community service as it emerges from actual practice. As results of recommendations are fed back to colleagues in the probation service they are in a better position to test out the potential of the scheme. Apart from ruling out offenders who are rootless, addicted to drugs or alcohol, or who are experiencing a multiplicity of problems which suggest supervision as a more appropriate measure, probation officers, have felt growing confidence in the scheme's capacity to absorb a variety of people, and have referred those with special difficulties such as the long term unemployed lacking occupational skills, the physically handicapped and those of low intelligence.

For the probation officer, one of the most instructive elements in this process of integrating clients with community groups is the recognition of the potential value of the community itself. In linking with other social networks in the community, from the neighbourhood level to the Area Health Authority community service schemes have reduced the isolation of the criminal justice system from other social systems. In doing so, as Professor de Smit suggested in a recent paper we are forging a new role for the probation officer as a social consultant for the offender whose social network is or has become closed to him (De Smit, 1976). De Smit does not see probation officers breaking with their casework role but becoming more aware of the need to open up resources for the offender within his own community. Community service organizers have, indeed, developed contacts with a variety of groups and organizations in the community with the aim of supplying satisfactory community service placements which are of benefit to both offender and user organization. However, the relevance of these community resources has not generally been translated by probation officers to other clients on their caseload who are not subject to community service orders. The extent to which probation officers are prepared to modify traditional views and practices may in the last resort depend on the way community service organizers make their new skills and insights available to colleagues in the probation service.

Most community service schemes are developed by community service organizers operating from specialist units. Whilst this single-minded approach was necessary in getting schemes underway, the perpetuation of specialist units could prolong the assimilation of

what the community service experience has to offer to other probation officers outside the specialist units. Where possible, it seems
desirable to de-centralize community service at the area team level
so that effective links can be made with a locally based officer. Thus
the area team community service specialist, whilst in the course of
identifying opportunities for those on community service, may pass
on relevant information to colleagues seeking help in their own
task of, say, finding recreational opportunities for the handicapped
son of a serving prisoner.

The Community

In analysing the impact of community service orders on the community, one immediately encounters some difficulty with the
amorphous and unspecific word 'community'. Although press and
media praise the scheme for its constructive attempt to re-integrate
the offender into the community, only certain sections of a community, namely those who are involved in working alongside an
offender, are able to speak in beneficial terms about the experience.
West, a former Community Service Organizer, suggests that the
beneficiary group which was nervous about using offenders before
the experience, is likely after the experience to be almost as nervous,
except in relation to the one individual they have come to like and
respect. Thus their 'own' offender will be split off from the rest as
untypical. West further believes that the offender is more capable
of generalizing from this experience than is the beneficiary, as the
offender's motivation may well involve a wish to be accepted as a
valuable member of the community, whereas society's instinct to
segregate the deviant remains a strong one. (West, 1976.) Even so,
there are increasing numbers of available schemes and of offenders
being absorbed in the community service experience—3,126 orders
in 1975 and 5,669 in the first eight months of 1976. As more schemes
become available to courts in England and Wales one can foresee
the development of an informed band of opinion within communities which have witnessed offenders performing service tasks
in a manner which makes nonsense of the human tendency to label
and stereotype.

Whatever the long-term effects of the scheme, new community
service organizers have not been disappointed by the initial response
of agencies and organizations to the scheme. Finding work has not
been a problem. Rather the reverse in some areas; too few orders

were being made to take advantage of all the job opportunities. Finding the right type of work has remained a difficulty in some areas e.g. limited scope in some rural areas, work available on Sundays, or in the client's local community. Overall, the range of tasks in most areas with a community service scheme has been impressive and imaginative. They include: helping the geriatric, mentally handicapped and physically handicapped in hospital and day centres, work with children in youth clubs, intermediate treatment projects and children's homes, helping old people and others in neighbourhood care groups, work in community associations, driving for the disabled, delivering furniture, constructing adventure playgrounds, restoring short-life property for the homeless, building maintenance, painting and decorating, etc.

Outright resistance to the scheme has been limited, and rarely has the community service organizer been rejected at the first approach. The main reason for agencies' reluctance to participate appears to be their feelings towards offenders working as volunteers; for example, one organization had had unhappy experiences using Borstal boys. Alternatively, as with some traditional voluntary organizations, they may feel threatened by the thought of using offenders, or that the good name of the agency will be contaminated by doing so. Some organizations, with justification, waited to see how the scheme would work out in operation before committing themselves.

What benefits, therefore, was the community expected to obtain from the help offered by the community service organizer? Organizers are usually in a position to offer manpower, tools and equipment in certain cases, and professional support and guidance where required. A considerable degree of control could be offered over the individual worker who could be removed if he did not prove satisfactory or if the agency did not find him sympathetic or helpful to their clients. Apart from these familiar expectations, Stephens, in a small study of inter-organizational relationships between the community service unit and voluntary agencies, has determined that benefits fall into four main categories. (Stephens, 1976.)

Personality and Leadership Factors. In his study Stephens identifies leading figures in agencies who showed considerable ability and qualities of altruism and understanding of human problems. Usually, such figures exercise great influence within the agencies and often show a strong commitment to protect or further the interests of the unfortunate or underprivileged in society. Their willingness to open up opportunities for offenders on placement often masked deep-seated reservations by subordinate staff. These leaders had the vision, particularly in situations of high risk, such as the supervision of handicapped children, children in care and the elderly, to see that community service workers, often disadvantaged themselves, could relate in meaningful terms to other members of the community who are similarly vulnerable.

To acquire skills or new experience. Stephens suggests that a number of agencies recognize the opportunities in community service for their staff to broaden their experience by having contact with offenders. Their range of accountability was widened in the sense that in return for the help offered by the community service worker they were expected to hand in time sheets, to evaluate worker performance and above all, to make constructive relationships with those for whom they were responsible.

To help further the objectives of the organization. Many agencies have expanded the scope of their work with the additional services of community service manpower and expertise. One can think of a small Housing Action project in Plymouth where a number of volunteers restored short life properties for homeless families under licence from the Housing Department of the City. Before the inception of community service the project volunteers were able to restore only a small number of properties a year. In the first year of partnership with the community service workers the number of houses available for homeless families trebled. At another level such a project has important side benefits in that the community service can readily form an identification with the homeless, often from personal experience.

In Nottingham, a small community care group on a council estate transformed the range of its services to the elderly, disabled and house-bound by the inclusion of ten offenders who helped in the daytime, evenings and weekends. They were mainly involved in providing 'bus trips, organizing a shopping service and a programme of household repairs for the house-bound. Most of the ten workers came from the locality and some were able to bring along friends and relatives to help with the task. This type of experience can be duplicated in most community service schemes as it provides a fitting example of the way a voluntary organization can extend its social service and the community service worker his social links.

To gain added status. Many of the organizations participating in community service gain publicity in a positive sense. The press and media often highlighted their achievement in working alongside community service offenders. They were additionally given a fresh opportunity to spread and publicize the aims of their organizations.

Obviously, the agencies' actual experience with offenders has not always been satisfactory, but the usual cause for the removal of an offender from a particular task has been the unreliability of attendance rather than unacceptable work or behaviour. This in itself demonstrates the high level of commitment of organizations to offenders under their supervision and the extent to which they must have modified their demands to the offenders' actual behaviour. As far as the offender is concerned, unreliability can usually be attributed to the deficiencies in the matching process or the original assessment of the offender. Unreliability may occur because the demands on the offender are too great or too little, or because of domestic health or employment factors, or travelling difficulties unconnected with the placement.

Instances of unacceptable behaviour by offenders at work locations are extremely rare, and it is usually possible to trace these to a history of mental instability or evidence of general unsuitability for community service. Some thefts have occurred, but on extremely isolated occasions. Such losses are thoroughly investigated by the community service staff, usually without any major breach occurring between the community service unit and the agency concerned.

Ironically, most of the messages from the agencies to the community service unit are concerned with their valuation and appreciation of the help that is offered by the person on community service. Half of the task of the unit is to ensure that the beneficiaries extend appreciation for what is done to the participants themselves. Invariably, this is of more lasting value than any endorsement from the community service staff. As a further indication of the way some offenders have benefited from their experiences within agencies, a number have volunteered to continue with the agency after termination of their community service orders.

The Participants

There have been a number of small surveys on views of community service offenders about their experience. The most far-reaching and helpful is undoubtedly that conducted by Deirdre Flegg and her probation officer colleagues in the Nottinghamshire area between 1973 and 1976. The survey represents the views of 100 people who completed community service orders. Interviewers usually arranged to see a person soon after completion of the order. The actual interviews were semi-structured, using questionnaires as a guide but exploring additional points if these were raised by the individual. There are obvious methodological weaknesses in the survey, but it does manage to capture the 'feel' of many interviews.

Of those interviewed, 67 per cent thought community service a fair sentence, while 73 per cent had expected a custodial sentence when they appeared before the court. When asked to compare community service with other sentences such as fines or probation orders the overwhelming majority preferred community service to a fine or probation. Many respondents referred to probation as a waste of time or 'it lasts for years'. Community service, by comparison, offered to many a fixed time commitment, a measure of purpose and, in some cases, a sense of satisfaction and achievement. These comments have been corroborated by a small survey which examined the reaction of six people who had failed community service orders and six who had succeeded (Ford, 1976). Ford's interviewees regarded community service a less 'hit or miss' situation; they felt the overall emphasis on giving them responsibility and in putting them in a position of some trust. If they failed on community service, they were likely to be willing to take the responsibility, but failure on the probation order was invariably blamed on the probation officer's inability to make an effective relationship. Although one cannot generalize too much from these interviews conducted in a relatively unstructured manner, it is clear that the probation experience does elicit some consistently negative and frustrated comment.

Offenders were able to identify with tasks so long as the need was clearly felt. For example, they did not begrudge painting and decorating an old lady's kitchen provided, of course, that there were not fit and able relatives living nearby who could have completed the task themselves. Similarly, they appreciated the matching of their skills or experience to the right situation. For example, a partially disabled young man helped at a club for the physically handicapped. Many gained pride and satisfaction from their work, and were critical of slapdash performances of others or the unavailability of the right equipment. Tasks also gave opportunities for offenders to identify skills and work interests which they themselves did not suspect or regard as useful. In some cases service work helped to identify entirely new skills, when existing ones were no longer appropriate or in demand, or to test an interest or aspiration before an offender committed himself to lengthy training or employment. Even those who admitted that they had simply been concerned to get their hours done wanted to do a good job.

Finally, those interviewed were asked whether it had been a worthwhile experience. Only four replied negatively. Some took a very personal view and commented on learning skills, on gaining self confidence, being valued, and others on the extent to which the helping was worthwhile.

'It broadened my outlook, made me respect people less fortunate than myself. I knew they were there, and had pity, but get involved —you knew them and did something good.'

For some community service was an eye opener to other people's struggle to survive: 'I saw her nearly every night for company and help. It was helping someone get through life as best as possible. The social people were supposed to send a home help but they didn't so I did it myself.'

Clearly the motivation to continue to be of service varied a great deal. A few had forged further opportunities for themselves as 'new careerists' in paid employment with various social work programmes, youth clubs, day centres and ancillary posts within the Probation Service. For others, change has been less dramatic but no less significant. Offenders with poor work records and little opportunity to test out social or practical skills are provided with settings in which they can re-appraise their own potential.

Twenty-nine of those interviewed wanted to carry on as volunteers. Forty-six were content to have completed their hours. But a warning note is sounded in the comment of a man who finished his order after working with old people: 'Matron wanted me to stay . . . as long as you are doing the sentence the probation officer is O.K. but after they don't want to know. You are made to feel—I'm a feather in their cap, that's all. I do a quick, quiet sentence.'

It is too early to suggest that community service will have any long-term impact on those who have undergone the experience. But there must be some satisfaction in knowing that the majority of those interviewed responded positively in terms of acceptance, trust and opportunity gained with community service. Flegg, finally, emphasizes the importance of its time boundaries, especially when compared with the rather amorphous experience of probation reporting for what seemed like life-long periods. In this respect, numbers of hours and working at jobs made sense.

Community Service: Alternative Options

It is tempting to confine one's comments on the development of community service to the statutory measure just described and ignore the less publicized, but no less significant, schemes that have been in operation since the early seventies. One of the first schemes to utilize the helping potential of the offender was started by the Community Service Volunteers (C.S.V.) Organization in 1971 with Borstal trainees aged between 17 to 21 from five selected Borstals. The scheme was initiated by Alec Dickson, himself a pioneer of voluntary movements, in particular, Voluntary Service Overseas. A hundred trainees were selected by the Home Office and C.S.V. to work in residential projects one whole month prior to discharge from the institution.

In its five-year duration the scheme has enjoyed considerable success, but the intake still remains at one hundred offenders a year despite a low failure rate. The project organizers have, however, raised several issues from their experience in running repeat pro- grammes for trainees over the years. They caution against raising a trainee's expectations about a career in the human service occupa- tions, particularly as employers from local authorities have been reluctant to take on as paid workers those with a prior history of delinquency (see Chapter 8 also). The lack of encouragement from this quarter finds similar echoes in the United States, where thousands of the urban poor and ex-offenders have been employed under federally aided New Careers programmes for varying periods of time. Less than 1 in 3 stand any chance of breaking away from para-professional status by gaining entry into a full-time social work education programme, leading to a professional qualification.

C.S.V. Organizers have also stressed the need for community service to become an integral part of the Borstal training curriculum rather than a token fringe activity, left to a hand-picked minority from a few Borstals. They would see the Borstal as becoming more of a resource centre to certain sections of the community, in parti- cular those with a high incidence of vulnerability such as the dis- abled, handicapped and elderly. Trainees could also be encouraged to tutor less able peers within the institution and perform community service placements on a daily basis or at weekends in the local town or village.

C.S.V. recently acquired experience of placing disadvantaged children in another pioneer project which was launched early in 1975. The project, known as the Children in Care Programme, has recruited 35 young people in the care of the local authority to take part in full-time community service assignments. The average age of these volunteers was sixteen, and all but four had spent substantial periods in care—the average stay in residential care being seven years. Twenty-four per cent of these volunteers came direct to C.S.V. from schools for the maladjusted, 21 per cent from community home schools and the remainder either from their own homes or from community homes. Sixty per cent were offenders. (Children in Care Programme, C.S.V., 1976.) The young volunteers who were placed by full-time C.S.V. Organizers working in local authorities stayed in projects for an average of five months. Volunteers worked residentially with children (deprived, physically and mentally handicapped, maladjusted and educationally sub-normal) or in day-care situations such as youth work, play schemes, adventure playgrounds and community centres. Seventy-five per cent of all placements were reported as mutually satisfactory. The organizers comment that local placements have appeared particularly appropriate for volunteers with a history of delinquent behaviour. Such an opportunity allows the volunteer to appreciate himself or herself in a new light, but also allows for some modification in attitude by the participant's peers, family and local neighbourhood.

Alec Dickson also reports some parallel experiments to the C.S.V. projects in a recent article describing a residential project for young offenders run by the California Youth Authority. (Dickson, 1973.) At O.H. Close school the Authority have designed a student aide programme whereby young adult offenders aged between eighteen to twenty-one are selected on the basis of background and education and voluntary choice to take on the responsibility of younger wards, some three years their junior. Such an undertaking has played havoc with those who believe that young offender institutions are populated by Artful Dodgers waiting to corrupt the minds of the less blooded newcomer. The aides, after a short induction programme, are expected to work as assistants to teachers and to undertake special activities in hobby crafts, entertainment, recreation, etc., for wards in a living unit. Implicit in all these tasks is the notion that aides will act as role models for the youngsters in their charge. They also serve as mediators between the value systems of wards coming from youth subcultures and those of middle-class-orientated staff. At the end of the six-month programme, the aide has gained experience and skills which, hopefully, might strengthen his chances of finding a social work assistant post or some related career in the community.

Community service has also emerged in recent months as an integral part of federally aided restitution programmes now being set up by a small number of Corrections Departments in the United States. The normal restitution practice in the United States is for the offender to make monetary payments backed by traditional probation supervision. Since the assignment of restitution is largely based on the perceived ability of the offender to pay, the restitution sanction is seldom available to members of lower income groups. The outcome has been that only predominantly middle-class offenders tend to get into restitution programmes, because judges consider the offender's ability to pay as the most important factor when considering whether restitution should be ordered. Thus, lower class, poor offenders are disproportionately excluded from the restitution sanction and are in effect often imprisoned for debt. Nader and Combs-Schilling believe that justice in the United States is operating on a model of internal colonialism, in which there are at least two legal systems operating—one for the upper income groups and the other for the lower income groups (Nader and Combs-Schilling, 1976). They suggest that such selected application of law along income lines further sabotages the very basis of respect for law and justice that is so necessary for crime prevention and/or rehabilitation by law. Grasping this point, programme planners in Georgia have extended the availability of the restitution sanction to those offenders who comprise the most significant percentage of our prison population—the lower-class poor—by devising new ways for such offenders to make restitution meaningfully. They have, accordingly, developed a community restitution concept, wherein lower-class poor offenders provide service restitution to their local communities in lieu of direct money restitution to the victims. Like the English community service programme, the Georgia experiment relies closely on the tapping of available citizen and community resources and a high degree of involvement from the offender.

The Restitution plan in Georgia starts with staff making an assessment either before sentencing or after a prison term on all offenders meeting the programme criteria. The Parole Board will grant a conditional release to all offenders for whom a restitution plan is approved. This plan will normally be developed within thirty days after arrival at the diagnostic centre. The restitution plan developed with a probation officer consists either of financial restitution, service restitution, or a combination of both. Unlike the British system, the dollar value of restitution owed will be converted to equivalent hours of service restitution, based on the type of service performed, in a manner which accurately reflects fair market value. Once the restitution of either kind is complete, there is no further obligation on the offender unless he wishes to continue with the organization to which he has been attached.

The other significant difference in the Georgia restitution programme, which started in September 1976, is the involvement of the scheme with the victim. Georgia officials rightly believe that the victim of crime is always the neglected factor in the criminal justice process. They maintain that the overwhelming victim need is to believe in the ability of their society to effect simple justice regardless of whether or not this justice involves personal victim compensation. They further argue that as the size of the population of crime victims continues growing the attitudes of crime victims as a further determinant of system maintenance or reform becomes even greater. Accordingly, while the offender is making restitution, the victim is kept informed regarding the offender's progress. If financial and/or service restitution is not made by the offender as scheduled, the victim will be notified by the restitution staff of the appropriate reasons and of the expected outcome (e.g. the offender is not keeping to his schedule for payment or the act of restitution proved unworkable).

It is far too early to comment on the success of this project, but the Georgia restitution programme, interestingly, reflects all points of the criminal justice process—the victim, the court, the offender and the involvement of the community as representatives of control and care. (Sole Sanction Restitution Programme, Georgia, 1976.)

Community Service has now gained an accepted place in sentencing policy both as a penalty and a form of rehabilitation in its own right. Offenders, through the medium of work, which is often creative and enhancing, have used the experience of community service to the point where self respect and the respect of others begins to run parallel. The Probation Service, too, in the course of developing community service schemes has exposed a range of community resources which are highly relevant to other sections of their responsibility. Outside the statutory framework, community service is equally applicable as part of the training programme for young people in care, trainees in institutions, hostel residents or simply as a re-integrating experience for someone who has recently undergone the confines of the total institution.

Above all, as Gilbert Geis, the American criminologist, recently reminded an audience, it offers some hope that an element of empathy might be introduced into the criminal justice business. By that, he meant that there is a perceived need of a healthy society to close the distance between its peoples; to create feelings of relationship and common purpose, so that one group does not consider itself free to exploit another. Community service, at its best, does at least offer a chance of creating some sympathetic bonds between offenders and the community as part of the criminal justice system which is desperate to find constructive alternatives to incarceration.

CHAPTER TEN

Strategies for Innovation

MARTIN WRIGHT

Assuming for a moment that there is room for improvement in the penal system, what is the best way to make it more likely that they will take place? It will be necessary to encourage people to conceive ideas; to attract funds; to win support and overcome resistance both within the system and among the general public, and to promote new legislation if needed; and, if new schemes prove sound, to ensure that they are continued and extended. In the short term it is a question of working within the existing structure; in the long term changes to the structure itself may help to improve its capacity to accept worth-while innovations.

We need to be clear about what our goals are. One ideal is reducing the amount of crime: a valuable objective indeed, but one which would involve far-reaching social and moral reforms to which the criminal justice system can make at best a marginal contribution (though its spokesmen sometimes imply that it has the power to stem the rising tide of crime). Even the more limited task of reducing reconvictions is difficult to achieve, and it is still more difficult to *show* that it has been achieved. That is not to say that it should not be attempted, provided that the efforts to do so are directed towards not only the offender but also towards his surroundings.

'Success' in this field does not necessarily mean a reduction in the recidivism rate. Success may also be measured by the effect on the penal system: keeping people out of prison, saving money or spending it better, or by the degree of public acceptance of a sanction which is based less on repression and more on constructive principles such as learning, reparation or reconciliation. These are all legitimate aims, provided they do not have undesirable side-effects such as an increase in the number of offences committed. The design for a project should state its aims and the methods intended to achieve them, as a yardstick for assessing the outcome.

186

This article, then, will proceed on the working assumptions that when an offence comes to light some form of social intervention is called for, and that the search for new forms of intervention is worthwhile. If these new methods prove better than the existing ones, and are ethically acceptable, they will be in the interests of both the offender and of society, helping the offender to make the most of his life without falling foul of fellow members of the community. Often it will be found that less intervention, and fewer removals of people from the community, are necessary than was previously thought, as the foregoing chapters of this book have shown.

Attracting ideas

A dynamic strategy in a complex society will not seek one ideal solution, a philosopher's stone, but will encourage people to be thinking constantly of new approaches and refining the old ones. The need to adapt to a state of constant change, and ways of encouraging creative adaptation, have been analysed by D. A. Schon (1971).

One way is to let it be known among people involved directly in trying to implement policy into practice, such as probation officers, teachers and others, that their ideas would be welcomed and that the means could be made available for them to test out the ideas. At a time of retrenchment in public spending, this policy is severely restricted. It may be possible to turn economic stringency to advantage, however, by using the probation subsidy approach, in which the money provided for schemes in the community is conditional upon a reduction in the number of committals to institutions. The case for this has been argued elsewhere (Howard League, 1975, Section I; Wright, 1976). Once this scheme has been used to the maximum in replacing institutions by community-based projects, it could perhaps begin by offering subsidies in proportion to the number of cases transferred from professional social services to volunteers. Several examples of volunteer involvement are given in the Proceedings of the N.A.C.R.O. European Conference, 1976 (in press). This method will not work, of course, where the preferred alternative is more costly than the present methods.

Ideas may also come from voluntary organizations (i.e. independently managed non-profit bodies, financed by donations or government grants or both). It is often said that many of the most valuable

N

social services have originated in this way, and a country which encourages these voluntary initiatives will improve the quality of life of its citizens—very likely at less cost to them in their rôle as taxpayers. It is, therefore, desirable that funds should be forth-coming to help private organizations with vision to realize their ideals. Sometimes courage will be needed to support unconventional schemes, which often only gain the confidence of their clients *because* they are 'off-beat' and even anti-authority. (One example would be the Harambee project for alienated black youngsters in North London.) Conversely, safeguards are needed in case a project leader proves lacking in administrative capacity (or even in integrity —but this is fortunately very rare). In the United States the avail-ability of money for these purposes has led to the formation of profit-making private organizations in this field; this may be an effective incentive to generating ideas, given adequate inspection and safeguards, though it would seem strange to some countries.

Included among the voluntary organizations which may produce proposals are self-help groups, such as associations of prisoners' wives, with a problem in common, which their own experience helps them to tackle. Much the same considerations apply to these groups as to other voluntary initiatives, though their ideas may be difficult for the official system to assimilate, because they start from different premises and on occasion, actively oppose official policy. The pit-falls of this approach have been chronicled in descriptions of the New Careers movement promoted in America by the Office of Economic Opportunity (Marris and Rein, 1975; Moynihan, 1969).

Another type of voluntary organization which produces ideas does not offer direct help to individuals, but acts as a 'think-tank' and pressure group, putting forward proposals and encouraging their adoption. Not being involved in the day-to-day exigencies of running projects the kind of group can also question and re-think the assumptions which underlie current practice. (Such is the ideal, but when the organizations are obliged to become pre-occupied with raising funds to keep themselves afloat, they cannot always live up to it.) Their rôle is in some ways similar to that of academics; they are vehicles for conveying academic thinking and the implica-tions of research findings to policy-makers, practitioners and the public. Some of the larger organizations of this type, like the National Children's Bureau, also undertake research themselves. They can stimulate interest in ideas from abroad. Day training centres, for example, on a model originating in the United States, were described at a Howard League conference in 1970, taken up by the Home Office, and introduced experimentally under the Criminal Justice Act 1972 (Moriarty, in Cambridge Institute, 1977). Several European projects were described in English for the first time at the N.A.C.R.O. conference in 1976 (N.A.C.R.O., in press).

The civil service itself is naturally an important source of ideas. In 1957 the Home Office set up a research unit, and more recently it has formed a Crime Policy Planning Unit insulated from day-to-day administrative pressures, with the aim of developing penal strategies (Moriarty, *op. cit.*). Ideas can also flow from adjuncts to government such as the Home Secretary's Advisory Council on the Penal System, if such bodies are given a brief to be creative; its present terms of reference, however, limit its rôle to an advisory one, and a suggestion for re-structuring is made below. It was the Advisory Council that proposed the Community Service Order (ACPS, 1970, and Chapter 9 above). Ministers' personal advisers, too, can serve as a sort of talent scout.

Finally, an active and comprehensive information service could collect ideas from a variety of sources, and draw them to the attention of those who may be able to use them. Of this, too, more below.

Attracting funds

From one point of view, obtaining the money to start a new project is a chore, consuming precious time which might be used in directly helping people. But the provision of finance can also be used as an instrument of policy to promote new initiatives. It is the policy of some grant-giving trusts to conceive their own ideas for promoting social betterment.

Other trusts invite proposals, and select those which they consider will be most beneficial. The American Ford Foundation collaborated with the President's Committee on Juvenile Delinquents and Youth Crime in the 1960s to consider how, by spending considerable sums of money, they could help towards making America a better place to live. (Marris and Rees, 1972; Moynihan, 1969.) The terms on which a grant is made can be a check on cost-effectiveness and a safeguard to ensure that the intended beneficiaries of the scheme receive a service of a satisfactory standard of competence. Both these aspects are exemplified in the probation subsidy scheme: the availability of the subsidy set probation officers thinking of ways of claiming it, but projects were not approved unless they were based on a clear hypotheses, adequately staffed, and provided with facilities for evaluation (Smith, 1972). The trusts, on the other hand, do not always insist firmly enough that the project should be independently evaluated, or at least that a descriptive report should be published so that others can learn from the experience. If this is to be done properly it will add to the cost of the project; but without it much of its value is lost. Projects categorized as 'action research' are able to obtain money from research budgets, which are sometimes more ample. The problem here is to ensure that the project, if it has merit, is continued. To take one example among many, the project described by Goetschius and Tash in *Working with Unattached Youth* seemed to be imaginative and worthwhile, and it is unfortunate that it was funded only for a fixed period, so that the last months had to be spent meticulously dismantling most of the enterprise instead of handing it over to a continuing source of funding (Goetschius and Tash, 1967).

Making sure that money is available in the right place is partly a matter of the structure and policy of public finance. As has been pointed out (Wright, 1976), misallocation of resources is likely to occur when the individual requiring services could be dealt with either expensively (e.g. in a prison or hospital) by one department of government, or at less cost (e.g. in the community with appropriate support or supervision) by another. For example, in 1976 3,340 youngsters in England and Wales aged 14 to 16 were sent to prison before trial, ostensibly because they were 'unruly'. The structure still exerts pressure in the wrong direction. Local Authority Social Service Departments are expected to devote time, imagination and money to devising better, and preferably non-custodial, ways of keeping track of youngsters awaiting trial. If they do so, and thereby reduce the numbers sent to Prison Department establishments, they are taking on an extra burden, but it is the Prison Department which reaps the benefit of having fewer cases to cope with. Conversely, if the SSDs fail to provide the necessary facilities, they are able to transfer their most difficult youngsters to the Prison Department by asking magistrates to declare them (the youngsters) 'unruly'. The method by which this abuse is being countered is a stricter definition of the criteria of 'unruliness' (Certificates of unruly character (conditions) order, 1977); a more effective method might be to change the structure and make Social Service Departments solely responsible for this age-group, as the Children and Young Persons Act 1969 intended. It was a transfer of resources *within the Social Service Department's own budget*, by closing residential establishments, that made possible the financing of the fostering scheme described in Chapter 5.

Where a service is provided by a voluntary organization it may, as we have seen, be paid for by fund-raising from trusts and the general public, or by public funds, or a combination of the two. Finding the right level and method of support will obviously be crucial. After-care hostels for ex-prisoners have been helped by a new and flexible grant scheme (Home Office, 1976). The Barbican Centre at Gloucester, of which Day Training Centres are variants, resolved its problem after the expiration of the initial grant from a charitable trust by arranging to be taken over by the local Probation Committee—but keeping its own management committee with an understanding that its autonomy would be respected. Another method is known in the United States as 'purchase of services', whereby the relevant authority pays a fee, for example, for each child sent to a school for maladjusted children. This offers a safeguard, provided that the authority keeps itself informed about the way the programme is run, since the child can be transferred elsewhere. According to the philosophy of free enterprise, the resulting element of insecurity might lead staff to try a little harder; alternatively it might discourage some good people from wanting to work there since career prospects are not readily obvious. Again, since the Children and Young Persons Act 1969, some community homes have been 'controlled', i.e. supported regardless of the number of children in them; others have been 'assisted', which means that they are paid a fee for each child. It would be interesting to know whether the difference in funding method leads to any differences in the running of the homes, such as the use made by the head of his right to refuse admittance to particular children. The effects of funding on performance should be studied if services are to be improved and innovation encouraged.

Attracting support

When an idea has been worked out and funding obtained, it remains to secure its implementation. This overlaps of course with the fund-raising process, but can be considered separately, both in the positive aspect of persuading people to give their support, and the negative one of overcoming opposition.

The first essential is that the idea should be explained in terms which conventional lay people can understand. The idea is deeply ingrained that the appropriate method to denounce wrongdoing is punishment, and anyone wanting to substitute any other response has to convince the public that it will be at least as effective or that it *is* punishment. Innovators are forced to show, for example, that the method forces the offender to face up to unpleasant realities instead of escaping into prison; or that it will have other effects preferable to those of punishment, such as assisting rehabilitation or enabling the offender to make reparation; or that the punishment used hitherto was excessive, inappropriate or too expensive (all of which apply to a substantial proportion of prison sentences).

The foregoing chapters describe a number of schemes which are in varying degrees substitutes for punishment. In some of them the public explanation and persuasion have been done successfully. In the case of the Community Service Order, precisely the combination of punishment, education and reparation which led some people initially to regard the suggestion as a philosophical hotch-potch appears to have led to its general acceptance—aided by the fact that initially it was used very selectively, and by the flair with which some of those who ran the pilot schemes explained them to the media. A sample of the way the message was put across is the pamphlet 'Community Service by Offenders' by Harding, (1974). Careful exposition paid off, too, in the introduction of the complex package of the probation subsidy in California (Smith, 1972). This package was also preceded by several years of problem-oriented research, so that its advocates could support their arguments with a better ratio of facts to hypotheses than is usually the case.

By contrast, Intermediate Treatment (Chapter 4) has not won nearly as much comprehension and acceptance. This is partly because the White Paper *Children in trouble* did not adequately define the method, and the Act of 1969 did not even refer to it by its rather uninformative name. Not until about five years after the Act were many signs discernible of a concerted attempt by those who believed in the concept to explain it and gain support for it. To some extent it was also a victim of the divided responsibility for the 14–17 age group. If Local Authorities had invested more heavily in Intermediate Treatment projects, juvenile courts could probably have been persuaded to use them, in some cases, in place of detention centres or borstals, and thus to check the rise in the number of juveniles in England and Wales sentenced to penal institutions from 2,682 in 1969 to 6,695 in 1976. This would have eased the pressure to build more institutions, especially junior detention centres; but the consequent savings would have accrued to the

Prison Department, and there seems to be no machinery for transferring money unspent from the Home Office budget to Local
Authorities, even though it would be used for the same youngsters,
in a way which is more in line with current thinking, and more
economical.

Another innovation which has so far not been 'sold' very successfully is the day training Centre. Four of these centres were set up
simultaneously with Community Service Orders, with the aim of
offering offenders, in a non-custodial setting, the opportunity to
acquire vocational and social skills, and the self-confidence and
motivation to use them. But no one seems to have hit on a simple—
if necessary over-simplified—way of conveying in one or two phases
what they are trying to do and why it is a relevant way of dealing
with people convicted of offences. Another drawback is that day
training centres are relatively expensive, especially when running
below capacity.

Sometimes an innovation meets not merely incomprehension but
open hostility. It is advisable not to dismiss the opposition as mere
unenlightened self-interest, on a par with the often-heard (and
occasionally well-founded) claim that 'a hostel is a good idea, but
our area is unsuitable'. Even if those who hold contrary views are
not convinced, they can at least be shown that there is a tenable
case for the proposal, and that many of their apprehensions are
based on misapprehensions: and the waverers may be won over.

But if philosophical (and emotional) agreement about the aims
of a penal system had to be obtained before anything was done, we
should still be in the Dark Ages. If a project is based on a clearly
thought out hypothesis, and includes proper provision for evaluation, an element of 'Do it first and argue about it afterwards' may
be no bad thing. In many cases (though not all) it will be possible
to show the critics that the project was well conceived.

The active involvement of members of the public is desirable
both because they can contribute their own professional and human
skills and because they will be able to explain the project to their
taxpaying friends, colleagues and neighbours and the local newspaper or radio station. They may be volunteers, personally offering
help and friendship to the participants, or they may serve on the
management committee (or both).

Participants are themselves members of the public, of course.
More and more schemes are being run in a way which involves
them in day-to-day decisions, and they are often employed as staff.
Their expression of the 'consumer' viewpoint can be useful in

showing outsiders the sense of the scheme: they can cut through
the abstract concepts and say 'Look what it did for me.' The media,
too, like to use actual examples to illustrate what is being done.
This can cause heart-searching about whether it is right to 'use'
participants for publicity purposes. But if the subjects are willing,
and are not led to imagine that they are about to become television
personalities, there seems no reason in principle why they should
not be invited to tell their 'success story' for the possible benefit of
others. However, highlighting a problem *before* a way out has been
found, by asking people to talk publicly while they are still 'down',
needs even more careful thought.

This problem is less acute for client groups who have come
together for the express purpose of securing better treatment for
themselves and people like them: they can decide for themselves
how far they are prepared to expose their own lives in the interests
of the cause. So far, client groups in this field have focussed mainly
on the problems of prisoners and their families, rather than on
non-custodial alternatives. There does not yet appear to be an
association for people who feel they are being pushed around by
social workers or probation officers, but as the number of community programmes increases for which the ultimate sanction for
non-compliance is being 'breached' (i.e. returned to court for breach
of conditions, and possibly imprisoned), the enforcement procedure
will become an important issue of legal and civil rights (English,
1975).

Support has to be won within the penal system, as well as outside.
Several projects have found that not only courts were slow to accept
them, but the idea had to be 'sold' even to probation officers and
social workers before they in turn would recommend it to magistrates and judges. The Day Training Centre in Camberwell is one
of those which has increased its intake of clients by inviting probation officers, magistrates and others to take part in some of its
typical activities on open days which give the outsiders some insight
into the centre's aims and its clients' responses. Caution is needed,
however: it is said that one senior Prison Departmental official,
invited to experience group counselling, left the session precipitately
and refused to have anything to do with the technique. One explanation of this alleged incident may be that he had personal problems
of his own; another may be that the method used was a potentially
intrusive one to which people should not be subjected against their
inclinations—a view with which some people who saw the film
One Flew Over the Cuckoo's Nest will have sympathy. Probably

the answer is that methods designed to enhance people's self-awareness and self-confidence are acceptable so long as they take into account the feelings of the person who is being asked to accept help as well as the motives of those who offer it (Keith-Lucas, 1966.)

Continuing and extending the new idea

If a new scheme is considered to have achieved at least some of its goals, the question will arise of extending it and assuring its future. Some of the problems have already been considered in the context of obtaining initial finance and local support, and the same principles can be applied on a larger scale; new ones arise, however, in securing acceptance at a national level. Parliament, the Home Office, the judiciary, the probation service, voluntary organizations and others all have parts to play which were reviewed at the recent Cropwood Conference on *Penal policy-making in England* (Cambridge Institute, 1977).

First it is necessary to have a blue-print for the continued implementation of the plan. Its funding has to be assured by one of the methods referred to above. A place has to be found for it within the existing system. This is possible at almost any stage, as the following list shows:

Before the police are involved (Manhattan Bowery Project, for skid-row alcoholics (Vera Institute, circa 1970))

In conjunction with police discretion not to prosecute (referral to detoxification centre under Section 34, Criminal Justice Act, 1972; Manhattan Court Employment Project (Vera Institute, 1970) and other applications of the concept of 'diversion' from the criminal justice system)

During a period of deferment of sentence (Newham Alternatives Project, 1976)

Under a conditional discharge

As a condition of probation (New Careers project, Chapter 8; Day Training Centres)

As a separate court order (Community Service Orders)

In the context of a court order handing over to executive discretion (Massachusetts juvenile institutions (Flacke, 1974, and Chapter 6); Intermediate Treatment (Chapter 4)

During discretionary release from a penal institution (to live in a hostel (Whitlam, 1975) or take part in community service (Kelmanson, 1975)).

As a condition of release on licence from a penal institution (Vacaville New Careers project (Briggs and Hodgkin, 1972))

Voluntarily (after a decision to take no further official action, e.g. in the Scottish scheme (Morris, 1976, and Chapter 3), or in a scheme available equally to non-offenders, probationers and ex-prisoners (Barbican Centre, 1976))

Some of these require no legislation and can be introduced by executive action, or voluntary initiative, or a combination. Others do need legislation; or it may be considered that to make a special court order will give the new measure a more secure place in the range of alternatives, as was done in the case of Community Service Orders in England and Wales, but not (so far) in Scotland. The method employed to extend the use of the idea will vary accordingly. If its introduction is to be left to local enterprise, whether of statutory or voluntary agencies, it should be someone's job to promote it; if it requires legislation, it is necessary to gain the support of the ministers and civil servants who are responsible for Criminal Justice Bills, or of Members of Parliament. In both cases the co-operation of those who will actually use the measure, courts, probation officers, social workers, and sometimes the prison and police services, will be indispensable.

One method described by Schon is for a charismatic 'Johnny Appleseed', perhaps the originator of the idea, to roam the country inspiring people's enthusiasm. (Schon, 1971.) This may lead to sporadic and unco-ordinated development, but it could be argued that in this field new inspirations are likely to depend on personal vision and leadership, and do not lend themselves to routine application (Chap. 1). The optimum, on this view, would be a succession of new concepts adapted to local circumstances and personalities and fuelled by pioneering commitment. But a policy of encouraging the fruit of this year's new thinking, while trying to breed a hardy strain incorporating the best features of last year's variety, would seem to offer a chance of getting the best of both worlds.

More prosaically, a development officer or 'sales division' could be appointed. The Advisory Committee on Alcoholism of the Department of Health and Social Security has appointed a sub-group to promote the development of services for homeless alcoholics, although its name and according to Campaign for the Homeless and Rootless (CHAR) (1976) its activity are somewhat lacking in urgency, and it was not set up until five years after the report on *Habitual drunken offenders*.

Will the report of the Advisory Council on the Penal System on *Young adult offenders* (1976) remain unimplemented? It would require changes in the law, and concomitant changes in the operation of young offenders' establishments and the probation service. The changes in the penal régimes could be brought about administratively by the Prison Department, with appropriate staff consultation and re-training; but the principles involved in the proposed new forms of sentence were criticized by a number of people such as magistrates and probation officers, the latter being particularly concerned about the possible effects on their relationships with their clients. It was not practicable to introduce legislation of this kind without a substantial measure of agreement by the practitioners who would be responsible for enforcing it. Members of the Advisory Council, especially the chairman, the late Sir Kenneth Younger, were conscientious in travelling round the country giving talks; but this was not enough to reach a consensus and make possible the result desired both by the Council and by most of its critics, namely to find a better way of dealing with young offenders than placing so many of them in institutions.

Perhaps a 'sales division' could identify areas of disagreement or misunderstanding, and elicit from probation officers, magistrates and others such modifications to the original proposals that legislation could proceed. A well-endowed voluntary organization could also take on the proselytizing rôle. Sometimes, of course, an idea develops its own momentum, as Community Service Orders have done and Victims Support Schemes may do; but they may be exceptions that prove the rule.

The government departments to which the campaign will generally be directed will be the Home Office, and, in the case of children, alcoholics and the mentally abnormal, the Department of Health and Social Security; these agencies are beginning to realize that vagrancy, for example, is related to homelessness and hence to housing, and truancy (with its links with delinquency) to education and family background. Similarly, joblessness and poverty have a bearing on crime, particularly among school leavers. The relevant departments (such as housing, education, employment, sport) should be concerned not merely with the functioning of these sectors of policy but also with the results of their malfunction and inadequacies, instead of leaving the social services and the penal system to provide a refuge for their casualties as well as each other's; they should therefore be involved to the full in any remedial action in their spheres.

In speaking of government departments, one is of course speaking of individuals within departments who are, as Musheno and others (1975) have pointed out, concerned not only with public-interest goals, but also with individual goals: the politician hopes to win votes, or at least commendation for assiduity; the administrator may aim for promotion or for a larger budget for his department, and the practitioner's concern for his relationship with his client may make him unwilling to adopt methods for which his training did not prepare him or to drop those to which he is accustomed. These personal goals are perfectly proper (similar ones can be detected among reformers), and indeed can contribute much to the attainment of public-interest ones, but they need to be borne in mind, especially when new proposals are not entirely consonant with them.

Creating a structure conducive to innovation

If there is to be a steady supply of ideas for making improvements, and a good number of them are to be brought to fruition, people who can help to cultivate them should be encouraged both outside and inside the statutory framework, and there may be advantages in modifying the framework itself.

Voluntary organizations can do much, provided they have adequate resources. They can run their own demonstration projects, as N.A.C.R.O. does, or collect and publicize information about other people's, and then press for the introduction of similar schemes. They can also, like the Howard League, contribute to the theoretical as well as the practical side of the system by bringing together, in conferences and working parties, people with academic and practical experience to review current thinking about problems related to social order in the light of research findings and make proposals. Those people of goodwill who agree that voluntary effort has a distinctive contribution to make towards social betterment should recognize that it can be achieved only in three ways: by grants from public funds, or by donations and subscriptions, or by unpaid work for the cause (or a combination of these). In the first case they pay through taxation, in the second they give voluntarily, and in the third they work voluntarily. Sympathy is not enough.

Basic to ideas and their realization, by voluntary and statutory agencies alike, is information exchange. The design of a new project requires information about how similar ones have fared elsewhere; its implementation requires that courts, social workers and defending lawyers should know what schemes are available and when it is appropriate to recommend or order their use. Evaluative reviews of the literature and the current state of knowledge have an important potential for policy, and practitioners would welcome a presentation of research findings in non-specialist language (Clarke, and Wootton, in Cambridge Institute, *op. cit.*). At present information is collected, notably by the library of the Cambridge Institute, but its dissemination is left to scatter its own small-scale efforts, and those of the Institute for the Study and Treatment of Delinquency, the Howard League, N.A.C.R.O. and others. In addition to internal papers for ministers and administrators, which unfortunately have not generally been published, the Home Office Research Unit has published an extensive series of reports; recently it has begun to issue Research Bulletins, which go some way towards meeting this need. But the extent to which this information reaches people who could use it is a subject which itself needs research.

Proposals have been made for better information for the probation and prison services, and most recently (by Lord Justice Bridge's Working Party on Judicial Information and Training) for judges; these have shown, incidentally, that the borderline between information and training is not clear-cut. These proposals have been brought together in the suggestion for a single co-ordinated information service (Elwyn-Jones, 1976; North East London Polytechnic, 1977). This could be catalysts, to the steady development of the criminal justice system. Probably it would be best if the information service were independent both of government and of voluntary organizations with the reputation of being committed to particular viewpoints, so that it would be seen to be free from political or ideological constraints.

There remains the question of whether the official structure is conducive to innovation. This can be considered under the general headings of research, thought and action.

Research in this area has in the past been to a substantial extent funded by the Home Office or carried out by the Home Office Research Unit; the latter in particular has been criticized for selecting, or being given, somewhat limited tasks. Dr R. V. G. Clarke, speaking as a researcher at the Cambridge Conference (1977) still felt that there should be a better dialogue between researchers and administrators. Researchers are now, however, looking at wider implications of penal measures. This should help policy-makers to make decisions, and if necessary justify them; in addition of course they have to take account of other questions such as ethical ones which research cannot answer, though it may help to pose them more clearly. New legislation should be brought into effect in such a way that its effects could be assessed. There have been moves in these directions—research-oriented policy, such as community service orders, and policy-oriented research, such as the IMPACT Intensive Matched Probation and After-Care Treatment (Home Office, 1976). The Crime Policy Planning Unit, described below, includes a member of staff with a research background, and research and statistical representation on its planning committee and statistical bodies. But the logical way to incorporate the fullest contribution that research offers to policy-making at all stages may be, as Clarke hinted, the complete integration of administrative, planning and research capabilities.

There are two organs of the penal system which have thought as their primary function. One is the planning organization, set up in 1974. It consists of the full-time Crime Policy Planning Unit and inter-linked committees of senior officials from all parts of the Home Office that are concerned with the analysis and co-ordination of policy. Its purpose is to think about longer-term problems that cross departmental boundaries (apparently with the Home Office) (Moriarty, in Cambridge Institute, *op. cit.*). In view of the inter-relatedness of crime problems, however, the ability to transcend established ways of thinking would be enhanced if members of other government departments were included in this body or a parallel one. Although there is already some machinery for consultation among central government departments (in addition to informal contact) and one should perhaps be wary of adding to it, it is possible that, for example, if officials from the Department of Education and Science and the Children's Department of the DHSS had regularly worked together over a period with their Home Office colleagues and developed a consensus or at least a fuller understanding of each other's standpoints, the 1976 White Paper on the Children and Young Persons Act would have had a less lingering birth and been a healthier infant. There are those who maintain that the Children's Department should never have been transferred from the Home Office to the DHSS in the first place.

The other unit for thinking about policy is the Advisory Council on the Penal System. Its terms of reference are much more limited, as is indicated by its title, restricting it to advising the Home Secretary, who either asks it to examine certain matters or accepts its own suggestions as to what it should consider. Its membership includes some distinguished names and represents a number of interests; its study of specific topics might well be carried out by sub-committees, as now, but the appointment of, and active endorsement by influential people from other. more diverse, fields of public life, could also help to secure their attention, understanding and support for its ideas.

It should not deal merely with the penal system (with the implication that therein alone lies the solution to the crime problem) but with all practical aspects of crime prevention and social control in a free society, and it should be entitled to advise not only the Home Secretary but any relevant minister. It should also be in a position to commission research to obtain necessary information. (It was the research by W. H. Hammond on *Persistent offenders*, commissioned by the former Advisory Council on the Treatment of Offenders, which played a large part in getting preventive detention abolished; and a statistical follow-up of robbers flogged and, not flogged in the past helped convince the Council, in the early 1960s, that corporal punishment should not be brought back.) This brief is not as wide as might appear, since it would obviously confine itself to areas where there was reason to believe its recommendations would be heeded.

There may also be a place for expanding the existing local crime prevention panels, which are mainly police-oriented, into regional or local crime prevention councils, with a similarly representative membership but a more practical bias, whose task would be to study local crime patterns and encourage schools, employers, and other local community resources to join forces in seeking preventative measures.

So much for ideas; what about action? It has been suggested above that the introduction of a new scheme could be more efficient if one person could be given the task of implementing it. Similarly, changes and innovations are more readily achieved if the head of the whole organization has as much flexibility as possible in the allocation of resources, combined with adequate statutory powers and high-level backing when using them. A much-quoted recent example is provided by the Department of Youth Services in Massachusetts, described above in Chapter 6: it is doubtful whether the drastic reduction in the use of juvenile correctional institutions and the development of community resources could have been achieved at all, let alone so quickly, had not Dr. Jerome Miller been in charge of both. In England, some years earlier, the great influence of Alexander Paterson on the ethos of the penal system was made possible partly by the semi-independent status of the Prison Commission of which he was a member. Although few people would now suggest the re-establishment of the Prison Commission, because that would perpetuate the division between custodial and non-custodial departments which still persists within the structure of the Home Office, perhaps it is time to look at the case for a board or commission responsible for all aspects of the treatment of offenders and crime prevention, which would have more scope to involve all the relevant services in shaping the system as a whole.

CHAPTER ELEVEN

The Future for Alternative Strategies

NICHOLAS HINTON

Sir Leon Radzinowicz divides the development of social policy with respect to crime and its prevention during the last one hundred and fifty years into three stages (Parole Board Report, 1968). During the first stage it was hoped that crime would be reduced by a measure of terror, during the second stage emphasis was placed on retribution, and during the third stage on rehabilitation. The rehabilitation ideal was at its most popular in the late 1960s, and it was during this period that much legislation with an emphasis on rehabilitation was introduced. Criticism of the philosophy of rehabilitation has been common in academic circles for many years, but has recently permeated practitioners and policy makers. Such doubts without any acceptable alternative philosophy must affect practitioner morale. For policy makers and planners doubts lead to indecisiveness.

This book, *Alternative Strategies*, by the very diversity of the ideas canvassed and the projects described, supports the view that no common philosophy, be it retribution, treatment, education, or rehabilitation, now provides a satisfactory single context for social policy with respect to the treatment of offenders. Much other evidence, too, suggests that we should abandon the tempting yet elusive search for a single formula through which to respond to all offenders. In an essay on the 'Ideology of Imprisonment' Gordon Hawkins (1975) has argued that in practical terms custodial resources may be used in relation to different groups of offenders for quite different objectives. For the minority of prisoners who fall into the maximum security category, the defined objective may be limited to containment within as humane an institution as possible.

o

For other people for whom imprisonment is deemed necessary, the particular objective may be defined as disciplinary, remedial, therapeutic, vocational, or educational. Such objectives, clearly stated, for the vast majority, can be better achieved outside prison.

If there is any common thread to initiatives in the penal field, it is that of reducing the numbers held in institutions to the minimum. In Britain, successive Home Secretaries have stressed that the use of imprisonment should be restricted to those from whom the public needs protection. More recently, the Lord Chancellor has exhorted sentencers to consider passing very short sentences of imprisonment—say fourteen days or a month instead of the more common three- or six-month sentences that they are imposing at present. Panel reformers might like to see such pronouncements as an indication of success; in reality, economic pressures have done more to persuade the minds, if not the hearts, of politicians.

Despite such exhortations, pressure brought to bear by reformers, or the success of this or that scheme, Britain and many other Western democracies are faced with critically high prison populations. The choice of solutions to this problem is limited. Traditionally Britain and many other countries have simply built more prisons—an option that is now prohibitively expensive and out of the question. In practice, therefore, we have either attempted to divert people from prison before they get there, or let them out earlier. In a somewhat piecemeal fashion most innovations of the past few decades can be seen to fall into one or other of these two categories. Legislation to curb the powers of the courts has as one of its main aims the diversion of people from prison. Early intervention schemes, particularly in other European countries, are concerned with providing practical assistance to men and women who risk receiving a custodial sentence for lack of the provision of basic help. Community Service Orders, probation hostels or day training centres are all recent examples of facilities being made available to discourage sentencers whenever possible from using custodial sentences. Suspended prison sentences and legislation to curb the use of remands in custody share the same basic aim. At the other end of the spectrum, remission of sentences exists, and parole has been introduced in many countries in order to reduce the length of time spent in prison. Conditional discharge schemes or early release schemes follow a similar pattern.

Undoubtedly, in England and Wales, Parliament and those agencies responsible for the treatment of offenders will continue to pass legislation and develop further schemes designed to divert people from custody or to release them earlier. For example, legislation may be introduced to remove the power of imprisonment for certain offences. Possible candidates might include default in the payment of maintenance, fine default, or soliciting, and certain offences such as vagrancy may be removed from the Statute Book altogether. Parliament may go further and introduce legislation which would require every court at the time of passing a sentence of imprisonment to state that in its opinion it is essential for the protection of the public that the offender goes to prison, adding that the court would be expected to give reasons for this judgement and that this part of the process would form grounds for appeal. Similarly, legislation may be introduced to shorten the amount of time that should be spent in prison: the parole scheme may be revised to enable all prisoners serving sentences of up to and including three years to be released automatically after serving one third of their sentences with supervision on licence up to the end of the sentence. Alternatively, an early release scheme may be introduced whereby all prisoners are released after serving half of the sentence, subject to good conduct, such a scheme has been in operation in Northern Ireland since mid 1976.

Legislation apart, the Home Secretary or his colleague, the Lord Chancellor, will continue to exhort magistrates and judges to pass shorter sentences, and to use alternatives to custody whenever possible. As time passes and confidence increases, it is likely that greater use will be made of existing non-custodial facilities. For example, the use of Community Service Orders as a direct alternative to prison will increase by forty or fifty per cent. As courts become familiar with probation hostels and other facilities that can be seen as a satisfactory alternative, their use may well become focussed on those who would certainly have received custodial sentences. An interest, largely stemming from the widespread appeal of Community Service, in the concept of reparation is likely to lead to an expansion of direct work projects for those who would otherwise have been sent to prison. Of the various pilot projects run by N.A.C.R.O. (The National Association for the Care and Resettlement of Offenders), the majority of which are designed as alternatives to prison, the most appealing to the courts is the experimental workshop in Manchester. Here offenders are offered the opportunity of a forty-hour-a-week job renovating and repairing furniture which is supplied to Department of Health and Social Security clients whose income level entitles them to certain items of house furnishings free of charge. It is feasible that this and similar experiments might develop into a national organization providing direct employment for offenders in much the same way that Remploy provides direct work for the disabled. (Remploy is an organization which employs physically handicapped workers to produce, distribute and market a wide range of consumer goods.)

The revival of housing associations in Britain provides the potential for a considerable growth in the number of housing projects which can provide for the army of offenders lacking adequate accommodation. Similarly, there is a growing awareness of the handicap of illiteracy for a considerable number among the offender population. Employment, accommodation, and education tailored to suit the needs of individual offenders can provide the necessary complex of resources to contain in the community the offender who would otherwise suffer imprisonment.

This growth in the number and variety of non-custodial facilities for offenders is encouraging. It inevitably means that more people and a more diverse range of agencies are involved in providing for offenders and in serving to remove some of the myths and fantasies that surround the offender and the prisoner. Anticipated adverse public reaction is the most frequently quoted obstacle to change.

In Britain, and to a lesser extent elsewhere in Europe and in America, many of the alternative programmes have developed as a result of the initiatives of non-government agencies. Accommodation projects in Britain owe their beginnings to, and many are still run by, voluntary or non-statutory organizations. All direct employment schemes are run by similar bodies, and voluntary organizations are in the forefront of attempts to provide education and literacy schemes, and to co-ordinate all of these for the benefit of the offender needing a network of provision in the community. In America, the Vera Institute of Justice in New York has played as great a part as any other non-government body in the country in pioneering work schemes, alternative programmes for habitual drunken offenders and the like. Voluntary organizations play a large part in the functioning of the Community Service schemes described by John Harding in this book. A voluntary organization runs the Bristol New Careers Scheme described by Spencer Millham, and voluntary organizations play a large part in the provision of Intermediate Treatment.

Most of the schemes described in this book came about as a reaction to an over-use of custody, and share a desire to provide alternatives to custodial care. The part that education can play in helping children at risk of appearing before the courts incurring a custodial sentence is described by David Reynolds. Allison Morris continues with an examination of schemes aimed at diverting children from the criminal justice system. Intermediate Treatment, described by David Thorpe, was introduced in the United Kingdom under the 1969 Children and Young Persons Act with the aim of containing as many children and young persons as possible within the community. The professional fostering project described by Nancy Hazel again came into being as a reaction against institutional care. The well-known Massachusetts experiment initiated by Jerome Miller is, perhaps more than any other scheme in this collection, a revolt against institutional treatment. One of the main objectives of the Bristol New Careers Project and Community Service on a wider scale is to provide alternatives to Borstal and prison.

The implementation of the schemes described in this book has depended on special circumstances, usually the fire and energy of an individual or a group of people. Would, for example, the Massachusetts experiment have come about without the force of Jerome Miller's personality? The Bristol New Careers Scheme was eventually born after hard negotiation by N.A.C.R.O. Community Service in England and Wales has been particularly fortunate in the quality and commitment of those probation officers (of whom John Harding was one) selected to mount the initial six pilot schemes. Similarly, those Intermediate Treatment schemes which have had a positive impact depend or have depended on the drive of a small number of people. Arguably, these efforts have created the momentum for reform and change in the offender field as in many others, but it underlines the fact that far from there being any common philosophy, there is little in the way of a common strategy other than a revulsion for institutions reinforced latterly by economic necessity.

One cannot avoid the fact that despite all these efforts and many others, the number of people incarcerated in prisons, borstals, detention centres, remand centres and any other version of custodial care has risen. This is a feature of all systems for the treatment of offenders throughout the western world. The rise in rates of recorded crime and the determination of sentencers are beating the attempts to reduce prison populations.

The criminal justice system itself, insofar as such an unconnected group of agencies can be seen to form one system, poses considerable obstacles to change. We value the independence of the judiciary, and the relative independence of the probation and after-care service and that of the county-based police forces. Yet the independence of any one agency may prove counterproductive to attempts by another to achieve change. For example, the probation service may take determined steps to reduce the prison population, only to find that its best efforts are frustrated by equally laudable efforts on the part of the police to increase their rate of detection, or by changed attitudes on the part of the police to their powers of discretion. Similarly, penal remedies prescribed by the legislature, access to legal representation and the sentencing practices of the judiciary will all have a direct bearing on the number of people in prison. At another level, any considerable growth in the use of alternatives to prison which affects the number of people in prison may well threaten the jobs and security of prison staff.

In summary, the chief preoccupation of many agencies concerned with the treatment of offenders is likely to remain that of reducing the prison population. Yet it is unlikely that any government or agency is likely to nail its flag firmly to a single strategy for achieving such a reduction. For government such a policy, so overtly expressed, is politically unpalatable, and no one agency, be it the prison service, probation service, police or judiciary, is in a position to command the necessary commitment and actual support of all the others. It does not follow, however, that change and evolution are impossible. Much can be learnt from the experience of the past thirty years, experience which indicates a number of strategies that must be pursued in parallel. It remains the responsibility of government, in particular the Home Office or its equivalent, to pursue these strategies, though we have seen that government's ability to act in this field is severely restrained by the nature of 'the system' itself.

On the basis of recent experience and in particular of the developments described in this book I would identify five strategies or areas where pressure might be applied and encouragement given, if we are to achieve a major shift of emphasis from custodial to non-custodial means of dealing with offenders.

The Sentencers

Steps should be taken to close the distance between the judiciary (and to a lesser extent the magistracy) and those agencies responsible for the treatment of offenders. In England and Wales the establishment of the Working Party on Judicial Training and Information under the chairmanship of Lord Justice Bridge is an important and positive move in this direction. The outcome of this Working Party should provide greater opportunities for members of the probation service, social workers, prison staff, offenders, and others to meet with representatives of the judiciary on a regular basis. There should be further opportunities for judges to visit prisons, to learn of new initiatives, and to be consulted about the management of local schemes for offenders. It is hoped that, in time, training wider than that required as a basis for entry into the legal profession, for example an understanding of criminological research and the prison system, would become mandatory for all newly-appointed judges. As a further step the door to judicial service could be opened to professions other than the legal profession.

The lay magistracy is open to certain criticisms in that it tends to draw from a narrow section of society. Is it not possible for employers, particularly in industry, to include a clause in their employees' contracts enabling a member of the staff or work force to take time off for public duties such as service as a magistrate? which has the effect of limiting the breadth of community representation amongst magistrates to those who are able to take time out of employment without financial loss. The recent appointment of an ex-offender as a judge in the United States is hardly typical or likely to set a trend. It does perhaps give some indication of a different attitude to the judiciary from that commonly found in Britain.

Voluntary Organizations

Central and local government should pay much closer attention to, and encourage the potential of, voluntary organizations working with offenders. Voluntary or non-government agencies can claim credit for paving the way for many of our modern statutory agencies, yet so often they are now treated as useful in practice though peripheral in the development of theory. This is hardly surprising if the architects of our welfare state assumed that the contribution of voluntary organizations would gradually wither and die. In practice this has not happened as can be seen from the number of projects discussed in this book that have their origins in voluntary organizations or indeed are still managed by voluntary organizations.

If voluntary agencies are to play their full part in the development of non-custodial measures, it is important that their potential be understood. The strength of voluntary agencies lies above all in their relative independence, both economic and constitutional.

Whether funded totally or only in part from government sources, a voluntary agency has considerably more freedom and flexibility in determining how services are delivered, and is relatively untrammelled by the creeping bureaucracy of many statutory agencies. Such flexibility is crucial since even the best-laid plans fall victim to change, change which frequently results from circumstances outside an agency's own control.

Among the current prison population of most countries there is an increasing stage army of men and some women who find themselves in custody for lack of any suitable non-custodial resource. Typically they are the petty recidivist offender with housing, income maintenance, employment and educational problems who might equally find himself caught up in the psychiatric network or accommodated in a commercial lodging house. Many would agree that prison is an expensive and totally inappropriate resource, for this group; yet they represent the most significant failure of our non-custodial agencies and systems. Their needs are multiple, demanding a use of resources drawn frequently from four or five statutory agencies. Voluntary organizations are particularly well placed to attract and deploy resources in this way. From where should the initiative come? Rather than the voluntary agency going cap-in-hand to government with its plans and requests for money, perhaps the statutory agencies could recognize where their shortcomings are to an extent complemented by the strengths of the voluntary sector. A partnership of the statutory and voluntary sectors would not only enrich the total service available, but also provide a bridge between the professional statutory agency and the community within which those agencies must operate.

The Involvement of Other Agencies

The responsibility for providing for offenders cannot rest solely within the criminal justice system and its agencies. We have seen how housing associations, employment agencies, or education services, often channelled through voluntary organizations, can offer a service to offenders. The tendency in the past has been that offenders' facilities have grown and developed quite separately from other systems in the community. Offenders are seen as special: if accommodation is needed, the Home Office or its equivalent must provide; if employment presents a problem, funding is sought for a special scheme for offenders. This is an expensive response and one that tends to perpetuate the isolation of the offender from others. Offenders' needs are shared by many other groups in the community. An education service, run by local or central government, has a responsibility for meeting the educational needs of offenders; if it does not acknowledge this responsibility it is discriminating against the offender.

The future pattern of non-custodial measures should restrict the tasks of the specialist offender agencies, notably the probation service, to providing a specialist service to the courts and the offender. They should become a gateway to a wide range of *other* voluntary and statutory agencies' facilities.

Earlier Intervention

A fourth strategy for reducing the prison population is that of increasing the opportunities for earlier intervention in the criminal justice process. Traditionally the helping agencies have preferred to wait until guilt has been established and the sentence passed. This pattern is changing. In England and Wales the probation officer is encouraged to make recommendations about the disposal of a case to the court within a social enquiry report. Similarly, although it has met with considerable resistance, the probation service is increasingly involved with men and women on bail. In parts of America and elsewhere in Europe earlier intervention is now an accepted part of the process. The advantages are clear: a man or woman is more amenable to assistance at the critical time between arrest and trial, and more important, effective assistance offered and accepted at that stage can affect the eventual decision between a custodial and non-custodial sentence. Critics argue that such intervention pre-judges the outcome; but it is hard to see why providing employment, for example, or accommodation for a homeless out-of-work person is materially different be he a defendant or convicted offender.

A Unified Offender Service

The *status quo* prevents change. Should the development of alternatives to prison begin to have an impact on the number of people in prison and consequently bring into question the level of prison staff, resistance from the organized labour force within prisons

212   *The Future for Alternative Strategies*

would not be long delayed. Andrew Rutherford describes how the Massachusetts Youth Authority continued to employ staff in institutions long after their charges had departed. This is one reason for embarking on a strategy to bring together those agencies responsible for the offender in custody and out of custody; in England the prison and probation services.

At present relationships between the two services are weak. The probation service is ambivalent about the fact that its members are employed as probation officers in prisons; the prison service often expresses resentment that its members' tasks are restricted to those of a turnkey with few opportunities for involvement in helping or caring tasks. Some European countries, but most notably Sweden, have brought their probation and prison agencies into a single service. They are now well placed to blur increasingly the differences between imprisonment and control in the community and also in a position to begin to transfer resources from the custodial to the non-custodial budget. The recent but unimplemented report by the British Advisory Council on the Penal System, the Young Adult Offender Report, suggested two new orders, both of which envisaged a more flexible use of both custody and supervision in the community. One of the main reasons why such proposals met with protest is that neither of the two main statutory agencies concerned is at present able to bridge the wide gulf between imprisonment and supervision in the community. So long as that gulf remains it is hard to see how alternatives to prison can be developed which actually reduce the use of custodial facilities. The success of the Massachusetts experiment lies not simply in the development of community programmes but that this was preceded by a decision to close the institutions. The creation of a unified service can provide the context for this to happen elsewhere. No single alternative strategy will reap success unless it is accompanied by a parallel move to reduce dramatically the number of prison places. Otherwise all that is likely to be achieved is an increase in the total number of people entwined in the criminal justice system.

Contributors

NORMAN TUTT has worked directly with delinquents as a clinical psychologist for a number of years. He has held a range of advisory posts in central and local government, and is the author of *Care or Custody*.

DAVID REYNOLDS is Lecturer in Social Administration at University College, Cardiff, and is an Honorary Lecturer at the Welsh National School of Medicine.

DEE JONES is on the scientific staff of the Medical Research Epidemiology Unit, Cardiff, where she took part in the research reported in this chapter.

ALLISON MORRIS is Lecturer in Criminology at the Institute of Criminology at Cambridge, and a fellow of Newnham college. She is a member of the Parole Board for England and Wales, and is also a Justice of the Peace.

DAVID THORPE has worked as a Probation Officer and social worker, and as a development officer with Nottinghamshire Social Services Department. He is now Lecturer in Social Work at the University of Lancaster.

NANCY HAZEL since 1975 has organized the Special Family Placement Project, a five-year experiment in the placement of adolescents with severe problems sponsored by the Kent Social Services Department, the University of Kent and the Gatsby Charitable Foundation. She was a member of the Council of Europe Co-ordinated Research Group on the use of foster care and community homes.

ANDREW RUTHERFORD has been Assistant Director of the Guggenheim Programme in Criminal Justice at the Yale Law School since 1973, where he is working in the field of serious youth crime. He was Deputy Governor of Everthorpe Borstal from 1970–3.

OTTO DRIEDGER is Director of the Human Justice Services Program at the University of Regina in Saskatchewan, where he is also

Associate Professor of Social Work. He has been Director of Child Welfare for the province.

SPENCER MILLHAM, ROGER BULLOCK and KENNETH HOSIE are members of the Social Research Unit at Dartington Hall, Devon, which began at King's College, Cambridge. Current projects of the unit include studies of secure provision for adolescents, training for residential social work and problems of maintaining ties between the child in care and his family.

JOHN HARDING is Assistant Chief Probation Officer in the Devon Probation and After-care Service, and is Chairman of the Editorial Board of B.A.S.W.'s *Social Work Today*.

MARTIN WRIGHT is Director of the Howard League for Penal Reform, and was Librarian at the Cambridge Institute of Criminology from 1964–71. He is a member of the executive committee of the Newnham Alternatives Project.

NICHOLAS HINTON is Director of the National Council of Social Services. He is a former Director of N.A.C.R.O.

Bibliography

Chapter 1

Department of Health and Social Security (1976), 'Social Services for Children in England and Wales 1973–1975'. London: Her Majesty's Stationery Office.
Home Office (1977), 'Criminal Statistics 1976'. London: Her Majesty's Stationery Office.
Home Office (1977), 'Annual Report of the Prison Department'. London: Her Majesty's Stationery Office.

Chapter 2

Aubert, W. (1965), 'Inmate Pride in Total Institutions', *American Journal of Sociology*, Vol. 71, p. 5.

Barker-Lunn, J. (1970), *Streaming in the Primary School*. Slough: N.F.E.R.
Bronfenbrenner, U. (1975), 'Reality and research in the ecology of human development'. *Proceedings of the American Philosophical Society*, Vol. 119, pp. 439–69.

Cicourel, A. V., and Kitsuse, J. I. (1963), *The Educational Decision Makers*. New York: Bobbs-Merrill.
Clegg, A., and Megson, B. (1968), *Children in Distress*. Harmondsworth: Penguin.
Cloward, R. A., and Ohlin, L. E. (1961), *Delinquency and Opportunity*. London: Routledge and Kegan Paul.
Cohen, A. K. (1955), *Delinquent Boys*. Chicago: Free Press.
Cox, C. B., and Dyson, A. E. (1975), *Black Paper 1975*. London: Dent.

216   *Bibliography*

Crowther Report (1959), '15 to 18'. London: Her Majesty's Station-
    ery Office.

Davie, R., *et. al.* (1972), *From Birth to Seven*. London: Longmans.
Davie, R. (1975), *Children and Families with Special Needs*. Cardiff:
    University College Press.
Department of Health and Social Security (1977), *Working Together
    for Children and their Families*. London: Her Majesty's
    Stationery Office.
Douglas, J. W. B. (1968), *All Our Future*. London: Panther.
Downes, D. (1968), *The Delinquent Solution*. London: Routledge
    and Kegan Paul.
Dyer, H. S. (1968), 'School factors and equal educational oppor-
    tunity'. *Harvard Educational Review*, Vol. 38, No. 1, pp. 38–
    56.

Finlayson, D. S., and Loughran, J. L. (1976), 'Pupils' perceptions in
    high and low delinquency schools'. *Educational Research*,
    Vol. 18, pp. 138–45.
Frease, D. (1972), 'The Schools, Self Concept and Juvenile Delin-
    quency'. *British Journal Criminology*, Vol. 12, No. 2, pp. 133–
    146.

Gath, D. (1972), 'Child guidance and delinquency in a London
    borough'. *Psychological Medicine*, Vol. 2, pp. 185–91.
Goldman, N. (1961), 'A Socio-Psychological Study of School
    Vandalism'. *Crime and Delinquency*, pp. 221–30.

Halsey, A. H. (1972), *Educational Priority*. London: Her Majesty's
    Stationery Office.
Hamblin, D. (1974), *The Teacher and Counselling*. Oxford: Black-
    well.
Hargreaves, D. H. (1967), *Social Relations in a Secondary School*.
    London: Routledge and Kegan Paul.
Hirschi, T. (1969), *Causes of Delinquency*. Berkeley: University of
    California Press.
Husan, T. (1974), *The Learning Society*. London: Methuen.

Jackson, B., and Marsden, D. (1962), *Education and the Working
    Class*. London: Routledge and Kegan Paul.
Johnson, P. (1977), 'Educational Policy and Social Control in Mid-
    Victorian England'. *Past and Present*, Vol. 49.

Jencks, C., *et al.* (1972), *Inequality*. London: Allen Lane.

Johnston, A., and Krovetz, L. (1976), 'Levels of aggression in a traditional and a pluralistic school'. *Educational Research*, Vol. 18, No. 2.

Kellmer-Pringle, M. (1973), *The Roots of Violence and Vandalism*. London: National Children's Bureau.

Little, A. (1977), 'Declining pupil performance and the urban environment' in Field, F. (ed.), *Education and the Urban Crisis*. London: Routledge and Kegan Paul.

Mays, J. B. (1964), *Growing Up in the City*. Liverpool: University Press.

McDill, E. L., and Rigsby, L. C. (1974), *Structure and Process in Secondary Schools*. Baltimore: Johns Hopkins Press.

Miller, W. B. (1958), 'Lower Class Culture as a Generating Milieu of Gang Delinquency'. *Journal of Social Issues*, Vol. 14, pp. 5–19.

Murgatroyd, S. J. (1975), 'School Centred Counselling'. *New Era*, Vol. 56, No. 4, pp. 90–1.

Murgatroyd, S. J. (1976), 'Ethical Issues in Secondary School Counselling'. *Journal of Moral Education*, Vol. 4, No. 1, pp. 27–37.

Newcomb, T. M. (1963), 'Student Peer-Group Influence', in Sanford, N. (ed.), *The American College*. New York: John Wiley.

Palmer, J. (1964), 'Smoking, Caning, and Delinquency in a Secondary Modern School'. *Brit. J. Prev. Soc. Med.*, Vol. 19, pp. 18–23.

Partridge, J. (1968), *Life in a Secondary Modern School*. Harmondsworth: Penguin.

Phillipson, C. M. (1971), 'Juvenile Delinquency and the School', in Carson, W. G., and Wiles, P. C. (eds), *Crime and Delinquency in Britain*. London: Martin Robertson.

Power, M. J., *et al.* (1967), 'Delinquent Schools?' *New Society*, 19 October.

Power, M. J., *et al.* (1972), 'Neighbourhood, School and Juveniles before the Courts'. *British Journal of Criminology*, Vol. 12, pp. 111–32.

President's Commission on Law Enforcement and Administration of Justice (1967), *Juvenile Delinquency and Youth Crime*. Washington: U.S. Government Printing Office.

Rafalides, M. and Hoy, W. K. (1971), 'Student Sense of Alienation and Pupil Control Orientation of High Schools'. *The High School Journal*, Vol. 55, pp. 101–11.

Reynolds, D., *et al.* (1976), 'Schools do Make a Difference'. *New Society*, 29 July.

Reynolds, D. (1977), 'The Delinquent School' in Hammersley, M., and Woods, P. (eds), *The Process of Schooling*. London: Routledge and Kegan Paul.

Reynolds, D., and Murgatroyd, S. J. (1974), 'Being Absent from School'. *British Journal of Law and Society*, Vol. 1, No. 1, pp. 78–81.

Rhodes, A. L., and Reiss, A. J. (1969), 'Apathy, Truancy and Delinquency as Adaptations to School Failure'. *Social Forces*, Vol. 48, No. 1.

Robbins Report (1963), *Higher Education*. London: Her Majesty's Stationery Office.

Rose, G. (1967), *Schools for Young Offenders*. London: Tavistock.

Rutter, M. (1973), 'Why are London children so disturbed?' *Proceedings of the Royal Society of Medicine*, Vol. 66, pp. 1221–5.

Rutter, M., and Madge, N. (1977), *Cycle of Disadvantage*. London: Heinemann.

Schools Council (1970), *Cross'd with Adversity*. London: Evans.

Searle, C. (1972), *This New Season*. London: Calder and Boyars.

Stinchcombe, A. L. (1964), *Rebellion in a High School*. Chicago: Quadrangle.

Stone, J., and Taylor, F. (1977), *Vandalism in Schools*. London: Save the Children Fund.

Sugarman, B. (1967), 'Involvement in youth culture, academic achievement and conformity in school; an empirical study of London schoolboys'. *British Journal of Sociology*, Vol. 18, pp. 151–64.

Tyerman, M. J. (1958), 'A Research Into Truancy'. *British Journal of Educational Psychology*, Vol. 28, pp. 217–25.

Tyerman, M. J. (1968), *Truancy*. London: University of London Press.

West, D. J. (1969), *Present Conduct and Future Delinquency*. London: Heinemann.

West, D. J. (1973), *Who Becomes Delinquent?* London: Heinemann.

West, E. G. (1970), *Education and the State*. London: Institute of Economic Affairs.

Werthman, C. (1967), 'The function of social definitions in the development of delinquent careers' in *Juvenile Delinquency and Youth Crime*. Washington: U.S. Government Printing Office.

Wootton, B. (1959), *Social Science and Social Pathology*. London: George Allen and Unwin.

Chapter 3

Association of Chief Police Officers (1974), 'Memorandum of the General Purposes Standing Committee'.

Bottoms, A. E., 'On the Decriminalisation of the English Juvenile Court', in Hood, R. (ed.) (1974), *Crime, Criminology, and Public Policy*. London: Heinemann.

Bruce, N., and Spencer, J. G. (1976), *Face to face with families: A report on the children's panels in Scotland*. Midlothian: Macdonald.

Canada Law Reform Commission (1975), 'Diversion', Working Paper No. 7. Ottawa.

Canada Ministry of Solicitor-General (1975), 'Young Persons in conflict with the law. A report of the Solicitor-General's Committee on proposals for new legislation to replace the Juvenile Delinquent Act'. Ottawa.

Committee on Children and Young Persons (The Ingleby Committee) (1960), 'Report'. Cmnd. 1191. London: Her Majesty's Stationery Office.

Creekmore, M. (1976), 'Case Processing: intake, adjudication, and disposition', in Sarri, R., and Hasenfeld, Y. (eds), *Brought to Justice? Juveniles, Courts, and the Law*. Ann Arbor: University of Michigan.

Cressey, D. R., and McDermott, R. A. (1973), *Diversion from the juvenile justice system*. Ann Arbor: University of Michigan, National Assessment of juvenile Corrections.

Farrington, D. (forthcoming), 'The Effect of Public Labelling', in Crim, B. J.

Home Office (1968), 'Children in trouble', Cmnd. 3601. London: Her Majesty's Stationary Office.
House of Commons (1975), 'Eleventh Report of the Expenditure Committee', Vol. 1. London: Her Majesty's Stationery Office.
Howlett, P. W. (1973), 'Is the YSB all it's cracked up to be?' *Crime and Delinquency*, 19, pp. 485–92.

Klapmuts, N. (1972), 'Children's Rights—the legal rights of minors in conflict with law or social custom', *Crime and Delinquency Literature*, September.

Lemert, E. M. (1971), 'Instead of court: diversion in juvenile justice', *Crime and Delinquency*, monograph series. National Institute of Mental Health, Center for Studies of Crime and Delinquency, 5454 Wisconsin Ave., Chevy Chase, Md.
—— (1972), *Human Deviance, Social Problems, and Social Control*. Englewood Cliffs, New Jersey: Prentice Hall.
—— (1975), Paper presented to conference at the University of Cardiff. Unpublished.

National Institute of Mental Health (1971), 'Diversions from the Criminal Justice System'. Washington, D.C.

Oliver, I. T. (1973), 'The Metropolitan Police Juvenile Bureau Scheme', *C.L. Review*, pp. 499–506.

Piliavin, I., and Briar, S. (1964–5), 'Police encounters with juveniles', *American Journal of Sociology*, Vol. 76, pp. 206–14.
Priestley, P. (1975), 'In the interests of the child'. Bristol: University Department of Social Administration. Unpublished.

Sarri, R. (1976), 'Service Technologies: Diversion, Probation, and Detention', in Sarri, R., and Hasenfeld, Y. (eds), *Brought to Justice? Juveniles, the Courts, and the Law*. Ann Arbor: University of Michigan.
Scottish Advisory Council (1945), 'Police Warnings'. A Report on the Treatment and Rehabilitation of Offenders. Edinburgh: Her Majesty's Stationery Office.
Scottish Home and Health Dept. and Scottish Education Dept.

(1964), 'Children and young persons in Scotland: report by the committee appointed by the Secretary of State for Scotland, etc.' Cmnd. 2306. (Chairman Lord Kilbrandon.) Edinburgh: Her Majesty's Stationery Office.

Sudnow, D. (1965), 'Normal Crimes: sociological features of the penal code in a public defender office', *Social Problems*, Vol. 12, pp. 255–76.

Sutherland, E., and Cressey, D. (1970), *Principles of Criminology*, 8th ed. Philadelphia: J. B. Lippincott.

Taylor, M. (1971), 'Study of the juvenile liaison scheme in West Ham 1961–63'. Home Office Research Unit. London: Her Majesty's Stationery Office.

United States President's Commission of Law Enforcement and Administration of Justice (1967), 'The challenge of crime in a free society'. Washington: U.S. Government Printing Office.

Chapter 4

Baddeley, F. (1975), 'Can we rise to the challenge of delinquency?' *Social Worker*, 16 Oct. 1975.

Davies, M. (1969), *Probationers in their social environment*. London: Her Majesty's Stationery Office.

Department of Health and Social Security (1971), *Intermediate Treatment: a guide for the regional planning of new forms of treatment for children in trouble*. London: Her Majesty's Stationery Office.

Empey, L. T., and Rabow, J. (1961), 'The Provo Experiment in delinquency rehabilitation', *American Sociological Review* 26.

Hirschi, T. (1969), *Causes of delinquency*. University of California Press, Berkeley.

Home Office (1968), *Children in Trouble*. London: Her Majesty's Stationery Office.

Home Office (1969), *Children and Young Persons Act 1969*. London: Her Majesty's Stationery Office.

Matza, D. (1964), *Delinquency and drift*. New York: John Wiley and Sons.

Paley, J., and Thorpe, D. (1974), *Children: handle with care.* Leicester: National Youth Bureau.

Polk, K., and Halferty, D. (1972), 'School cultures, Adolescent Commitments, and delinquency' in Polk, K., and Halferty, D. (eds), *Schools and delinquency.* Englewood Cliffs, N.J.: Prentice-Hall.

Ryall, R. (1974), 'Delinquency: the problem for treatment', *Social work today* 5 (4).

Schur, E. M. (1973), *Radical non-intervention: rethinking the delinquency problem.* New Jersey: Prentice-Hall.

Stephenson, R. M., and Scarpitti, F. R. (1974), *Group interaction as therapy.* Connecticut: Greenwood Press.

West, D. J. (1969), *Present conduct and future delinquency.* London: Heinemann.

West, D. J. (1973), *Who becomes delinquent.* London: Heinemann.

Chapter 5

Bonhoeffer, M., and Widemann, P. (1974), *Kinder in Ersatzfamilien.* Stuttgart, Germany: Ernst Klett Verlag.

Caplan, G. (1964), *Principles of Preventive Psychiatry.* London: Tavistock.

Cornish, D. B., and Clarke, R. V. G. (1975), 'Residential treatment and its effects on delinquency'. London: Her Majesty's Stationery Office.

Department of Health and Social Security. Annual publication, 'Children in care in England and Wales'. London: Her Majesty's Stationery Office.

Department of Health and Social Security, Social Work Development Group, N. Tutt (ed.), 'Violence'. London: Her Majesty's Stationery Office.

Department of Health and Social Security (1976), *Priorities for health and personal social services in England.* London: Her Majesty's Stationery Office.

Hartnell, M. (1974), 'The professional foster parent', *Health and Social Services*, Vol. LXXXIV No. 4396.

Hazel, N. (1975), 'Residential Care as the Key to Fostering', *Social Work Today*, Vol. 5 No. 25.

Hazel, N., and Cox, R. (1976), 'First progress report of the special family placement project'. Maidstone, Kent: Kent County Council.

Kälveston, A. L. (1976), *Caring for children with special needs*. Marcinelle, Belgium: Institut Inter-Universitaire de l'action sociale, 179 rue du Debarcadere.

National Children's Bureau (1973), *Highlight no. 6*. N.C.B. London.

Rowe, J., and Lambert, L. (1973), 'Children who wait'. London: Association of British Adoption Agencies.

Chapter 6

Anderson, Karen (1976), 'Monitoring Deinstitutionalized Youth Services', unpublished paper, Yale University.

Bartollas, Clemens, Miller, Stuart J. and Dinitz, Simon (1976), *Juvenile Victimization: The Institutional Paradox*. New York: Sage Publications.

Behn, Robert D. (1976), 'Closing the Massachusetts Public Training Schools', *Policy Sciences* 7, (2), pp. 151–71.

Coates, Robert B. (1974), 'A Working Paper on Community Based Corrections: Concept, Historical Development, Impact and Potential Dangers', unpublished paper, Harvard Center for Criminal Justice.

Coates, Robert B., and Miller, Alden D. (1975), 'Evaluating Large Scale Social Service Systems in Changing Environments: The Case of Correctional Agencies', *Journal of Research in Crime and Delinquency*, 12 (2), pp. 92–106.

Coates, Robert B., Miller, Alden D. and Ohlin, Lloyd E. (1973), 'Strategic Innovation in the Process of Deinstitutionalization: The University of Massachusetts Conference', in Bakal, Y. (ed.), *Closing Correctional Institutions*, Lexington, Mass.: D. C. Heath.

—— (1975), 'Juvenile Detention and Its Consequences', unpublished paper, Harvard Center for Criminal Justice.

—— (1975), 'Exploratory Analysis of Recidivism in the Massachusetts Youth Correctional System', unpublished report, Harvard Center for Criminal Justice.

—— (1976), 'Social Climate, Extent of Community Linkages and Quality of Community Linkages: The Institutionalization-Normalization Continuum', unpublished report, Harvard Center for Criminal Justice.

Department of Youth Services, Commonwealth of Massachusetts (1976), 'Task Force on Secure Facilities: Preliminary Report to Commissioner John A. Calhoun', Boston.

Harvard Center for Criminal Justice (1975), 'Preliminary Analysis Relating to the Generalizibility of the Massachusetts Experience in Juvenile Corrections Reform', unpublished paper.

Institute of Judicial Administration/American Bar Association (1976), *Standards Relating to Juvenile Delinquency and Sanctions*, draft. New York: National Justice Standards Project.

McGillis, Daniel, and Spangenberg, Robert (1976), 'The Camp Hill Project: An Assessment', report prepared for the National Institute for Juvenile Justice and Delinquency Prevention, Law Enforcement Assistance Administration by Abt Associates.

Miller, Jerome G. (1973), 'The Politics of Change: Correctional Reform' in Bakal, Y. (ed.), *Closing Correctional Institutions*, Lexington, Mass.: D. C. Heath.

National Advisory Commission on Criminal Justice Standards Goals (1973), *A National Strategy To Reduce Crime*, Washington, D.C.: USGPO.

Polsky, Howard (1962), *Cottage Six*. New York: Russel Sage Foundation.

Rutherford, Andrew (1974), *The Dissolution of the Training Schools in Massachusetts*. Columbus, Ohio: The Academy for Contemporary Problems.

Rutherford, Andrew (1977), *Youth Crime Policy in the United States*. London: Institute for the Study and Treatment of Delinquency.

Wooden, Kenneth (1976), *Weeping in the Playtime of Others*. New York: McGraw-Hill.

Chapter 7

Canadian Criminology and Corrections Association (1970), Ottawa.

Francis, W. R. (1973), 'Corrections—Community Resources in the North'. Proceedings of the 1973 Canadian Congress on Crime and Corrections.

Information and Public Programs Office, Attorney General's Department (1976), 'Justice 1975'. British Columbia.
Information Canada. 'The Criminal in Canadian Society—A Perspective on Corrections'. Ottawa.

Liaison (1976), A monthly newsletter for the criminal justice system, Vol. 2 No. 9.

McGrath, W. T. (1968), *Crime and Treatment in Canada*. Ministry of the Solicitor General, Communication Division. 'Young Persons in Conflict with the Law'.

National Advisory Commission on Criminal Justice Standards and Goals (1973).

Probation and After-Care Department (1971), Habitual Drunken Offenders. London: Her Majesty's Stationery Office.

Report of the Saskatchewan Penal Commission (1976). Regina: Queen's Printer.

Saskatchewan Corrections Committee (1971), Study Report. Regina: Queen's Printer.
Statistics Canada Service Bulletin (1975), Law Enforcement Judicial and Correctional Statistics, Vol. 3 No. 1.

Titmuss, R. (1974), Social Policy: An Introduction. London: Allen and Unwin.

Chapter 8

Briggs, D. (1975), *In Place of Prison*. London: Temple Smith.

Flackett, J. M. (1973), 'Juvenile offenders in the community: some recent experiences in the United States', *Howard Journal*, XIV, pp. 22–37.

Griffiths, W. A. (1969), 'The development of an after-care hostel', *British Journal of Criminology*, IX, pp. 312–43.

Hayes, J. (1976), 'Organisational development: a group centred approach to improving the effectiveness of after-care hostels', *British Journal of Social Work*, VI, pp. 465–80.
Her Majesty's Stationery Office (1975), 'Report on the Work of the Prison Department'. London: Cmnd. 6152.
Hodgkin, N. (1972), 'The "New Careers" Project at Vacaville: a California experiment', *New Careers for ex-Offenders*. London: Howard League for Penal Reform.

Joint Commission on Correctional Manpower and Training (1968), 'Offenders as a Correctional Manpower Resource'. Washington, D.C.

N.A.C.R.O. (1973), *New Careers Information Bulletin*. London.

Pearl, A., and Riessman, F. (1965), *New Careers for the Poor*. New York: Free Press.

Sinclair, I. (1971), 'Hostels for Probationers'. London: Her Majesty's Stationery Office.
Social Action Research Center (1973), 'New Careers Evaluation Project: Report on Recruitment and Selection of New Careerists'. Berkeley.

Chapter 9

Children-in-Care Programme, C.S.V. (1976), C.S.V., 237 Pentonville Road, London, N1 9NJ.
'Community Service Orders' (1975). London: Her Majesty's Stationery Office.

Dickson, A. (1973), 'Delinquents into Donors'. *Prison Service Journal*, 1973 (2).

Flegg, D., *et al.* (1976), 'Community Service Consumer Survey 1973–76'. Nottinghamshire Probation and After-Care Service.
Ford, C. B. (1976), 'A Project on the Community Service by Offenders Scheme'. Unpublished.

Harding, J. K. (1974), 'Community Service by Offenders—the Nottinghamshire Experiment'. London: N.A.C.R.O. and Howard League for Penal Reform.

Nader, L., and Combs-Schilling, E. (1976), 'Restitution in Cross Cultural Perspective', in Hudson, J. (ed.), *Restitution in Criminal Justice*. L.E.A.A. Grant No. 76ED–99–0004, 1976.

Pease, K. (1975), 'Community Service Orders'—Address to British Society of Criminology'. Unpublished.

Sole Sanction Restitution Programme (1976), Georgia Department of Corrections, 800 Peachtree Street N.W., Atlanta, Georgia.
de Smit, N. W. (1976), 'Involvement of the Public in the Administration of Justice'. N.A.C.R.O. European Crime Conference.
Stephens, F. (1976), 'Within a County Probation Area: A Study of Interorganisational Relationships between the Community Service Unit and Voluntary Agencies providing field placements for Community Service workers'. A Project Report for the National Institute of Social Work, 5 Tavistock Place, London.
West, J. S. M. (1976), 'Community Service Orders', in King, J. F. S. (ed.), *Control without Custody*. Cambridge: Institute of Criminology.

Chapter 10

Advisory Council on the Penal System (1970), *Non-custodial and semi-custodial penalties*. London: Her Majesty's Stationery Office.
Advisory Council on the Penal System (1974), *Young adult offenders*. London: Her Majesty's Stationery Office.

Barbican Centre (1976). The Barbican Centre: an experiment in self-help with socially disadvantaged people. Progress report 1973–5. Gloucester: the Centre

Briggs, D., and Hodgkin, N. (1972), *New Careers for ex-offenders.* London: Howard League for Penal Reform.

Cambridge Institute of Criminology (1977), *Penal policy-making in England.* (Cropwood Series No. 9.) Edited by Nigel Walker with the assistance of Henri Giller.

CHAR (1976), *Habitual drunken neglect.* London: Campaign for the Homeless and Rootless.

Elwyn-Jones, Lord (1976), 'Putting knowledge to work'. *Howard Journal*, Vol. 15 No. 2, pp. 1–5.

English, P. (1975), 'Rights of the offender in the non-custodial setting'. Paper to National Criminological Conference, Cambridge, 1975.

Flackett, J. (1974), *Juvenile offenders in the community: some recent experiences in the United States.* London: Howard League.

Goetschius, G., and Tash, M. J. (1967), *Working with unattached youth.* London: Routledge.

Harding, J. (1974), *Community service by offenders.* London: Howard League and N.A.C.R.O.

Home Office (1976), 'Home Office after-care hostel grant scheme: a new approach'. Home Office Probation Department Circular No. 39 (1976).

Home Office Research Study, 36 (1976), 'IMPACT—the result of the experiment', Vol. 2.

Howard League for Penal Reform (1975), *Between probation and custody.*

Keith-Lucas, A. (1966), 'The art and science of helping', *Case Conference*, Vol. 13 No. 5.

Kelmanson, A. (1975), *The experience of giving: borstal boys in full-time community service.* London: Community Service Volunteers.

Klockars, C. B. (1976), 'The true limits of *The effectiveness of correctional treatment*', *Prison Journal*, Vol. 55 No. 1, pp. 53–66.

Lipton, D.; Martinson, R.; and Wilks, J. (1975), *The effectiveness of correctional treatment*. New York: Praeger.

Marris, P., and Rein, M. (1975), *Dilemmas of social reform: poverty and community action in the United States*. Second ed. London: Routledge.

Martinson, R. (1974), 'What works? Questions and answers about prison reform', *Public Interest*, Spring, pp. 22–54.

Morris, A. (1976), 'Juvenile justice: where next?' *Howard Journal*, Vol. 15 No. 1, pp. 26–37.

Moynihan, D. P. (1969), *Maximum feasible misunderstanding*. New York: Free Press.

Musheno, M., *et al.* (1976), 'Evaluating alternatives in criminal justice: a policy-impact model', *Crime and Delinquency*, Vol. 22 No. 3, July, pp. 265–83.

N.A.C.R.O. (in press), Proceedings of European Conference, London, December 1976.

N.A.P. (1976), *Newham Alternatives Project*. London: Radical Alternatives to Prison.

N.E.L.P. (1977), Proceedings of conference *Information vs. crime*, April 1976. London: North East London Polytechnic.

Palmer, T. (1975), 'Martinson revisited', *Journal of Research in Crime and Delinquency*, Vol. 12, July, pp. 133–52.

Rutherford, A. (1975), 'Taylor House: an example of penal tokenism', *Howard Journal*, Vol. 14 No. 2, pp. 46–9.

Schon, D. A. (1971), *Beyond the stable state: public and private learning in a changing society*. London: Temple Smith.

Smith, Robert L. (1972), 'A quiet revolution: probation subsidy'. U.S. Department of Health, Education and Welfare, publication No. (SRS) 72–26011. Washington: USGPO.

Vera Institute of Justice (1970), *The Manhattan Court Employment Project*. New York: Vera Institute.

Vera Institute of Justice (circa 1970), *In lieu of arrest: the Manhattan Bowery Project*. New York City Criminal Justice Coordinating Council.

Whitlam, M. (1975), 'Taylor House: an experiment in borstal Hostels'. *Howard Journal*, Vol. 14 No. 2, pp. 43–6.

Wright, Martin (1976), 'The benefits of keeping offenders out of prison', *Times*, 19 August.

Chapter 11

'Parole Board Report' (1968). London: Her Majesty's Stationery Office.
Hawkins, Gordon (1975), *Ideology of Imprisonment. Progress in Penal Reform*. Oxford: Oxford University Press.